*French*
*Symbolist*
*Poetry*

# French Symbolist Poetry

AN ANTHOLOGY

Selected and Translated by

John Porter Houston and Mona Tobin Houston

Indiana

Bloomington University

Press

First Midland Book Edition 1980

Copyright © 1980 by John Porter Houston and Mona Tobin Houston

Manufactured in the United States of America

**Library of Congress Cataloging in Publication Data**
Main entry under title:

French symbolist poetry.

English and French.
1. French poetry—Translations into English.
2. English prose literature—Translations from French.
3. French poetry. 4. Symbolism (Literary movement)—
France. I. Houston, John Porter. II. Houston, Mona
Tobin, 1935-
PQ1170.E6F69   1980      841'.8'08   79-3381
ISBN 0-253-16725-6      1  2  3  4  5  84  83  82  81  80
ISBN 0-253-20250-7 (pbk.)

*184282*

# Contents

# TRISTAN CORBIERE

# ARTHUR RIMBAUD

# GEORGES RODENBACH

# EMILE VERHAEREN

# JEAN LORRAIN

# JEAN MOREAS

# REMY de GOURMONT

# ALBERT SAMAIN

## GUSTAVE KAHN

## ALBERT GIRAUD

## JULES LAFORGUE

## SAINT-POL ROUX

## CHARLES van LERBERGHE

## MAX ELSKAMP

## RENE GHIL

## LOUIS Le CARDONNEL

## GREGOIRE Le ROY

# MAURICE MAETERLINCK

# STUART MERRILL

# ADOLPHE RETTE

# PIERRE QUILLARD

# HENRI de REGNIER

# EPHRAIM MIKHAEL

# PIERRE LOUYS

# PAUL VALERY

# HENRY BATAILLE

# OSCAR-VENCESLAS de MILOSZ

# GUILLAUME APOLLINAIRE

*French*
*Symbolist*
*Poetry*

# INTRODUCTION

More than other literatures, that of France has traditionally been notable for the production of manifestoes and for the formation of movements growing out of sometimes violent literary polemics. Symbolism is just such a movement: it suddenly took shape owing to the appearance, in the early 1880s, of a large number of younger poets, soon to be in an experimental mood, and to the founding of the first of a number of small reviews dedicated, at least in part, to new literature. Equally influential was the return to prominence of an important older poet, Verlaine, who emerged from obscurity to publish not only his own verse in *Jadis et Naguère* (1884) but also a series of essays, appearing in the little review *Lutèce,* on Rimbaud, Corbière, and Mallarmé, whom he designated as "accursed poets." Not only were the poets he revealed forgotten or unknown, and fascinating in the "accursed" aspects of their careers, but they were highly adventurous in style and in no way concerned with avoiding hermeticism. They wrote largely for themselves, ignoring what they considered a monumentally stupid and frivolous reading public, in which, moreover, these poets included all the well-known writers of their day as well as the bourgeois audience. The *poètes maudits* thus provided younger poets a model both in strictly poetic matters and in the attitude to take toward society.

The *poètes maudits* had started out in different ways. Corbière, isolated from the literary world, was, by temperament and by the misfortune of his chronic illness, inclined toward an ironic, scoffing view of things. He assumed the mask of a much older man in his verse, unlike the youthful voice of poetic tradition. The self-consciously sacerdotal view of the poet, increasingly widespread in the nineteenth century, was not his; he lacked the conventional high seriousness of his calling. Mallarmé, on the other hand, was a hieratic figure, evermore isolated from the literary world by too extreme a priestly vision of his role. Only when it became possible to accept poetry as a sacred mystery, a replacement for religion, did his central position in the world of letters become recognized. Rimbaud, finally, was a thorough revolutionary, seeking to destroy nineteenth-century poetic conventions; he brought out the iconoclast in Verlaine during their homosexual liaison in 1872–73, and the latter's verse then reached its greatest brilliance. What

3

emerges from the collocation of these four poets is that conventional poetry, best represented by Leconte de Lisle, had for them a solemn bookishness but was basically not serious. It lacked the ironic dimension that even Mallarmé and Rimbaud found in the poet's position, and yet it did not go far enough in transmuting life into something strange and absolute.

The lesson of Verlaine's essays on the *poètes maudits* was immediately reinforced by the publication of Huysmans's novel *A rebours* (1884). The sole figure in it is an esthete, Des Esseintes, who has withdrawn from the world and whose reflections on society, painting, sex, literature ancient and modern, religion, music, and so forth, make of the work a kind of encyclopedia of "decadent" taste. There is much that is tongue-in-cheek about Des Esseintes and his opinions, but the discussion of Baudelaire, Verlaine, Corbière, and Mallarmé is thoroughly serious, as is the characterization of contemporary society in terms of adulteration and genetic decline. The significance of Huysmans's novel in the spread of the new taste in poetry—the popularity of the book astonished everyone—is confirmed by the dedication to Des Esseintes of Mallarmé's poem "Prose," which is an *ars poetica*.

The number of remarkably original volumes of verse by younger poets published between 1884 and the early '90s in France was quite without precedent, and nothing comparable has been seen since. The little reviews—*La Revue Indépendante, La Vogue, La Pléiade,* and others—had some impressive issues, especially perhaps *La Vogue,* which printed Rimbaud's *Une Saison en enfer* and *Illuminations,* then unknown. At first the term *decadent* was applied to the new literature: the word had been increasingly used to describe modern writing in the preceding decades. While *decadent* is not an altogether inappropriate word for the styles and subjects of the younger poets, the word *symbolist* came into favor after the publication in 1886 of Jean Moréas's *Symbolist Manifesto,* and it seemed better, more neutrally, to describe what the new poetry was aiming at. The notion and term of *decadence* went on to enjoy much currency in other countries, and if we speak of symbolism as a poetic manner, it would not be out of place to speak of a decadent view of the world behind much symbolist poetry and one related extensively to literature outside of France.

In any case, the real history of the symbolist movement lies not in the date this or that little review began or ceased publication but in the formation of the idea of a literature for an elite, and in the modernist acceptance of obscurity as a perhaps necessary part of a work of art.

This sense of separateness from the larger public arose at a time when poets, although uninfluenced by great events the way certain romantics had been affected by the French Revolution and Napoleon's career, found themselves nonetheless in a distinctive, new era in the history of French society and one which marked them. A recent French historian, Emmanuel Todd, has said in an interview:

> If the French of 1979 were confronted with their ancestors of 1914, they might well consider them mad. Men and women of that day, while living in a politically liberal society, had imprisoned themselves in a moral system almost pathological in its rigidity: bourgeois virtues. They saved, they accumulated gold; they were terrorized and obsessed by sexuality. . . . In France between 1835 and 1910 the suicide rate grew by 260 percent, the number of mental patients by 310 percent, the per capita consumption of alcohol by 100 percent. . . . Toward 1900, the middle classes were the ones which produced the mentally ill, the alcoholics, the suicides.*

These social facts suggest the measure of alienation, constraint, and despair obtaining in the "Belle Epoque" and the impression this period might make on a sensitive individual. The sociology of late nineteenth-century literature has scarcely been touched on, but it appears to be such that systematic pessimism on the part of poets should hardly surprise us, and we shall turn now to its philosophical aspects.

## II

One of the most useful ways to look at decadent-symbolist themes is in terms of Arthur Schopenhauer's thought, although his direct influence is not easy to establish. Schopenhauer consciously examined and rationally analyzed all manner of ideas which are found in symbolist poetry expressed with varying degrees of philosophical generality and explicitness. The world of active life was for Schopenhauer the realm of blind will, a largely unconscious force by which we, as subject, constantly reach out to seize on the objects of phenomena, which we propose to ourselves as goals. The process of living propels one continually toward unwanted death; while the will is purposeless in general, it shows up in each individual as a determining, fatalistic force. Sexuality is its most obvious form, and the decadent imagination makes much over this "fruit of death on the tree of life," as Samain called it. The prostitute is an important figure, as in Verhaeren's "Dame en noir,"

---

*"Le Fou et le Prolétaire," *L'Express*, no. 1440 (February 17, 1979).

and in her mythic form she is Salome, as in Samain's "Des soirs fiév-
reux . . ." or Milosz's "Salomé."

It is characteristic of symbolist technique to represent a theme in var-
ious conventions of realism or imaginativeness. We move up the scale
from the mimetic representation of the prostitute in the city to the
medievalizing, symbolic realms of Retté's "Bâille la haute salle . . ."
and Régnier's "Salut à l'étrangère," in which we see the fatal woman
associated with that other object of libido, glory. The Chimaera is a
frequent accompanying symbol of insane illusions. We are here on the
grander, tragic level, where sexuality is merely part of the unfulfillment
inevitable in the world of will. Retté's allegory "Sillages," in which
man is the Eternal Beggar, dispenses with the prostitute, as does Ré-
gnier's "Motifs de légende et de mélancolie," a purely symbolic poem,
whose tone might be characterized with Schopenhauer's comment:

> Thus between desiring and attaining all human life flows on throughout.
> The wish is, in its nature, pain; the attainment soon begets satiety: the end
> was only apparent; possession takes away the charm; the wish, the need,
> presents itself under a new form; when it does not, then follows desolate-
> ness, emptiness, ennui, against which the conflict is just as painful as
> against want.*

There are shorter poems in which the world of will is depicted by a
symbol: the city in Verhaeren's work or the violent, erotic, or death-
giving sunset in Giraud and Rodenbach. Mikhaël's "Le Mage" is an
especially interesting ironic poem on glory: the Barbarians, whose com-
ing is the subject of various decadent poems, turn out to be really impo-
tent, sexually as well as figuratively. The illusion of vitality is a false
one: there are no conquerors of man's infirmity in the world of will.

Jules Laforgue, who makes highly conscious references to
Schopenhauer and to the latter's disciple Hartmann, transposes decadent
thematic material into a mode which is variously ironic, lyrical, and
realistic. In the "Complainte des pianos," young girls of the bourgeoisie
are under the sway of the will; "Complainte du printemps" comments
further on the erotic urge in spring. Laforgue alludes to the late
nineteenth century's obsessive scientific ideas of heredity, and we see
how Schopenhauer's categories of thought can be nicely adjusted to dif-
ferent degrees of practical or imaginative, comic or serious representa-

---

*This and subsequent Schopenhauer quotations are from *The World as Will and Idea*, trans.
R. B. Haldane and J. Kemp, I (London: Kegan Paul, Trench, Trübner, 1896), pp. 404–
405, 397, 494–95, 524, 532.

tion in literature. The world of blind will, of sexuality and the life cycle, in which the will to live is actually the will to die, may seem at first to comprehend the whole range of human existence, but the symbolists found a great source of inspiration in its opposite: the denial of the will.

It is often in slim, symbolic lyrics that we find a striking image of a world other than that of the will. The refining process of illness, as in Rodenbach's "Les Malades aux fenêtres," the revelation of the exquisite essence of a dying flower in Lorrain's "Effeuillement," the sublimation of real women in a perfect dream of beauty in Van Lerberghe's "La Jonchée," the angel-woman of Mallarmé's "Soupir," the presentation in Maeterlinck and Rodenbach of the soul as being in a hothouse or aquarium, Valéry's dream of "Blanc"—all these are symbolic ways of depicting the individual free of sexual impulses, unwanted death, and unfulfilled desires. The imagery of attenuation—"formes grêles" as Samain put it—characterizes them. Such poems represent not only a release, but by their quiet nature recall the technical definition of beauty in Schopenhauer's thought: the individual ceases to be a *willing* subject grasping after the fleeting objects of phenomena and becomes the contemplator of Platonic Ideas, in a relation free from the subject-object tension of the world of will.

Purity might be said to be the positive characterization of the state of being free from will, and purity has in many symbolist works a nexus of spiritual, esthetic, and chaste-erotic connotations which make it rather elusive. In an allegorical convention, we find it embodied by Mallarmé's Hérodiade. At the opposite, realistic pole, *Le Grand Meaulnes* shows a superb use of an experience of ineffable purity in the context of narrative; the mysterious contrast of Meaulnes's experience in the lost domain with the practical, provincial world of his schoolboy life makes this work an exemplary case of the simultaneously erotic, esthetic, and spiritual whole which cuts across philosophical categories and defies naming in any rational way. Finally, Laforgue, with his usual fondness for irony, presents one of his young poet figures mocking his own obsession with purity in "Complainte à Notre-Dame des soirs."

Purity is achieved through renunciation. When man arrives at philosophical awareness, he has a choice:

This freedom . . . can now, at the point at which in its most perfect manifestation it has attained to the completely adequate knowledge of its own nature, express itself anew in two ways. Either it wills here, at the summit of mental endowment and self-consciousness, simply what it willed before blindly and unconsciously, and if so, knowledge always re-

mains a *moving force* for it. . . . Or conversely, this knowledge becomes for
it a *quieter,* which appeases and suppresses all willing.

One of the famous renunciations in symbolist poetry is that of Mal-
larmé's swan, despising the "région où vivre," but a more elaborate one
can be found in the same poet's triptych of sonnets ("Tout Orgueil . . . ,"
"Surgi de la croupe . . . ," and "Une dentelle . . ."). There, we find the
important symbolist motif of the last heir to the manor, who has
realized that reproduction is the madness of the world of blind will and
who dreams only of entering the realm of purity, symbolized by rebirth
from a musical instrument. More explicit developments of the same
theme are to be found in *A rebours,* where Des Esseintes, the last of his
line, surveys the wretchedness of the world of will, and in *Axël,* Villiers
de l'Isle-Adam's striking play:

> C'est elle [la Terre], ne le vois-tu pas, qui est devenue l'Illusion!
> Reconnais-le, Sara: nous avons détruit, dans nos étranges coeurs, l'amour
> de la vie—et c'est bien en REALITE que nous sommes devenus nos âmes!
> Accepter, désormais, de vivre, ne serait plus qu'un sacrilège envers nous-
> mêmes. Vivre? les serviteurs feront cela pour nous.
>
> Vieille terre, je ne bâtirai pas les palais de mes rêves sur ton sol ingrat: je ne
> porterai pas de flambeau, je ne frapperai pas d'ennemis. Puisse la race
> humaine, désabusée de ses vaines chimères, de ses vains désespoirs, et de
> tous les mensonges qui éblouissent les yeux faits pour s'éteindre—ne con-
> sentant plus au jeu de cette morne énigme,—oui, puisse-t-elle finir, en
> s'enfuyant indifférente, à notre exemple, sans t'adresser même un adieu.

Axël's image of becoming one's own soul is a perfect example of the
vocabulary of attenuation and sloughing off the material associated with
the theme of purity. Renunciation, on the practical level of sexuality, is
the subject of Laforgue's "Dimanches," "O Géraniums . . . ," and
"Noire bise . . . ," except that in the last poem, the conclusion, follow-
ing Hartmann's correction of Schopenhauer, is that one must be recon-
ciled to the world of will or the unconscious.

The greatest of myths of renunciation is that of Parsifal (always
spelled in Wagnerian fashion by the symbolists). Schopenhauer explains
saints' lives in philosophical terms:

> Thus it may be that the inner nature of holiness, self-renunciation, mor-
> tification of our own will, asceticism, is here for the first time expressed
> abstractly, and free from all mythical elements, as *denial of the will to live,*
> appearing after the complete knowledge of its own nature has become a
> quieter of all volition.

We see here why, from the mystical imagery of Rimbaud's "Fêtes de la patience" to the frequent liturgical references of Laforgue, Christianity plays such a large role in the work of poets who, with rare exceptions like Saint-Pol Roux, were no longer Christians. Purity is a sacred concept in connotation, even when no theology lies behind it. Merrill's "Chrysostome" is an especially relevant example of the transfer of the religious to poetic purity. The peculiar concept of sin we encounter in the symbolists is also made quite clear by Schopenhauer:

> Certainly the doctrine of original sin (assertion of the will) and of salvation (denial of the will) is the great truth which constitutes the essence of Christianity, while most of what remains is only the clothing of it, the husk or accessories.

We see the significance of "regrets primordiaux" (Kahn's "Vers le plain ciel . . .") and the enormous difference separating the symbolists from Baudelaire, who, however erring, thought in modes clearly reflecting orthodox theology. Baudelaire's poetry is highly ethical in import, whereas for the symbolists good and evil are not in themselves notions of significance; what counts is the metaphysical distinction epitomized by Schopenhauer's willing and non-willing. There is no question of an afterlife for the symbolists: imagination and renunciation replace any life beyond death. Redemption is a poetic idea. These themes constitute, in a sense, a kind of mystique, making up for what Schopenhauer admits to be the inability of philosophy to achieve more than negative knowledge, at most a hint of peace in a will-less state. Essentially, one can only choose between conditions defined largely as to what they are free of:

> We freely acknowledge that what remains after the entire abolition of will is, for all those who are still full of will, certainly nothing; but, conversely, to those in whom the will has turned and has denied itself, this our world, which is so real, with all its suns and milky-ways—is nothing.

Both the life-in-death of the world of the will and the death-in-life of purity are denials of all fecundity except, perhaps, artistic creation. The peculiar character of Schopenhauerian and symbolist pessimism comes from this opposition of two realms which, from an outside point of view, may seem to add up to very much the same thing in the end.

## III

The rendering of such things as ineffable states of purity would seem to demand a new conception of poetry, and indeed the symbolists did a considerable amount of theorizing. Aside from Mallarmé's writings, however, most of the theory is vague and wordy, with much talk of the symbol but little clarity about the actual choice and treatment of symbols. (A selection of theoretical texts may be found in La Doctrine symboliste, ed. Guy Michaud [Paris: A.G. Nizet, 1947].)

It is not perhaps an exaggeration to see in the desire to obscure poetry, to attenuate its sense, a manner of conveying quiet, will-less contemplation: the only way hermetic poetry can be read is with a certain initial indifference to the goal of understanding. Mallarmé spoke on more than one occasion of poetry as a kind of dark evocation or suggestion of something—but not so dark that there was not some "reminiscence of the object." He varied in his notions as to whether this was a really creative artistic mode. In any case, we see that he is defining poetry in the mimetic or representational tradition but drawing as far away as possible from the actual representation of life, without completely breaking with it. Thus the renunciation of the practical world of will corresponds to a diminished perception of objects.

Mallarmé's attempt to define poetry in regard to traditional mimetic terms is not his only major way of conceiving of poetry. He also put forth a much more modern notion of poetry as a structure in which the words "illuminate one another reciprocally," that is, function in relation to each other and not denotatively. This is the "Idea," "music in the Greek sense," "a rhythm of relations." This purely structural idea of poetry is what Mallarmé refers to when he speaks of "taking back poetry's own from music," the nonrepresentational art. Mallarmé had, knowing virtually nothing about music, intuited that what makes music an art is a complex of harmonic, rhythmic, and melodic relationships among notes and that any art, beyond accessory representational values, must be analogous to music.

Mallarmé sometimes specifically states that when he speaks of music he means an ideal, silent music, which is why he also refers to Greek music, of which we have little practical knowledge. He did, however, in his early years, before the elaboration of his ultimate theories about art, make comparisons between symphonic music and complex poetry and express his admiration for the cryptic beauty of musical notes on

paper: a properly esoteric means of expression for art. Mallarmé's con-
temporaries also were much given to musical analogies and the back-
ground to this way of thinking deserves a word or two.

Music has, to a greater or lesser degree, an intellectual and emotional
content which is difficult to paraphrase in words. We can see that this
elusiveness could be felt as comparable to the effect of hermetic poetry,
an even excellent translation of which always seems to leave a large gap
between explanation and the original statement. Notions like ineffable
purity obviously suggest the analogy with unparaphrasable music.
When Mallarmé spoke of music and poetry as two forms of an essential
mystery, he doubtless had in mind not all music and poetry but some
specific passages in each where one has an intense feeling of perfect
communication without denotational values.

At the same time, Mallarmé and his contemporaries were influenced
by the peculiar development of program music and music drama in the
late nineteenth century, which were much discussed in the symbolist
*Revue Wagnérienne*. Wagner had attacked pure music and held out as
ideal a mixed mode of musical expression in which the literary element
and the musical one combine in what some found to be an uneasy rela-
tion. There was a great deal of ambiguity about such music and many
variations in technique (even among, for example, Wagner's operas) for
conveying the programmatic aspect of it. Mahler and Debussy, who
were generally identified with this movement, found themselves de-
stroying programs or putting titles at the ends of pieces so as not to
limit music through words and literality. It is obvious that poets would
find, in any case, a greater degree of analogy between this new musical
mode and their own art and that, without the manifestations of a kind
of music one could tax with impurity and unfaithfulness to itself, the
symbolist comparison between music and poetry would probably not
have been pursued to any great length.

In practical terms, poets could hear only commonplace selections
from Wagner in Paris around 1885; most of the symbolists were quite
ignorant of music, and their thinking on it derived from written sources,
such as the *Revue Wagnérienne,* rather than from any contact with music
itself. Wagner as a *literary* inspiration, however, is not without impor-
tance, as one can see from precise references in poems to the libretto
and stage action of *Parsifal*. In any case, Mallarmé, always more subtle
than his contemporaries, criticized Wagner's music for being too grossly
material, too loud or sensuous, too little the pure manifestation of the
Idea.

After Mallarmé, Verlaine in his "Art poétique" made the most fa-
mous statement of the necessity of music in poetry. His equating of
music with the nine-syllable line and its soft contours suggests the
Wagnerian idea of the endless melody, and his rejection of rhetoric can
be compared with the abandonment of conventionalized sonata form
and other hackneyed musical models—except for the fact that Verlaine
wrote his "Art poétique" years before such things were discussed in
Paris, and he himself had no particular musical culture. Analogies be-
tween music and poetry always run the risk of being purely fanciful
rapprochements, but it remains a profoundly interesting fact that both
Verlaine and Mallarmé, long before they had the faintest inkling of the
new European music of their day, when Offenbach was probably more
familiar to them than even Beethoven, felt the need of a nonrepresenta-
tional way of describing poetry and sensed that music would provide
such a vocabulary.

## IV

While music drama may be impure music, the poetry that was com-
pared in France to contemporary music was felt to be considerably
purer in more than one sense than what had preceded it. An obvious
case is description: Mallarmé, Verlaine, and Rimbaud had defined their
styles in contrast to the orderly, pictorial, mimetic poetry of Leconte de
Lisle and other poets usually called Parnassians. Not raw sense data, but
the sensation of the sensation, or a purified form of sensory experience
was their preference, and we see how poetry drawing on such material
can be compared with experience conveyed through the quintessential
form of music. The vaguely medieval setting of many symbolist poems
results from an attempt to achieve both sensory and metaphysical im-
mediacy without describing anything remotely real. Mallarmé's angel
who gives a purer sense to the words of the tribe is attempting to dis-
sociate words from the practical world of individual material things.

*Eloquence* or rhetoric was the general term Verlaine used in his "Art
poétique" to describe what poetry should not be, and we must under-
stand rhetoric in the general sense of an art of rational, measured, sys-
tematic presentation and development of subject matter or themes.
Most of Baudelaire's poetry, for example, reflects, in a very high form,
the sense of order and division inherent in the spirit of rhetoric. Verlaine
calls *literature,* in a pejorative sense, whatever obeys such principles, and
we find in his work and in that of later poets some new matter and

techniques which were counter to rhetoric such as it had existed up to then in French. Irrational mental phenomena presented in all their disarray constituted a new domain: a strange state of half-dreaming in Verlaine's "Kaléidoscope," delirium in Maeterlinck's "Hôpital," madness in Verhaeren's "Chanson de fou." In Verlaine's "L'espoir luit . . ." and certain of Kahn's poems there seems to be some sort of plot concealed, which we can scarcely make out. Fragments without commentary are used by Laforgue, as in "Complainte de l'orgue de Barbarie," and often syntax is fragmented, as in "Complainte de l'automne monotone." A general lack of explicit articulation between parts gives a certain mystery to Rimbaud's "Mémoire" or Kahn's "Je suis rentré . . ." The patterns of Rimbaud's "Bateau ivre" and Mallarmé's "Ses purs ongles . . ." are not the ordinary kinds of traditional allegorical-symbolic structures to which one can easily assign a single general meaning. Finally, allusion is handled in a new, surprising way in such a poem as Laforgue's "Complainte du roi de Thulé," with its pertinent but indirect reference to Goethe's ballad. In all of these cases we must do without the fullness and univocity of sense that rhetoric traditionally assured.

The form which offers the most striking potential for elliptical or implicit meaning is probably the song. While real songs, of course, may vary a great deal in the completeness and overtness of their meaning, the symbolists had as their ideal a kind of slim, allusive, even obscure song such as might have come from centuries of erosion of sense in the singing of it. Verlaine provided the model in his "songs without words," inexplicit as the expression suggests, and Rimbaud worked along with him in the same mode. In Moréas, Kahn, Merrill, and others we find attempts to create this kind of song, which seems to have been unknown, in any folkloric form it had in France, to city-bred poets. The symbolists actually felt their model was more a German one and occasionally designated their poems as *Lieder*.

It was not only the imitation of folk song which led away from the traditional rhetoric of French poetry; song poems drawing on a more urban or proletarian inspiration brought in new subject matter and forms of expression in Elskamp and Laforgue. They imported into poetry material outside the traditional domain of high culture, and in this they had a striking predecessor in Corbière, with his bohemian, argot-colored manner. This surprising range of late nineteenth-century French poetry from the exquisite, the precious even, to the popular is one of the most remarkable things about it and reminds us of the coexistence with symbolism in France of the taste for literary realism. All these forms of the antirhetorical contribute to the formation of modernist esthetics, which, we must remember, have their origins in the symbolist period: Corbière and Laforgue's use of slang obeys basically the same rejection of academic verse styles as does Mallarmé's hermetic manner, and brings us back to that contempt for the public generally considered literate which we noted at the beginning of this account of the decadent-symbolist movement.

# V

In strictly formal matters the banishment of rhetoric brought about an intensification of tendencies already at work in French poetry. The history of French versification since the late seventeenth century might be described as a process of progressive destruction of the symmetrical patterns associated with high neoclassicism. The ideal of the closed alexandrine couplet with medial caesuras and similarly strict, balanced patterns represents the extreme form of the principle of regularity. The innovations of the romantic era—frequent enjambment, free strong pauses within the line, the alexandrine divided into three equal parts—tend toward unpredictability of form. The work of the symbolists, after Hugo's example, continues this tendency, but in many ways their most innovative poems may be said to pass beyond the point where the classic structure of French verse remains perceptible. They wrote entire poems in lines of nine, eleven, and thirteen syllables, which are difficult for the ear to seize on and classify. Besides the romantic alexandrine (4/4/4), they extensively used one, found occasionally in Hugo, of three irregular sections (3/4/5) arranged in any order. Strange stanzas were invented, especially by Laforgue: 9/9/5/12/12/9 in the "Complainte de l'automne monotone" or 10/10/7/3/14 in the "Complainte du pauvre chevalier-errant." Extremely short lines are frequent, valued for their fluid quality.

Rhyme theory may be said to follow the evolution of poetic vocabulary: as the vocabulary increased, rare rhyme and rich rhyme came to be admired, beginning with the romantics. The symbolists likewise prized extraordinary combinations such as *désir, Idées/des Iridées, anses/Hanses,* and *lactescent/descend.* Repeating a word instead of making a rhyme constitutes another full use of recurring sounds. The tendency away from rhyme, however, is also present: there are blank lines, as in Moréas's "Agnès," or whole stanzas of them, as in Rimbaud's "Bannières de mai." Assonance was also used by Rimbaud instead of rhyme: *auberge/ perche*. In other words, the new poetry aimed at great variety of effects rather than pursuing one kind exclusively. Old rules were broken: poems were written all in masculine or all in feminine rhymes (Verlaine's "Bruxelles" I and II); masculine and feminine forms were made to rhyme together (*tel/immortelle*). This profusion of devices diminishes any element of predictability in versification, as does the use of *rimes mêlées* or irregular rhymes. The confining of repeated sounds to the end of the line, that is, regular end-rhyme, is abandoned: "Des lointains, des teints, des pantins," "la nuance seule fiance/Le rêve au rêve." With sounds recurring sporadically, the whole symmetrical idea of rhyme is destroyed. Much use of alliteration ("Je me mire et me vois ange! et j'aime . . ."), as well as of inner rhyme, further impairs the neat traditional pattern of confining repetitions to the ends of lines. We see an extremely fluid approach to the whole question of sound in poetry. Puns are used, like Corbière's employment of *âme* in the sense of "sounding-post" (of a violin, guitar) as well as "soul," or Apollinaire's "Les humains savent tant de jeux, l'amour, la mourre," in which the rare *la mourre* designates a children's game played with the fingers (*la mora* in Italian). All these manifold devices bring us closer to the elaborate prosody of the late Middle Ages and of the poets called *les grands rhétoriqueurs* or to the sound patterns of Renaissance theory of figures.

Free verse was the ultimate outcome of symbolist experiments in prosody. It is usually rhymed, but in an often irregular fashion. Lines must often be scanned dropping certain mute *e*'s, the pronunciation of which sounds too strange by spoken standards, although others are kept which have a merely formal effect. In this way, many lines that at first appear to be odd in length become familiar ones. Yet there are in these poets very odd lines indeed, ranging from thirteen to twenty-one syllables. Each free-verse poet, furthermore, tends to have an esthetic of his own in regard to his choice of elements of prosody.

# VI

The following selections do not include the work of all poets associated with symbolism but only of those who have recognizable voices of their own. The amount of space accorded each poet depends not only on the amount of verse of reasonable quality he wrote, but also on peculiarities of genre: Régnier, for example, is most distinctive in certain long poems, hence the number of pages he receives; Rodenbach and Kahn, on the other hand, both very interesting poets, worked in the short lyric almost exclusively and do not occupy so much space. No poem has been given in a cut form, although that meant leaving out Albert Mockel's curious *Chantefable un peu naïve*. Prose poems are excluded, since, in the period in question, not enough poets wrote good ones for a real picture of the genre to emerge. Poets of the 1880's and '90s who simply have little to do with the symbolist manner, like Vielé-Griffin, are also omitted. The work of the great precursors, Mallarmé, Verlaine, and Rimbaud, is presented in only those aspects of their work which have the most significance for later poetry. Finally, Valéry and Apollinaire are only minimally represented: their work is, of course, most pertinent to the history of symbolism and could have been extensively drawn upon, but that would have distorted the temporal focus we have maintained.

For further reading see:

Anna Balakian, *The Symbolist Movement: A Critical Appraisal* (New York: Random House, 1967).

John Porter Houston, *French Symbolism and the Modernist Movement: A Study of Poetic Structures* (Baton Rouge: Louisiana State University Press, 1980).

James R. Lawler, *The Language of French Symbolism* (Princeton: Princeton University Press,1969).

Henri Peyre, *Qu'est-ce que le symbolisme?* (Paris: Presses universitaires de France, 1974).

Roger Shattuck, *The Banquet Years: The Origins of the Avant Garde in France, 1885 to World War I*, rev. ed. (New York: Vintage Books, 1968).

For the related movement in painting see:

Philippe Jullian, *Dreamers of Decadence* (New York: Praeger, 1971).

# STEPHANE MALLARME

## Soupir

Mon âme vers ton front où rêve, ô calme soeur,
Un automne jonché de taches de rousseur,
Et vers le ciel errant de ton oeil angélique
Monte, comme dans un jardin mélancolique,
Fidèle, un blanc jet d'eau soupire vers l'Azur!
—Vers l'Azur attendri d'Octobre pâle et pur
Qui mire aux grands bassins sa langueur infinie
Et laisse, sur l'eau morte où la fauve agonie
Des feuilles erre au vent et creuse un froid sillon,
Se traîner le soleil jaune d'un long rayon.

*Poésies*

## Sigh

My soul rises toward your brow, O calm sister, on which dreams a
bespeckled autumn, and toward the changing sky of your angelic eye; it
rises, as in a melancholy garden a faithful white fountain spray sighs
toward the blue sky—toward the tender blue sky of October, pale and
clear, reflecting its infinite languor in the great pools of the fountain and
trailing a long languid yellow sunbeam on the still water, where leaves
in their tawny death drift before the wind and trace a cold wake.

## Les Fenêtres

Las du triste hôpital, et de l'encens fétide
Qui monte en la blancheur banale des rideaux
Vers le grand crucifix ennuyé du mur vide,
Le moribond sournois y redresse un vieux dos,

Se traîne et va, moins pour chauffer sa pourriture
Que pour voir du soleil sur les pierres, coller
Les poils blancs et les os de la maigre figure
Aux fenêtres qu'un beau rayon clair veut hâler.

Et la bouche, fiévreuse et d'azur bleu vorace,
Telle, jeune, elle alla respirer son trésor,
Une peau virginale et de jadis! encrasse
D'un long baiser amer les tièdes carreaux d'or.

Ivre, il vit, oubliant l'horreur des saintes huiles,
Les tisanes, l'horloge et le lit infligé,
La toux; et quand le soir saigne parmi les tuiles,
Son oeil, à l'horizon de lumière gorgé,

Voit des galères d'or, belles comme des cygnes
Sur un fleuve de pourpre et de parfums dormir
En berçant l'éclair fauve et riche de leurs lignes
Dans un grand nonchaloir chargé de souvenir!

Ainsi, pris du dégoût de l'homme à l'âme dure
Vautré dans le bonheur, où ses seuls appétits
Mangent, et qui s'entête à chercher cette ordure
Pour l'offrir à la femme allaitant ses petits,

Je fuis et je m'accroche à toutes les croisées
D'où l'on tourne l'épaule à la vie, et, béni,
Dans leur verre, lavé d'éternelles rosées,
Que dore le matin chaste de l'Infini

Je me mire et me vois ange! et je meurs, et j'aime
—Que la vitre soit l'art, soit la mysticité—
A renaître, portant mon rêve en diadème,
Au ciel antérieur où fleurit la Beauté!

Mais, hélas! Ici-bas est maître: sa hantise
Vient m'écoeurer parfois jusqu'en cet abri sûr,
Et le vomissement impur de la Bêtise
Me force à me boucher le nez devant l'azur.

Est-il moyen, ô Moi qui connais l'amertume,
D'enfoncer le cristal par le monstre insulté
Et de m'enfuir, avec mes deux ailes sans plume
—Au risque de tomber pendant l'éternité?

*Poésies*

## The Windows

Tired of the gloomy hospital and of the fetid incense rising along the banal white curtains toward the great weary crucifix on the bare wall, the sly dying man straightens up his aged back, drags himself along, and, less to warm his rotting body than to see sunlight on the stones, goes to the windows that a bright beam is toasting and against which he glues his white hair and bones of his thin face. And his mouth, feverish and hungry for blue sky, such as his mouth was, when, as a young man, he went to smell his treasure, a virgin skin of the old days—his mouth soils the warm gold panes with a long bitter kiss. Intoxicated, he lives and forgets the horrible holy unction, the medicinal teas, the clock, the bed forced on him, and his cough. And when evening bleeds over the roofs, his eye, devouring light along the horizon, sees golden galleys, beautiful as swans, dozing on a river of purple and perfumes, gently rocking their brilliant, rich, tawny lines in a great calm laden with memories. So I, disgusted at hard-souled men wallowing in happiness, where their appetites alone feed, and stubbornly seeking this filth to offer their females suckling their young, so I flee and hang onto any window from which one can turn one's back on life, and, blessed, I look at myself in the window-glass washed by eternal dew and gilded by the chaste dawn of eternity, I look at myself and I am an angel! and I die and I am enraptured—whether the window be art or mysticism—at being reborn, with my dream like a diadem on my forehead, under the primeval sky where beauty flowers. But, alas, this earth is master: it haunts me and nauseates me sometimes even in this safe shelter, and the vile vomit of stupidity makes me hold my nose as I contemplate the azure. Is there a way that I, who know bitterness, could break through the crystal befouled by the monster and flee with my two featherless wings—at the risk of falling for all eternity?

## Hérodiade—Scène

### La Nourrice—Hérodiade

#### N.

Tu vis! ou vois-je ici l'ombre d'une princesse?
A mes lèvres tes doigts et leurs bagues et cesse
De marcher dans un âge ignoré...

#### H.

                              Reculez.
Le blond torrent de mes cheveux immaculés
Quand il baigne mon corps solitaire le glace
D'horreur, et mes cheveux que la lumière enlace

Sont immortels. O femme, un baiser me tûrait
Si la beauté n'était la mort...

                       Par quel attrait
Menée et quel matin oublié des prophètes
Verse, sur les lointains mourants, ses tristes fêtes,
Le sais-je? tu m'as vue, ô nourrice d'hiver,
Sous la lourde prison de pierres et de fer
Où de mes vieux lions traînent les siècles fauves
Entrer, et je marchais, fatale, les mains sauves,
Dans le parfum désert de ces anciens rois:
Mais encore as-tu vu quels furent mes effrois?
Je m'arrête rêvant aux exils, et j'effeuille,
Comme près d'un bassin dont le jet d'eau m'accueille,
Les pâles lys qui sont en moi, tandis qu'épris
De suivre du regard les languides débris
Descendre, à travers ma rêverie, en silence,
Les lions, de ma robe écartent l'indolence
Et regardent mes pieds qui calmeraient la mer.
Calme, toi, les frissons de ta sénile chair,
Viens et ma chevelure imitant les manières
Trop farouches qui font votre peur des crinières,
Aide-moi, puisqu'ainsi tu n'oses plus me voir,
A me peigner nonchalamment dans un miroir.

### N.

Sinon la myrrhe gaie en ses bouteilles closes,
De l'essence ravie aux vieillesses de roses,
Voulez-vous, mon enfant, essayer la vertu
Funèbre?

### H.

                 Laisse là ces parfums! ne sais-tu
Que je les hais, nourrice, et veux-tu que je sente
Leur ivresse noyer ma tête languissante?
Je veux que mes cheveux qui ne sont pas des fleurs
A répandre l'oubli des humaines douleurs,
Mais de l'or, à jamais vierge des aromates,
Dans leurs éclairs cruels et dans leurs pâleurs mates,
Observent la froideur stérile du métal,
Vous ayant reflétés, joyaux du mur natal,
Armes, vases depuis ma solitaire enfance.

N.

Pardon! l'âge effaçait, reine, votre défense
De mon esprit pâli comme un vieux livre ou noir...

H.

Assez! Tiens devant moi ce miroir.

O miroir!

Eau froide par l'ennui dans ton cadre gelée
Que de fois et pendant des heures, désolée
Des songes et cherchant mes souvenirs qui sont
Comme des feuilles sous ta glace au trou profond,
Je m'apparus en toi comme une ombre lointaine,
Mais, horreur! des soirs, dans ta sévère fontaine,
J'ai de mon rêve épars connu la nudité!

Nourrice, suis-je belle?

N.

Un astre, en vérité
Mais cette tresse tombe...

H.

Arrête dans ton crime
Qui refroidit mon sang vers sa source, et réprime
Ce geste, impiété fameuse: ah! conte-moi
Quel sûr démon te jette en le sinistre émoi,
Ce baiser, ces parfums offerts et, le dirai-je?
O mon coeur, cette main encore sacrilège,
Car tu voulais, je crois, me toucher, sont un jour
Qui ne finira pas sans malheur sur la tour...
O jour qu'Hérodiade avec effroi regarde!

N.

Temps bizarre, en effet, de quoi le ciel vous garde!
Vous errez, ombre seule et nouvelle fureur,
Et regardant en vous précoce avec terreur;
Mais toujours adorable autant qu'une immortelle,
O mon enfant, et belle affreusement et telle
Que...

H.

Mais n'allais-tu pas me toucher?

N.

...J'aimerais
Etre à qui le destin réserve vos secrets.

H.

Oh! tais-toi!

N.

Viendra-t-il parfois?

H.

Étoiles pures,

N'entendez pas!

N.

Comment, sinon parmi d'obscures
Épouvantes, songer plus implacable encor
Et comme suppliant le dieu que le trésor
De votre grâce attend! et pour qui, dévorée
D'angoisses, gardez-vous la splendeur ignorée
Et le mystère vain de votre être?

H.

Pour moi.

N.

Triste fleur qui croît seule et n'a pas d'autre émoi
Que son ombre dans l'eau vue avec atonie.

H.

Va, garde ta pitié comme ton ironie.

N.

Toutefois expliquez: oh! non, naïve enfant,
Décroîtra, quelque jour, ce dédain triomphant.

H.

Mais qui me toucherait, des lions respectée?
Du reste, je ne veux rien d'humain et, sculptée,
Si tu me vois les yeux perdus au paradis,
C'est quand je me souviens de ton lait bu jadis.

N.

Victime lamentable à son destin offerte!

## H.

Oui, c'est pour moi, pour moi, que je fleuris, déserte!
Vous le savez, jardins d'améthyste, enfouis
Sans fin dans de savants abîmes éblouis,
Ors ignorés, gardant votre antique lumière
Sous le sombre sommeil d'une terre première,
Vous, pierres où mes yeux comme de purs bijoux
Empruntent leur clarté mélodieuse, et vous
Métaux qui donnez à ma jeune chevelure
Une splendeur fatale et sa massive allure!
Quant à toi, femme née en des siècles malins
Pour la méchanceté des antres sibyllins,
Qui parles d'un mortel! selon qui, des calices
De mes robes, arôme aux farouches délices,
Sortirait le frisson blanc de ma nudité,
Prophétise que si le tiède azur d'été,
Vers lui nativement la femme se dévoile,
Me voit dans ma pudeur grelottante d'étoile,
Je meurs!
        J'aime l'horreur d'être vierge et je veux
Vivre parmi l'effroi que me font mes cheveux
Pour, le soir, retirée en ma couche, reptile
Inviolé sentir en la chair inutile
Le froid scintillement de ta pâle clarté
Toi qui te meurs, toi qui brûles de chasteté
Nuit blanche de glaçons et de neige cruelle!
Et ta soeur solitaire, ô ma soeur éternelle
Mon rêve montera vers toi: telle déjà,
Rare limpidité d'un coeur qui le songea,
Je me crois seule en ma monotone patrie
Et tout, autour de moi, vit dans l'idolâtrie
D'un miroir qui reflète en son calme dormant
Hérodiade au clair regard de diamant...
O charme dernier, oui! je le sens, je suis seule.

## N.

Madame, allez-vous donc mourir?

## H.

        Non, pauvre aïeule,
Sois calme et, t'éloignant, pardonne à ce coeur dur,

Mais avant, si tu veux, clos les volets, l'azur
Séraphique sourit dans les vitres profondes,
Et je déteste, moi, le bel azur!

                    Des ondes
Se bercent et, là-bas, sais-tu pas un pays
Où le sinistre ciel ait les regards haïs
De Vénus qui, le soir, brûle dans le feuillage:
J'y partirais.

               Allume encore, enfantillage
Dis-tu, ces flambeaux où la cire au feu léger
Pleure parmi l'or vain quelque pleur étranger
Et...

N.

Maintenant?

H.
Adieu.

                 Vous mentez, ô fleur nue
De mes lèvres.

             J'attends une chose inconnue
Ou peut-être, ignorant le mystère et vos cris,
Jetez-vous les sanglots suprêmes et meurtris
D'une enfance sentant parmi les rêveries
Se séparer enfin ses froides pierreries.

*Poésies*

## Herodias—Scene

The Nurse, Herodias. N: You are still alive! Or am I seeing the ghost of a princess? Let me kiss your fingers and their rings, and cease your wandering through some unknown world. H: Do not touch my hand. The blond torrent of my spotless hair, as it envelops my solitary body, freezes it with horror, and my hair, laced with light, is immortal. O woman, a kiss would kill me, if beauty were not already death. Do I know what drew me on or what special day, forgotten by the prophets, this is, which in the dying distance displays its sad festivities? But, wintry nurse, you did indeed see me go down into the heavy prison of iron and stone where my old lions spend their tawny years, and drawn by fate, my hands perfectly safe, I wandered amidst the deserted scent of these former kings. But did you perceive my terror? I stopped, thinking of exile, and, as if by the edge of a fountain whose spray welcomed me, I stripped the petals from the pale lilies of my thought, while, fascinated at watching the debris of the flowers slowly, silently float down, the lions nuzzled open the folds of my robe and looked upon my feet which could calm the sea. Quiet the urges of your aged flesh to kiss me. Come, and since my hair has that wild, disheveled look which makes you terrified of the lions' manes, since you cannot bear to see me looking thus, help me to comb myself tranquilly in a mirror. N: My child, would you like to try the funereal scent of essence of old roses, if you cannot bear the perfume of myrrh, cheerful in its tight bottles? H: Enough of perfumes. Do you not know, nurse, that I hate them? And do you want me to feel my languishing head succumb to their intoxication? My hair is not a flower wafting oblivion of human ills but gold, and I want it, forever virgin of aromatics, with its cruel highlights and mat pallors, to borrow the sterile chill of metal, since from my childhood on, it has reflected you, O jewels, arms, vases on the wall of my native castle! N: Pardon, Queen. Age had erased your injunction from my memory grown pale or dark like some old book. H: Enough. Hold this mirror before me. O mirror! Frigid water frozen in your frame by ennui! How many times and for how many hours, when I was despairing at dreams and searching for my memories which are like leaves under your ice with its gaping hole, I appeared in you like some distant shadow—but, O horror, on certain evenings, in your merciless spring, I have come to know in its nakedness my dream, otherwise fragmented and dispersed. Nurse, am I beautiful? N: A star, in truth! But that tress is falling down. H: Cease before you commit the crime of touching me, a crime which chills my blood to my very heart, and control your hand in its great impious gesture. Ah! tell me what sinister demon is impelling you today, that you tried to kiss my hand, offer me perfumes, and, dare I mention it, O my heart, extend your sacrilegious hand toward my hair! For I actually believe you wanted to touch me! All these signs indicate that this is a day that will not end without some dire event on the tower! O day Herodias contemplates with terror! N: These are strange times indeed, and I hope they will bring you no harm. You are wandering about like a lonely ghost or a new fury, gazing into your precocious self with terror—but still as worthy of worship as a goddess, O my child, and dreadfully beautiful and looking such that. . . . H: But were you not going to touch me? N: I should like to be the man for whom destiny is saving your secrets. H: Silence! N: Will he come sometime? H: Pure stars, do not hear! N: How can I imagine him, the god whom the treasure of your grace awaits, how could I imagine him other than as more implacable for being surrounded by mysterious terrors and yet, as it were, a suppliant? For whom else do you, devoured by anguish, preserve the unknown splendor and useless mystery of your being? H: For myself. N: That would make you a sad flower growing alone, with no other source of feelings than its own shadow glimpsed listlessly in the water. H: Enough. Keep your pity to yourself as well as your irony. N: But explain to me your notion—ah, no, naïve child, some day your haughty disdain will diminish. H: But who would dare to touch me, whom the lions respect? Moreover, I wish for nothing human, and, if you see me, like a statue, with my eyes glazedly looking to heaven, that is when I recall your milk drunk long ago. N: Pitiable victim offered up to her destiny. H: Yes, it is for me, for me that I flower alone! You know it, O amethyst gardens buried endlessly deep, in cunning radiant chasms, O gold unknown, preserving your ancient light under the dark sleep of a primeval land; you know it, stones from which my eyes like pure gems borrow their melodious brilliance, and you, O metals which give my young hair a fateful splendor and its massive air. As for you, woman born in evil times to match the spiteful sibyls in their caves, you, who talk of a mortal and suppose that my shuddering white naked body would emerge from the calyx of my robes like some aroma elusive in its delightfulness, I tell you to prophesy that if the warm blue sky of summer (before which women instinctively bare themselves) sees me like a naked star shivering with shame, I shall die! I love the horror of being virgin, and I want to live in the terror my hair conveys to me and in the evening, withdrawn into my couch, like an inviolate reptile, to feel in my useless flesh the cold sparkle of your pale brilliance, O night white with ice and cruel snow, night dying and burning with chastity! And your solitary sister, O my eternal sister, O moon, my dream will rise toward you. Like you and with the strange clarity needed to conceive it, I believe myself alone in my monotonous land, and the whole world around me lives to idolize the mirror which reflects, in its somnolent calm, Herodias and her bright diamondlike gaze. O ultimate enchantment, yes, I feel it, I am alone. N: Madam, are you going to die? H: No, poor crone. Be calm and, as you go, pardon my hard heart. But first, if you will, close the shutters; the seraphic blue sky smiles in the deep windows, and I hate the beautiful blue. Waves are undulating, and far away you know there is a country whose sinister sky has the face of Venus, which I hate, Venus, who in the evening smoulders in the woods. I might go there. Please, even if you think it is childish, light those tapers, whose wax, in the light fire, will form an alien tear dropping on the useless gold receptacle. N: Now? H: Farewell. You lie, O bare flower of my lips. I am expecting something unknown. Or perhaps you are uttering the last, injured sob of my childhood, which, ignorant of the nature of the mystery and of your cries, is feeling, in the midst of its reveries, its cold jewels finally part.

## Le Tombeau d'Edgar Poe

Tel qu'en Lui-même enfin l'éternité le change,
Le Poëte suscite avec un glaive nu
Son siècle épouvanté de n'avoir pas connu
Que la mort triomphait dans cette voix étrange!

Eux, comme un vil sursaut d'hydre oyant jadis l'ange
Donner un sens plus pur aux mots de la tribu
Proclamèrent très haut le sortilège bu
Dans le flot sans honneur de quelque noir mélange.

Du sol et de la nue hostiles, ô grief!
Si notre idée avec ne sculpte un bas-relief
Dont la tombe de Poe éblouissante s'orne,

Calme bloc ici-bas chu d'un désastre obscur,
Que ce granit du moins montre à jamais sa borne
Aux noirs vols du Blasphème épars dans le futur.

*Poésies*

## The Tomb of Edgar Allan Poe

Appearing such as eternity has transformed him into his real self, the poet awakens with a bare sword his century terrified at not having recognized that death triumphed in his strange voice. Like some vile writhing hydra long ago hearing the angel give a purer sense to the words of the tribe, they proclaimed his magic came from drinking some base black potion. O lament over the mutual hostility of heaven and earth! If, with it, our idea doesn't succeed in sculpting a bas-relief to adorn Poe's dazzling tomb, let this granite, a calm block fallen on earth from some obscure disaster among the stars, establish forever a limit for the black flights of blasphemy scattered in the future.

# Prose

*pour des Esseintes.*

Hyperbole! de ma mémoire
Triomphalement ne sais-tu
Te lever, aujourd'hui grimoire
Dans un livre de fer vêtu:

Car j'installe, par la science,
L'hymne des coeurs spirituels
En l'oeuvre de ma patience,
Atlas, herbiers et rituels.

Nous promenions notre visage
(Nous fûmes deux, je le maintiens)
Sur maints charmes de paysage,
O soeur, y comparant les tiens.

L'ère d'autorité se trouble
Lorsque, sans nul motif, on dit
De ce midi que notre double
Inconscience approfondit

Que, sol des cent iris, son site,
Ils savent s'il a bien été,
Ne porte pas de nom que cite
L'or de la trompette d'Eté.

Oui, dans une île que l'air charge
De vue et non de visions
Toute fleur s'étalait plus large
Sans que nous en devisions.

Telles, immenses, que chacune
Ordinairement se para
D'un lucide contour, lacune,
Qui des jardins la sépara.

Gloire du long désir, Idées
Tout en moi s'exaltait de voir
La famille des iridées
Surgir à ce nouveau devoir,

Mais cette soeur sensée et tendre
Ne porta son regard plus loin

Que sourire et, comme à l'entendre
J'occupe mon antique soin.

Oh! sache l'Esprit de litige,
A cette heure où nous nous taisons,
Que de lis multiples la tige
Grandissait trop pour nos raisons

Et non comme pleure la rive,
Quand son jeu monotone ment
A vouloir que l'ampleur arrive
Parmi mon jeune étonnement

D'ouïr tout le ciel et la carte
Sans fin attestés sur mes pas,
Par le flot même qui s'écarte,
Que ce pays n'exista pas.

L'enfant abdique son extase
Et docte déjà par chemins
Elle dit le mot: Anastase!
Né pour d'éternels parchemins,

Avant qu'un sépulcre ne rie
Sous aucun climat, son aïeul,
De porter ce nom: Pulchérie!
Caché par le trop grand glaïeul.

*Poésies*

## Hymn for Des Esseintes

Hyperbole! can you not rise triumphantly from my memory, now that you are a book of magic with iron clasps? For I install, through science, the hymn of spiritual hearts in the work of my patience: atlases, herbals, and rituals. We were gazing about (I insist there were two of us) on many a charm of the landscape and comparing your charms, O sister, to them. The age of profane authority is disturbed when, for no reason, we say that this south which we both unconsciously absorbed, that this land of a hundred iris, that this site bears no name recorded by summer's golden trumpet. (But they know whether it really existed.) Yes, in an island whose air was heavy with sight—and not mere visions—all the flowers grew bigger without our saying a thing about it. They were immense and such that each one, for the most part, was decorated with a shining halo, a kind of hole, which separated it from the rest of the garden. Glory of our long desire, Ideas! I was completely enraptured to see the iridaceae rise to this new challenge. But my sensible and tender sister did not stare but merely smiled, and as if I heard her speak, I busied myself with my old task. Oh, let the spirit of contention know that at that hour when we were silent, the many lilies on their stems grew too huge for our comprehension, and let it not say that that country did not exist—as the people on the shore seem to moan, when its monotonous water falsely suggests that the whole ample island was an illusion coming from my naïve astonishment at hearing the parting waves at my feet seemingly attest to the existence of every kind of heaven and earth. My sister renounces her ecstasy and, learned already in the ways of creation, said the word Arise!, born for eternal parchments. She spoke before the sight could vanish and there be left only the grave of beauty in its ancestral land, ironically bearing the name Pulcheria and half-hidden by some too huge gladiolus.

Quand l'ombre menaça de la fatale loi
Tel vieux Rêve, désir et mal de mes vertèbres,
Affligé de périr sous les plafonds funèbres
Il a ployé son aile indubitable en moi.

Luxe, ô salle d'ébène où, pour séduire un roi
Se tordent dans leur mort des guirlandes célèbres,
Vous n'êtes qu'un orgueil menti par les ténèbres
Aux yeux du solitaire ébloui de sa foi.

Oui, je sais qu'au lointain de cette nuit, la Terre
Jette d'un grand éclat l'insolite mystère,
Sous les siècles hideux qui l'obscurcissent moins.

L'espace à soi pareil qu'il s'accroisse ou se nie
Roule dans cet ennui des feux vils pour témoins
Que s'est d'un astre en fête allumé le génie.

*Poésies*

When, with its fateful regularity, the shadow of night threatened some old dream, which is like a painful desire at the back of my neck, my dream like a bird, desolate at dying under the funereal ceiling of night, folded in me its wings, real and suffering. O Night, ebony hall, where dying constellations of royal splendor writhe like luxurious and famous garlands, you are only a lie, the false pride of the shadow, in the eyes of the solitary poet dazzled by his faith in his art. Yes, I know that seen from far in this night, the earth casts the rare mystery of a great brillance in the hideous realms of time, which can no longer darken it as before. Space, always the same whether its existence is magnified or denied, rolls wearily with its vile stars, bearing witness that the genius of a festive planet has lit up.

Le vierge, le vivace et le bel aujourd'hui
Va-t-il nous déchirer avec un coup d'aile ivre
Ce lac dur oublié que hante sous le givre
Le transparent glacier des vols qui n'ont pas fui!

Un cygne d'autrefois se souvient que c'est lui
Magnifique mais qui sans espoir se délivre
Pour n'avoir pas chanté la région où vivre
Quand du stérile hiver a resplendi l'ennui.

Tout son col secouera cette blanche agonie
Par l'espace infligée à l'oiseau qui le nie,
Mais non l'horreur du sol où le plumage est pris.

Fantôme qu'à ce lieu son pur éclat assigne,
Il s'immobilise au songe froid de mépris
Que vêt parmi l'exil inutile le Cygne.

*Poésies*

"Will the pure, hardy, beautiful new day tear me free, with a drunken slap of its wing, from this hard forgotten lake, where I am haunted, under the frost, by the thought, like a transparent glacier, of flights I did not make?" A swan of old times remembers that, though a mighty creature, he struggles vainly to free himself, a prisoner because he did not sing or flee to the regions of life, when weary, sterile winter shone. He will shake off the death agony of snow from his long neck, the agony inflicted on him by the regions of space whose existence he denies, but he cannot shake himself loose from the horrible ground where his wings are caught. He is now a ghost, assigned to this spot by his pure brilliance, and remains motionless in his cold dream of contempt for other regions, the dream he is wrapped in during his useless exile.

Victorieusement fui le suicide beau
Tison de gloire, sang par écume, or, tempête!
O rire si là-bas une pourpre s'apprête
A ne tendre royal que mon absent tombeau.

Quoi! de tout cet éclat pas même le lambeau
S'attarde, il est minuit, à l'ombre qui nous fête
Excepté qu'un trésor présomptueux de tête
Verse son caressé nonchaloir sans flambeau,

La tienne si toujours le délice! la tienne
Oui seule qui du ciel évanoui retienne
Un peu de puéril triomphe en t'en coiffant

Avec clarté quand sur les coussins tu la poses
Comme un casque guerrier d'impératrice enfant
Dont pour te figurer il tomberait des roses.

*Poésies*

I have victoriously avoided the same suicide as the sun—that glorious fire-brand, foaming blood, gold, storm!—and I laugh if in the distance the evening purple is beginning to drape my royal tomb—which doesn't exist! What! Now that it is midnight not one shred remains, in this festive shadow, of all that brilliant light—except that your precious head, presumptuous in competing with the sun, pours out its torchless cool light, which I caress—your head, always so much my delight, your head, yes, which alone preserves a bit of juvenilely triumphant light from the vanished sunset and thus coifs you with radiance when you lay your head on a pillow, like some child empress's battle helmet, from which roses fall to form your face.

Ses purs ongles très haut dédiant leur onyx,
L'Angoisse, ce minuit, soutient, lampadophore,
Maint rêve vespéral brûlé par le Phénix
Que ne recueille pas de cinéraire amphore

Sur les crédences, au salon vide: nul ptyx,
Aboli bibelot d'inanité sonore,
(Car le Maître est allé puiser des pleurs au Styx
Avec ce seul objet dont le Néant s'honore).

Mais proche la croisée au nord vacante, un or
Agonise selon peut-être le décor
Des licornes ruant du feu contre une nixe,

Elle, défunte nue en le miroir, encor
Que, dans l'oubli fermé par le cadre, se fixe
De scintillations sitôt le septuor.

*Poésies*

In an act of consecration, this midnight, the lamp-statue of Anguish raises high its pure black fingernails, as if supporting the ashen remains of many an evening dream burnt up by the Phoenix of the sunset and not gathered in any funereal urn. On the sideboards, in the empty salon, there is no ptyx, a suppressed knick-knack in which emptiness echoes—for the Master has gone to seek tears from the Styx with this object which, alone, nothingness will recognize. But near the window opening onto the north, there is dying gold light, perhaps from the representation in relief, on the frame of a mirror, of unicorns throwing fire at a watersprite. The image of the naked sprite has vanished in the mirror, although, in the oblivion the frame encloses, soon there will be fixed the seven sparkling stars of the Big Dipper.

I

Tout Orgueil fume-t-il du soir,
Torche dans un branle étouffée
Sans que l'immortelle bouffée
Ne puisse à l'abandon surseoir!

La chambre ancienne de l'hoir
De maint riche mais chu trophée
Ne serait pas même chauffée
S'il survenait par le couloir.

Affres du passé nécessaires
Agrippant comme avec des serres
Le sépulcre de désaveu,

Sous un marbre lourd qu'elle isole
Ne s'allume pas d'autre feu
Que la fulgurante console.

## II

Surgi de la croupe et du bond
D'une verrerie éphémère
Sans fleurir la veillée amère
Le col ignoré s'interrompt.

Je crois bien que deux bouches n'ont
Bu, ni son amant ni ma mère,
Jamais à la même Chimère,
Moi, sylphe de ce froid plafond!

Le pur vase d'aucun breuvage
Que l'inexhaustible veuvage
Agonise mais ne consent,

Naïf baiser des plus funèbres!
A rien expirer annonçant
Une rose dans les ténèbres.

## III

Une dentelle s'abolit
Dans le doute du Jeu suprême
A n'entr'ouvrir comme un blasphème
Qu'absence éternelle de lit.

Cet unanime blanc conflit
D'une guirlande avec la même,
Enfui contre la vitre blême
Flotte plus qu'il n'ensevelit.

Mais, chez qui du rêve se dore
Tristement dort une mandore
Au creux néant musicien

Telle que vers quelque fenêtre
Selon nul ventre que le sien,
Filial on aurait pu naître.

*Poésies*

I. All family pride is glorious as a sunset, and, extinguished as one shakes and smothers a torch, it gives off an immortal puff of smoke, which, however, cannot survive neglect. If the heir of many a rich trophy, fallen from the walls, came back through the hallway into his room, he would not find it even heated. There is no light from a fire, but merely the last glint of sun on the dazzling gilt legs of the console, on which lions' claws grasp the heavy marble top, which is like the tombstone of the heir's disavowal, in this spectacle of the inevitable death-throes of the past. II. Rising steeply from the base of an ephemeral glass vase, which no one has paid any attention to, the neck stops abruptly, for it is not continued by the stem of any flower, relieving the bitterness of the evening. I, the sylph painted on this cold ceiling, am sure neither my mother nor her lover ever drank from the same dream. The vase empty of any liquid other than endless widowhood is dying but will not consent even to suggest anything so much as a rose in the darkness, like some naïve kiss of the moribund. III. A lace curtain blows aside at the moment of the doubtful dawn struggle of day and night; it only reveals that there is no bed of human birth in the room, a blasphemy. This white on white conflict of two garland-like curtains is blown over to the pale window and waves about more than it actually hides anything. But in him whose mind is gilded by his dream, a mandolin with its hollow musical sound chamber sadly sleeps. A mandolin such that, near some window, one could have been born a poet from its belly.

A la nue accablante tu
Basse de basalte et de laves
A même les échos esclaves
Par une trompe sans vertu

Quel sépulcral naufrage (tu
Le sais, écume, mais y baves)
Suprême une entre les épaves
Abolit le mât dévêtu

Ou cela que furibond faute
De quelque perdition haute
Tout l'abîme vain éployé

Dans le si blanc cheveu qui traîne
Avarement aura noyé
Le flanc enfant d'une sirène.

*Poésies*

Under the overwhelming storm cloud, in a shoal of basalt and lava, right at the level of the enslaved waves' echo, what ghostly shipwreck, unreported by a useless horn, destroyed the stripped mast which is the last piece of wreckage to float on the top of the waves (you know, foam, but only slaver), or what appearance of shipwreck concealed the fact that, in fury, in the absence of any higher order of destruction visited on a ship, the whole empty vast abyss of water probably drowned, as if hungry, only a child siren, in the white streak of foam remaining?

# PAUL VERLAINE

## Chanson d'automne

Les sanglots longs
Des violons
    De l'automne
Blessent mon cœur
D'une langueur
    Monotone.

Tout suffocant
Et blême, quand
    Sonne l'heure,
Je me souviens
Des jours anciens
    Et je pleure;

Et je m'en vais
Au vent mauvais
    Qui m'emporte
Deçà, delà,
Pareil à la
    Feuille morte.

*Poèmes saturniens*

## Autumn Song

The long sobs of the autumn violins wound my heart with a melancholy languor. Suffocating and ghastly pale when I hear the hour ring, I remember the old days and I weep. And I go off in an evil wind, which bears me now here, now there, like a dead leaf.


La lune blanche
Luit dans les bois;
De chaque branche
Part une voix
Sous la ramée...

O bien-aimée.

L'étang reflète,
Profond miroir,
La silhouette
Du saule noir
Où le vent pleure...

Rêvons, c'est l'heure.

Un vaste et tendre
Apaisement
Semble descendre
Du firmament
Que l'astre irise...

C'est l'heure exquise.

*La Bonne Chanson*

The white moon shines in the woods; from each bough comes a voice under the branches—O beloved. The pond, like a deep mirror, reflects the outline of the black willow, where the wind weeps—let us dream; it is the hour. A great tender peace seems to descend from the firmament in which the star glimmers—it is the exquisite hour.

## Bruxelles

### Simples Fresques

I

La fuite est verdâtre et rose
Des collines et des rampes,
Dans un demi-jour de lampes
Qui vient brouiller toute chose.

L'or, sur les humbles abîmes,
Tout doucement s'ensanglante,
Des petits arbres sans cimes,
Où quelque oiseau faible chante.

Triste à peine tant s'effacent
Ces apparences d'automne.
Toutes mes langueurs rêvassent,
Que berce l'air monotone.

II
L'allée est sans fin
Sous le ciel, divin
D'être pâle ainsi!
Sais-tu qu'on serait
Bien sous le secret
De ces arbres-ci?

Des messieurs bien mis,
Sans nul doute amis
Des Royers Collards,
Vont vers le château.
J'estimerais beau
D'être ces vieillards.

Le château, tout blanc
Avec, à son flanc,
Le soleil couché.
Les champs à l'entour...
Oh! que notre amour
N'est-il là niché!

*Romances sans paroles*

## Brussels

### Simple Frescoes

I. The fleeting hills and slopes are pink and greenish, in a half-light of streetlamps which come on and scramble all appearances. The golden light over humble hollows softly grows blood red—topless little trees in which some bird sings weakly. I am scarcely sad, so evanescent are these autumnal signs. In my languor I dream confusedly, cradled by the monotonous air. II. The tree-lined walk is endless under the sky, divine in its present paleness. You know, we would be cozy hidden under those trees. Well-dressed men, doubtless friends of Royer-Collard and his colleagues, are going toward the chateau. I think it would be nice to be those old men. The chateau, all white, with the last rays of sun at its side. The fields around—Oh! why is our love not nestled there!

Tournez, tournez, bons chevaux de bois,
Tournez cent tours, tournez mille tours,

Tournez souvent et tournez toujours,
Tournez, tournez au son des hautbois.

L'enfant tout rouge et la mère blanche,
Le gars en noir et la fille en rose,
L'une à la chose et l'autre à la pose,
Chacun se paie un sou de dimanche.

Tournez, tournez, chevaux de leur coeur,
Tandis qu'autour de tous vos tournois
Clignote l'oeil du filou sournois,
Tournez au son du piston vainqueur!

C'est étonnant comme ça vous soûle
D'aller ainsi dans ce cirque bête:
Bien dans le ventre et mal dans la tête,
Du mal en masse et du bien en foule.

Tournez au son de l'accordéon,
Du violon, du trombone fous,
Chevaux plus doux que des moutons, doux
Comme un peuple en révolution.

Le vent fouettant la tente, les verres,
Les zincs et le drapeau tricolore,
Et les jupons, et que sais-je encore?
Fait un fracas de cinq cents tonnerres.

Tournez, dadas, sans qu'il soit besoin
D'user jamais de nuls éperons
Pour commander à vos galops ronds:
Tournez, tournez, sans espoir de foin.

Et dépêchez, chevaux de leur âme:
Déjà voici que sonne à la soupe
La nuit qui tombe et chasse la troupe
De gais buveurs que leur soif affame.

Tournez, tournez! le ciel en velours
D'astres en or se vêt lentement.
L'église tinte un glas tristement.
Tournez au son joyeux des tambours!

*Sagesse*

Turn, turn, good wooden horses, turn a hundred times, a thousand times, turn often and evermore, turn, turn to the sound of the oboes.

The red child and the white mother, the guy in black and the girl in pink—she eager for him, he eager to make an impression—treat themselves to a penny's worth of Sunday. Turn, turn, horses of their heart, while around all your gyrations the sly pickpocket's eye winks. Turn to the sound of the conquering cornet! It's astonishing how it makes you drunk, going around like that in this stupid merry-go-round. Feeling good in the belly and bad in the head. Masses of bad and crowds of good. Turn to the sound of the crazy accordion, violin, trumpet, horses gentler than sheep, gentle like a people in a state of revolution. Wind, whipping the tent, glasses, bars, and the red-and-white-and-blue flag and petticoats and God knows what else, makes a sound worse than crashing thunder. Turn, hobbyhorses, without the need of spurs to send you galloping in a round; turn, turn with no hope of fodder. And hurry up, horses of their souls; now night with its dinner bell is falling and driving home the cheery crowd of drinkers made hungry by their thirst. Turn, turn! The velvet sky is gradually putting on gold stars. The church rings a sad knell. Turn to the joyous sound of drums!

L'espoir luit comme un brin de paille dans l'étable.
Que crains-tu de la guêpe ivre de son vol fou?
Vois, le soleil toujours poudroie à quelque trou.
Que ne t'endormais-tu, le coude sur la table?

Pauvre âme pâle, au moins cette eau du puits glacé,
Bois-la. Puis dors après. Allons, tu vois, je reste,
Et je dorloterai les rêves de ta sieste,
Et tu chantonneras comme un enfant bercé.

Midi sonne. De grâce, éloignez-vous, madame.
Il dort. C'est étonnant comme les pas de femme
Résonnent au cerveau des pauvres malheureux.

Midi sonne. J'ai fait arroser dans la chambre.
Va, dors! L'espoir luit comme un caillou dans un creux.
Ah! quand refleuriront les roses de septembre!

*Sagesse*

Hope shines like a wisp of straw in the stable. What do you fear from the wasp drunken with its own erratic flight? See, the sun still sends its dusty light through some hole. Why didn't you try to fall asleep with your elbow on the table? Poor pale soul, at least drink this icy water from the well. Then sleep afterwards. Come now, I will stay, you see,

and cradle the dreams of your nap, and you will hum like a child being
rocked. Noon is ringing. Please, go away, Madam. He is sleeping. It is
astonishing how womens' footsteps echo in the head of poor invalids.
Noon is ringing. I've had the room sprayed with water. Come, sleep.
Hope shines like a stone in a hole on the road. Ah, when will the Sep-
tember roses flower again!

## Sonnet boiteux

Ah! vraiment c'est triste, ah! vraiment ça finit trop mal.
Il n'est pas permis d'être à ce point infortuné.
Ah! vraiment c'est trop la mort du naïf animal
Qui voit tout son sang couler sous son regard fané.

Londres fume et crie. O quelle ville de la Bible!
Le gaz flambe et nage et les enseignes sont vermeilles.
Et les maisons dans leur ratatinement terrible
Épouvantent comme un sénat de petites vieilles.

Tout l'affreux passé saute, piaule, miaule et glapit
Dans le brouillard rose et jaune et sale des *sohos*
Avec des *indeeds* et des *all rights* et des *haôs*.

Non vraiment c'est trop un martyre sans espérance,
Non vraiment cela finit trop mal, vraiment c'est triste:
O le feu du ciel sur cette ville de la Bible!

*Jadis et Naguère*

## Lame Sonnet

Ah, it's really sad, ah, really it's ending too badly. It shouldn't be
allowed to be unfortunate to that point. Ah, really, it's too much the
death of a naïve animal seeing, with its dim eye, all its blood flowing
out. London smokes and screams. O what a city from the Bible! The
gas flares and trembles and the signs are gold. And the houses, with
their horrible shriveled look, are as terrifying as a senate of little old
women. All the dreadful past leaps, clucks, mews, and screeches in the
pink and yellow and dirty fog of Sohos, with *indeeds* and *all rights* and
*ohs*. No, really, it's too much a hopeless martyrdom, no, really, it's
ending too badly, it's sad. O the fire from heaven on this city from the
Bible!

## Vers pour être calomnié

Ce soir je m'étais penché sur ton sommeil.
Tout ton corps dormait chaste sur l'humble lit,
Et j'ai vu, comme un qui s'applique et qui lit,
Ah! j'ai vu que tout est vain sous le soleil!

Qu'on vive, ô quelle délicate merveille,
Tant notre appareil est une fleur qui plie!
O pensée aboutissant à la folie!
Va, pauvre, dors! moi, l'effroi pour toi m'éveille.

Ah! misère de t'aimer, mon frêle amour
Qui vas respirant comme on expire un jour!
O regard fermé que la mort fera tel!

O bouche qui ris en songe sur ma bouche,
En attendant l'autre rire plus farouche!
Vite, éveille-toi. Dis, l'âme est immortelle?

*Jadis et Naguère*

## Verses to be Slandered

This evening I bent over you in your sleep. Your whole body slept
chastely in the humble bed, and I saw, like one who with diligence
manages to read and make out the sense, I saw that all is vain under the
sun. What a delicate marvel that one is alive! Our mechanism is so like a
flower bending before the wind! O thought leading to madness! Come,
poor thing, sleep; fear for you keeps me awake. Ah, the wretchedness
of loving you, my fragile love, who breathe in the same way as in
dying. Oh closed eyes such as death will leave them! Oh mouth laugh-
ing in a dream against my mouth, until the time of the other, terrified
laugh. Quick, wake up! Tell me, is the soul immortal?

## Luxures

Chair! ô seul fruit mordu des vergers d'ici-bas,
Fruit amer et sucré qui jutes aux dents seules
Des affamés du seul amour, bouches ou gueules,
Et bon dessert des forts, et leurs joyeux repas,

Amour! le seul émoi de ceux que n'émeut pas
L'horreur de vivre. Amour qui presses sous tes meules

Les scrupules des libertins et des bégueules
Pour le pain des damnés qu'élisent les sabbats,

Amour, tu m'apparais aussi comme un beau pâtre
Dont rêve la fileuse assise auprès de l'âtre
Les soirs d'hiver dans la chaleur d'un sarment clair,

Et la fileuse c'est la Chair, et l'heure tinte
Où le rêve étreindra la rêveuse,—heure sainte
Ou non! qu'importe à votre extase, Amour et Chair!

*Jadis et Naguère*

## Lust

Flesh, sole fruit tasted of earthly orchards, bitter and sweet fruit that
spurts only for the teeth of those famished for the only love, their
mouths or maws, and delicious dessert of the strong, and their joyous
meal, love! the only emotion left to those unmoved by the horror of
life. Love, crushing in your millstones the scruples of prudes and liber-
tines for the bread of the damned, chosen for their sabbath, love, you
appear to me also like a beautiful shepherd dreamed of by a girl spin-
ning beside the hearth, on winter evenings in the heat of a bright log,
and the spinner is the flesh, and the hour sounds when the dream will
overcome the dreamer, a holy hour or not, what does it matter to your
ecstasy, love and flesh?

## Images d'un sou

De toutes les douleurs douces
Je compose mes magies!
Paul, les paupières rougies,
Erre seul aux Pamplemousses.
La Folle-par-amour chante
Une ariette touchante.
C'est la mère qui s'alarme
De sa fille fiancée.
C'est l'épouse délaissée
Qui prend un sévère charme
A s'exagérer l'attente
Et demeure palpitante.

C'est l'amitié qu'on néglige
Et qui se croit méconnue.
C'est toute angoisse ingénue,
C'est tout bonheur qui s'afflige:
L'enfant qui s'éveille et pleure,
Le prisonnier qui voit l'heure,
Les sanglots des tourterelles,
La plainte des jeunes filles.
C'est l'appel des Inésilles
—Que gardent dans des tourelles
De bons vieux oncles avares—
A tous sonneurs de guitares.
Voici Damon qui soupire
Sa tendresse à Geneviève
De Brabant qui fait ce rêve
D'exercer un chaste empire
Dont elle-même se pâme
Sur la veuve de Pyrame
Tout exprès ressuscitée,
Et la forêt des Ardennes
Sent circuler dans ses veines
La flamme persécutée
De ces princesses errantes
Sous les branches murmurantes,
Et madame Malbrouck monte
A sa tour pour mieux entendre
La viole et la voix tendre
De ce cher trompeur de Comte
Ory qui revient d'Espagne
Sans qu'un doublon l'accompagne.
Mais il s'est couvert de gloire
Aux gorges des Pyrénées
Et combien d'infortunées
Au teint de lys et d'ivoire
Ne fit-il pas à tous risques
Là-bas, parmi les Morisques!...
Toute histoire qui se mouille
De délicieuses larmes,
Fut-ce à travers chocs d'armes,
Aussitôt chez moi s'embrouille,

Se mêle à d'autres encore,
Finalement s'évapore
En capricieuses nues,
Laissant à travers des filtres
Subtils talismans et philtres
Au fin fond de mes cornues
Au feu de l'amour rougies.
Accourez à mes magies!
C'est très beau. Venez, d'aucunes
Et d'aucuns. Entrrez, bagasse!
Cadet-Roussel est paillasse
Et vous dira vos fortunes.
C'est Crédit qui tient la caisse.
Allons vite qu'on se presse!

*Jadis et Naguère*

## Penny Pictures

From all sweet sorrows I put together my magic! Paul, with red eyelids, wanders without Virginie in the Quartier des Pamplemousses. The woman crazy from love sings a touching arietta. The mother grows alarmed over her engaged daughter. The abandoned wife finds an austere charm in exaggerating the time she has been waiting and is still eager. Friendship is neglected and feels itself ignored. There is ingenuous fear and wretched happiness: the child who wakes and fears, the prisoner looking at the clock, sobs of turtledoves, laments of young girls. There is the call of the soubrette Inesilla—whom good old stingy uncles keep shut up in a tower—directed toward all serenaders. There is Damon who sighs his love for Genevieve of Brabant, who, in turn, dreams ecstatically of holding in chaste sway the widow of Pyramus, expressly resurrected, and the Forest of Arden feels in its veins the flaming persecuted love of these wandering princesses under its murmuring boughs, and Madame Malbrough of the song goes up into her tower the better to hear the viol and the tender voice of Count Ory, returning from Spain without a single doubloon. But he won glory in the gorges of the Pyrenees, and how many pining ladies, with skin of ivory and lily, he left, after much risk, among the infidel converts! Any story to be deliciously wept over, even if it involved battles, immediately gets confused in my telling, gets mingled with still others and finally evaporates in fanciful clouds, letting subtle talismans and philters pass through the filters of my apparatus into the bottom of the retorts red-hot from love. Come see my magic! It's very beautiful, come one and all. Come in, tart! Cadet-Roussel is a clown and will tell your fortunes. Credit is in charge of ticket sales. Step right up!

## Kaléidoscope

Dans une rue, au coeur d'une ville de rêve,
Ce sera comme quand on a déjà vécu:
Un instant à la fois très vague et très aigu...
O ce soleil parmi la brume qui se lève!

O ce cri sur la mer, cette voix dans les bois!
Ce sera comme quand on ignore des causes;
Un lent réveil après bien des métempsychoses:
Les choses seront plus les mêmes qu'autrefois

Dans cette rue, au coeur de la ville magique
Où des orgues moudront des gigues dans les soirs,
Où les cafés auront des chats sur les dressoirs,
Et que traverseront des bandes de musique.

Ce sera si fatal qu'on en croira mourir:
Des larmes ruisselant douces le long des joues,
Des rires sanglotés dans le fracas des roues,
Des invocations à la mort de venir,

Des mots anciens comme un bouquet de fleurs fanées!
Les bruits aigres des bals publics arriveront,
Et des veuves avec du cuivre après leur front,
Paysannes, fendront la foule des traînées

Qui flânent là, causant avec d'affreux moutards
Et des vieux sans sourcils que la dartre enfarine,
Cependant qu'à deux pas, dans des senteurs d'urine,
Quelque fête publique enverra des pétards.

Ce sera comme quand on rêve et qu'on s'éveille,
Et que l'on se rendort et que l'on rêve encor
De la même féerie et du même décor,
L'été, dans l'herbe, au bruit moiré d'un vol d'abeille.

*Jadis et Naguère*

## Kaleidoscope

On a street in the heart of a dream city, it will be just as if one had already lived there: at once a very vague and very piercing moment— Oh the sun in the clearing mist! Oh the cry on the sea, the voice in the woods! It will be as if one understood the causes of nothing: a slow awakening after many incarnations: things will be more the same than they ever were. On this street, in the heart of the magic city, where barrel organs will grind out jigs in the evenings, where cafes will have cats on the sideboards, and streaks of music will drift through the street. It will be so fated, that you feel it will kill you: gentle tears streaming along cheeks, sobbing laughs in the clatter of wheels, summonses of death to come, old words like a bouquet of faded flowers! The piercing sounds of dance halls will reach you, and widows with copper headbands, peasant women, will force their way through the crowd of whores idling there, talking with horrible children, and eyebrowless old men with white scaly faces, while nearby, amid the smell of urine, rockets are being fired off for some celebration. It will be the way it is when you dream and wake up, and fall asleep and dream again of the same fantastic story and setting, in summer, on the grass, against the shimmering sound of a bee in flight.

Un grand sommeil noir
Tombe sur ma vie:
Dormez, tout espoir,
Dormez, toute envie!

Je ne vois plus rien,
Je perds la mémoire
Du mal et du bien...
O la triste histoire!

Je suis un berceau
Qu'une main balance
Au creux d'un caveau:
Silence, silence!

*Sagesse*

A great black somnolence falls over my life. Sleep, all hope! Sleep, all envy! I see nothing any longer; I am losing all memory of good and bad—such a misfortune! I am a cradle rocked by a hand in the depths of a vault. Silence, silence!

## Art poétique

De la musique avant toute chose,
Et pour cela préfère l'Impair
Plus vague et plus soluble dans l'air,
Sans rien en lui qui pèse ou qui pose.

Il faut aussi que tu n'ailles point
Choisir tes mots sans quelque méprise:
Rien de plus cher que la chanson grise
Où l'Indécis au Précis se joint.

C'est des beaux yeux derrière des voiles,
C'est le grand jour tremblant de midi,
C'est, par un ciel d'automne attiédi,
Le bleu fouillis des claires étoiles!

Car nous voulons la Nuance encor,
Pas la Couleur, rien que la nuance!
Oh! la nuance seule fiance
Le rêve au rêve et la flûte au cor!

Fuis du plus loin la Pointe assassine,
L'Esprit cruel et le Rire impur,
Qui font pleurer les yeux de l'Azur,
Et tout cet ail de basse cuisine!

Prends l'éloquence et tords-lui son cou!
Tu feras bien, en train d'énergie,
De rendre un peu la Rime assagie.
Si l'on n'y veille, elle ira jusqu'où?

O qui dira les torts de la Rime?
Quel enfant sourd ou quel nègre fou
Nous a forgé ce bijou d'un sou
Qui sonne creux et faux sous la lime?

De la musique encore et toujours!
Que ton vers soit la chose envolée
Qu'on sent qui fuit d'une âme en allée
Vers d'autres cieux à d'autres amours.

Que ton vers soit la bonne aventure
Eparse au vent crispé du matin
Qui va fleurant la menthe et le thym...
Et tout le reste est littérature.

*Jadis et Naguère*

## Art of Poetry

Music before everything, and for that reason, prefer lines of an uneven number of syllables, vaguer and dissolving better into air, with nothing in them that is weighty or comes to a stop. You must also choose your words with a certain negligence: nothing dearer than the tipsy song where the indeterminate and the exact are joined. It's like beautiful eyes behind a veil, the great quivering light of noon; it's like, in a warmish autumn sky, the blue heap of bright stars! For we still want shades, not plain color, nothing but shades! Oh, a subtle shade alone weds dream to dream and the flute to the horn. Flee as far as possible from murderous epigram, cruel wit, and sullied laughter, which make the eyes of the divine blue weep; avoid all such garlic for crude dishes. Take rhetoric and wring its neck! You would do well, while you're at it, to chasten rhyme somewhat; if you don't watch it, it may do God knows what! Oh who can tell of the misdeeds of rhyme? What deaf child or crazy savage forged that penny ornament, which sounds false and hollow when you attempt to file it? Music again and always! Let your verse be something in flight, fleeing from a soul on its way toward other heavens and other loves. Let your verse be the prediction of good fortune disseminated by the crisp morning wind, which smells of mint and thyme—and anything else is literature.

Écoutez la chanson bien douce
Qui ne pleure que pour vous plaire.
Elle est discrète, elle est légère:
Un frisson d'eau sur de la mousse!

La voix vous fut connue (et chère?)
Mais à présent elle est voilée
Comme une veuve désolée,
Pourtant comme elle encore fière.

Et dans les longs plis de son voile
Qui palpite aux brises d'automne,

Cache et montre au coeur qui s'étonne
La vérité comme une étoile.

Elle dit, la voix reconnue,
Que la bonté c'est notre vie,
Que de la haine et de l'envie
Rien ne reste, la mort venue.

Elle parle aussi de la gloire
D'être simple sans plus attendre,
Et de noces d'or et du tendre
Bonheur d'une paix sans victoire.

Accueillez la voix qui persiste
Dans son naïf épithalame.
Allez, rien n'est meilleur à l'âme
Que de faire une âme moins triste!

Elle est *en peine et de passage*,
L'âme qui souffre sans colère,
Et comme sa morale est claire!...
Écoutez la chanson bien sage.

*Sagesse*

Listen to the gentle song, which weeps only to please you. It is discreet, it is light: water quivering on moss. The voice was known to you (and dear?), but at present it is veiled like a disconsolate widow, and yet, like her, it is still proud. And in the long folds of its veil, rustling in the autumn breeze, it conceals and shows truth like a star to the astonished heart. It says, the voice you recognize, that goodness is our life, that when death comes nothing is left of hatred and envy. It also speaks of the glory of being simple and expecting little, of golden wedding anniversaries and the tender happiness of peace without conquest. Welcome the voice, persisting in its naïve marriage song. Come, nothing is better for the soul than to make another soul less sad! The soul suffering without anger is in pain and on its way, and how its message is clear. Listen to the wise song.

# Langueur

Je suis l'Empire à la fin de la décadence,
Qui regarde passer les grands Barbares blancs

En composant des acrostiches indolents
D'un style d'or où la langueur du soleil danse.

L'âme seulette a mal au coeur d'un ennui dense.
Là-bas on dit qu'il est de longs combats sanglants.
O n'y pouvoir, étant si faible aux voeux si lents,
O n'y vouloir fleurir un peu cette existence!

O n'y vouloir, ô n'y pouvoir mourir un peu!
Ah! tout est bu! Bathylle, as-tu fini de rire?
Ah! tout est bu, tout est mangé! Plus rien à dire!

Seul, un poème un peu niais qu'on jette au feu,
Seul, un esclave un peu coureur qui vous néglige,
Seul, un ennui d'on ne sait quoi qui vous afflige!

*Jadis et Naguère*

## Languor

I am the Empire at the end of the decadence, watching the tall white Barbarians go by and composing indolent acrostics in a golden style like languorously dancing sunlight. The lonely soul is heartsick from dense weariness. In the distance they tell me there are long bloody battles. Ah, to be unable, so weak, with such lazy desires, ah, not to want to enliven a bit this existence. Ah, not to want, not to be able to die a little. Ah, I have drunk everything; Bathyllus, will you stop laughing? Ah, I have drunk everything, eaten everything; there is nothing left to say. Nothing but a silly poem I'll throw into the fire, nothing but a lascivious slave who neglects me, nothing but a weariness of heaven-knows-what afflicting me.

## Parsifal

Parsifal a vaincu les Filles, leur gentil
Babil et la luxure amusante—et sa pente
Vers la Chair de garçon vierge que cela tente
D'aimer les seins légers et ce gentil babil;

Il a vaincu la Femme belle, au coeur subtil,
Étalant ses bras frais et sa gorge excitante;
Il a vaincu l'Enfer et rentre sous sa tente
Avec un lourd trophée à son bras puéril,

Avec la lance qui perça le Flanc suprême!
Il a guéri le roi, le voici roi lui-même,
Et prêtre du très saint Trésor essentiel.

En robe d'or il adore, gloire et symbole,
Le vase pur où resplendit le Sang réel,
—Et, ô ces voix d'enfants chantant dans la coupole!

*Amour*

## Parsifal

Parsifal has vanquished the maidens, their sweet chatter and amusing lust, and his virgin boy's inclination toward the flesh, his temptation to love light breasts and sweet chatter. He has vanquished the beautiful woman with her devious heart, displaying her cool arms and exciting bosom. He has vanquished hell and returns to his tent, with a heavy trophy on his boyish arm, with the lance that pierced the sublime Side. He has cured the king and is now king himself and priest of the most holy and essential treasure. In a golden robe he worships the pure cup, glory and symbol, in which the real Blood shines—and, oh those boys' voices singing in the dome!

# TRISTAN CORBIERE

## Epitaphe

Il se tua d'ardeur, ou mourut de paresse.
S'il vit, c'est par oubli; voici ce qu'il se laisse:
—Son seul regret fut de n'être pas sa maîtresse.

Il ne naquit par aucun bout,
Fut toujours poussé vent-de-bout,
Et fut un arlequin-ragoût,
Mélange adultère de tout.

Du *je-ne-sais-quoi.*—Mais ne sachant où;
De l'or,—mais avec pas le sou;
Des nerfs,—sans nerf. Vigueur sans force;
De l'élan,—avec une entorse;
De l'âme—et pas de violon;
De l'amour,—mais pire étalon.
—Trop de noms pour avoir un nom.—

Coureur d'idéal,—sans idée;
Rime riche,—et jamais rimée;
Sans avoir été,—revenu;
Se retrouvant partout perdu.

Poète, en dépit de ses vers;
Artiste sans art,—à l'envers,
Philosophe,—à tort à travers.

Un drôle sérieux,—pas drôle.
Acteur, il ne sut pas son rôle;
Peintre: il jouait de la musette;
Et musicien: de la palette.

Une tête!—mais pas de tête;
Trop fou pour savoir être bête;
Prenant pour un trait le mot *très.*
—Ses vers faux furent ses seuls vrais.

Oiseau rare—et de pacotille;
Très mâle...et quelquefois très *fille:*

Capable de tout,—bon à rien;
Gâchant bien le mal, mal le bien.
Prodigue comme était l'enfant
Du Testament,—sans testament.
Brave, et souvent, par peur du plat,
Mettant ses deux pieds dans le plat.

Coloriste enragé,—mais blême;
Incompris...—surtout de lui-même;
Il pleura, chanta juste faux;
—Et fut un défaut sans défauts.

Ne fut *quelqu'un*, ni quelque chose
Son naturel était la *pose*.
Pas poseur,—posant pour *l'unique*;
Trop naïf, étant trop cynique;
Ne croyant à rien, croyant tout.
—Son goût était dans le dégoût.

Trop cru,—parce qu'il fut trop cuit,
Ressemblant à rien moins qu'à lui,
Il s'amusa de son ennui,
Jusqu'à s'en réveiller la nuit.
Flâneur au large,—à la dérive,
Epave qui jamais n'arrive...

Trop *Soi* pour se pouvoir souffrir,
L'esprit à sec et la tête ivre,
Fini, mais ne sachant finir,
Il mourut en s'attendant vivre
Et vécut, s'attendant mourir.

Ci-gît,—coeur sans coeur, mal planté,
Trop réussi,—comme *raté*.

*Les Amours jaunes*

## Epitaph

He killed himself with ardor or died of laziness. If he's alive, it's by inadvertence. Here is what he bequeaths himself. His only regret was not having slept with himself. He wasn't born in any advantageous position, always had the wind in his face, and was a second-hand dish of various foods, an adulterous mixture of everything. He had a certain

I-know-not-what, but didn't know where; gold but without a cent, nerves but no nerve, strength without force, a running leap but with a sprain, a sound-post without a violin, love but a terrible stud. Too many nouns to be renowned; running after the ideal without an idea; a rich rhyme never matched, back without having been, always finding himself lost. A poet despite his verse, an artless artist, backwards; a philosopher, helter-skelter. A serious rogue, unfunny; as an actor, he never knew his lines; as a painter, he played the bagpipe; as a musician, he played the palette. A mind but mindless, too crazy to be a fool, taking some thing as something, his false lines were his only true ones. A rare bird sold by every peddler, very male and sometimes very girlish, capable of anything and good for nothing, skillfully spoiling the bad and clumsily the good, prodigal like the son in the story, but without a story; he was brave, and often, thinking it dull to have both feet on the ground, he put a foot in his mouth. A wild user of color but ghostly pale; misunderstood, especially by himself, he wept and sang on pitch off key, and was an impeccable flaw. Never *some one* nor some thing, imposture was his natural self. He didn't assume various postures, posing as unique; he was cynical to the point of naïveté; believing in nothing, he believed in everything; his taste was for distaste. Too crude and raw because his goose was too often cooked, resembling nothing less than himself, he was amused by his boredom to the point it kept him up at night. He ventured out of his depths, then drifted, flotsam that failed to float. Too much himself for him to endure it, his mind sober and his head drunk, finished but not knowing how to wind things up, he died expecting to live and lived expecting to die. Here lies a heartless heart, not very firm on his feet, so much a success he was, so to speak, a failure.

## A l'éternel Madame

Mannequin idéal, tête-de-turc du leurre,
Éternel Féminin!...repasse tes fichus;
Et viens sur mes genoux, quand je marquerai l'heure,
Me montrer comme on fait chez vous, anges déchus.

Sois pire, et fais pour nous la joie à la malheure,
Piaffe d'un pied léger dans les sentiers ardus.
Damne-toi, pure idole! et ris! et chante! et pleure,
Amante! Et meurs d'amour!...à nos moments perdus

Fille de marbre! en rut! sois folâtre!...et pensive
Maîtresse, chair de moi! fais-toi vierge et lascive...
Féroce, sainte, et bête, en me cherchant un coeur...

Sois femelle de l'homme, et sers de Muse, ô femme
Quand le poète brame en *Ame,* en *Lame,* en *Flamme*!
Puis—quand il ronflera—viens baiser ton Vainqueur!

## To the Eternal Madam

Mannequin of the Ideal! Half whipping boy, half bait! Eternal
Feminine! Iron your kerchiefs! And come get on my lap when I say it's
time, and show me how you do it your way, fallen angels! Be worse,
and make our joy wretched! Stamp lightly along love's arduous paths!
Bring damnation on yourself, chaste idol! And laugh and sing and
weep! Lover! And die of love! When we've nothing better to do, marble
maiden, in heat! Be frolicsome and pensive! Mistress, flesh of my flesh!
Be a lascivious virgin! Ferocious, holy, and stupid when you search for
my heart! Be the female of the male and serve as Muse, O Woman,
when the poet is bellowing *heart, smart,* and *dart*! Then, while he's snor-
ing, come kiss your Conqueror!

## A la mémoire de Zulma
### Vierge-folle hors barrière
### et d'un louis

Elle était riche de vingt ans,
Moi j'étais jeune de vingt francs,
Et nous fîmes bourse commune,
Placée, à fonds perdu, dans une
Infidèle nuit de printemps...

La lune a fait un trou dedans,
Rond comme un écu de cinq francs,
Par où passa notre fortune:
Vingt ans! vingt francs!...et puis la lune!

—En monnaie—hélas—les vingt francs!
En monnaie aussi les vingt ans!
Toujours de trous en trous de lune,
Et de bourse en bourse commune...
—C'est à peu près même fortune!

. . . . . . . . . . . . . . . . . . . . . . .

—Je la trouvai—bien des printemps,
Bien des vingt ans, bien des vingt francs,
Bien des trous et bien de la lune
Après—Toujours vierge et vingt ans,
Et...colonelle à la Commune!

. . . . . . . . . . . . . . . . . . .

—Puis après: la chasse aux passants,
Aux vingt sols, et plus aux vingt francs...
Puis après: la fosse commune,
Nuit gratuite sans trou de lune.

*Les Amours jaunes*

## To the Memory of Zulma

*(One of the Roving Kind—
Outside of Police Jurisdiction)
And of Twenty Francs*

She was age twenty rich, I was twenty francs young. We pooled our
resources and invested them for a lifetime's income in a faithless spring
night. The moon made a hole in this arrangement, round as a five-franc
piece, through which passed our whole fortune: twenty years old,
twenty francs, plus the moon! Broken up and in change the twenty
francs, alas! The same with age twenty years. From one moonhole to
another and from pooled resources to pooled resources, we had about
the same luck. I found her again, many springs, age twenty many times
over, and many twenty-franc pieces later—still virgin and twenty—
and a female colonel in the Commune! Afterward: hustling the
passers-by, hustling for twenty sous now and not twenty francs. Then:
a pauper's grave, a night for free, and no moonholes. N.B.—*voir la
lune*: have sexual intercourse; *faire un trou à la lune*: not pay one's debts.

## Fleur d'art

Oui—Quel art jaloux dans Ta fine histoire!
Quels bibelots chers! Un bout de sonnet,
Un coeur gravé dans ta manière noire,
Des traits de canif à coups de stylet.—

Tout fier mon coeur porte à la boutonnière
Que tu lui taillas, un petit bouquet
D'immortelle rouge—Encor ta manière—
C'est du sang en fleur. Souvenir coquet.

Allons, pas de pleurs à notre mémoire!
—C'est la mâle-mort de l'amour ici—
Foin du myosotis, vieux sachet d'armoire!

Double femme, va!... Qu'un âne te braie!
Si tu n'étais fausse, eh serais-tu vraie?...
L'amour est un duel: —Bien touché! Merci.

*Les Amours jaunes*

## Art-Flower

Yes. What painstaking art in your subtle story. What precious bric-
a-brac. A bit of sonnet, a heart engraved in your Black Manner, the
stiletto used as a penknife. Proudly my heart wears, in the buttonhole
you incised for it, a little bouquet of red strawflowers. More of your
style. It's blood in flower. A pretty souvenir. Come, no tears in mem-
ory of us; this is the ill end of love. Enough forget-me-nots, fit only to
be a sachet in a closet. Double-faced woman, enough! Let an ass bray
you! If you weren't false, would you be any the more true? Love is a
duel: touché, thanks.

## Laisser-courre

### Musique *de Isaac Laquedem*

J'ai laissé la potence
Après tous les pendus,
Andouilles de naissance,
Maigres fruits défendus;
Les plumes aux canards
Et la queue aux renards...

Au Diable aussi sa queue
Et ses cornes aussi,
Au ciel sa chose bleue
Et la Planète—ici—
Et puis tout: n'importe où
Dans le désert au clou.

J'ai laissé dans l'Espagne
Le reste et mon château;
Ailleurs, à la campagne,
Ma tête et son chapeau;
J'ai laissé mes souliers,
Sirènes, à vos pieds!

J'ai laissé par les mondes,
Parmi tous les frisons
Des chauves, brunes, blondes
Et rousses... mes toisons.
Mon épée aux vaincus,
Ma maîtresse aux cocus...

Aux portes les portières,
La portière au portier,
Le bouton aux rosières,
Les roses au rosier,
A l'huys les huissiers,
Créance aux créanciers...

Dans mes veines ma veine,
Mon rayon au soleil,
Ma dégaine en sa gaine,
Mon lézard au sommeil;
J'ai laissé mes amours
Dans les tours, dans les fours...

Et ma cotte de maille
Aux artichauts de fer
Qui sont à la muraille
Des jardins de l'Enfer;
Après chaque oripeau
J'ai laissé de ma peau.

J'ai laissé toute chose
Me retirer du nez
Des vers, en vers, en prose...
Aux bornes, les bornés;
A tous les jeux partout,
Des rois et de l'atout.

J'ai laissé la police
Captive en liberté,

J'ai laissé La Palisse
Dire la verité...
Laissé courre le sort
Et ce qui court encor.

J'ai laissé l'Espérance,
Vieillissant doucement,
Retomber en enfance,
Vierge folle sans dent.
J'ai laissé tous les Dieux,
J'ai laissé pire et mieux.

J'ai laissé bien tranquilles
Ceux qui ne l'étaient pas;
Aux pattes imbéciles
J'ai laissé tous les plats;
Aux poètes la foi...
Puis me suis laissé moi.

Sous le temps, sans égides
M'a mal mené fort bien
La vie à grandes guides...
Au bout des guides —rien—
...Laissé, blasé, passé,
Rien ne m'a rien laissé...

*Les Amours jaunes*


## Letting the Pack Run

### *with Music by the Wandering Jew*

I have left the gallows to all the hanged men, fools from birth, eager for wizened forbidden fruit. I have left the feathers to the ducks, and the tail to the foxes. To the devil his tail also, and his horns as well; to the sky its azure and this planet and everything; any place in the wilderness of the pawnshop. The rest I have left in Spain along with my castle. Elsewhere, in the countryside, my head and its hat. Sirens, I have left my shoes at your feet! I have left throughout the world, among all possible curls, bald women, brunettes, blonds, and redheads, my golden fleece. I have left my sword to the conquered, my mistress to cuckolds. I have left the doorkeepers to the doors, the doorkeeper to her husband, the bud to the winner of the rose of virtue, the roses on the rosebush, bail to the bailiff, credit to creditors. In my veins my luck, my beam to the sun, my awkward slouch in its corset, my lizard to sleep; I have left in towers my waking love, or my baking love. And my coat of mail on the iron rosettes on the wall of Hell's gardens. On every sequin I have left some skin. I have allowed them to wring out of me what they wanted to hear, in ringing verse or prose. To milestones the retarded, to all games anyplace, kings and the ace. I have left the captive police free; I have left the truth to truism, left fate to run loose and whatever is still running. I have let gently aging hope enter its second childhood, a toothless hoyden. I have left all gods, I have left the better and the worse. I have left alone those who weren't. I have left mess to those who make a mess of things; to poets faith, then I left myself. Out in all weather, with no protection, life has ill-treated me well, leaving me much leeway—with nothing on the lee. Abandoned, blunted, obsolescent, nothing has left me anything.


## Heures

Aumône au malandrin en chasse
Mauvais oeil à l'oeil assassin!
Fer contre fer au spadassin!
—Mon âme n'est pas en état de grâce!—

Je suis le fou de Pampelune,
J'ai peur du rire de la Lune,
Cafarde, avec son crêpe noir...
Horreur! tout est donc sous un éteignoir.

J'entends comme un bruit de crécelle...
C'est la male heure qui m'appelle.
Dans le creux des nuits tombe: un glas...deux glas

J'ai compté plus de quatorze heures...
L'heure est une larme—Tu pleures,
Mon coeur!...Chante encor, va—Ne compte pas.

*Les Amours jaunes*


## Time

Alms for the hunting highwayman, an evil eye for the murderer's eye! Sword against the sword of the cutthroat for hire! My soul is not in a state of grace. I am the madman of Pamplona; I am afraid of the moon's laugh, the moon, with its black crepe. Horror! the world is under a candle-snuffer. I hear something like the noise of a rattle; it's misfortune summoning me. In the emptiness of the night falls one knell, two...I have counted more than fourteen tolls. The hour is a tear. You weep, my heart! Come on, sing some more—don't count.

## A un Juvénal de lait

A grands coups d'avirons de douze pieds, tu rames
En vers...et contre tout—Hommes, auvergnats, femmes.—
Tu n'as pas vu l'endroit et tu cherches l'envers.
Jeune renard en chasse...Ils sont trop verts—tes vers.

C'est le *vers solitaire.*—On le purge.—*Ces Dames*
Sont le remède. Après tu feras de tes nerfs
Des cordes-à-boyau; quand, guitares sans âmes,
Les vers te reviendront déchantés et soufferts.

Hystérique à rebours, ta Muse est trop superbe,
Petit cochon de lait, qui n'as goûté qu'en herbe,
L'âcre saveur du fruit encor défendu.

Plus tard, tu colleras sur papier tes pensées,
Fleurs d'herboriste, mais, autrefois ramassées...
Quand il faisait beau temps au paradis perdu.

*Les Amours jaunes*

## To a Suckling Satirist

With wild hexametric oars, you row in verse and versus everyone, men, peasants, women. You haven't seen things right side up and you're looking for the in-verse. Young fox in heat! The grapes of your rhymes are too green! You have a Bad-verse Habit! But there is a purge for poetry. Ladies of the night will take care of it. Afterward, you'll turn your nerves into catgut, when, like guitars without a sound-post, your rhymes will come back dis-chanted and agonized. Like a backwards hysteric, your Muse is too proud, little suckling pig; you have only tasted the green shoots of the tree with the bitter and still forbidden fruit. Later, you'll paste in an album your naturalist's flower-thoughts, gathered long before, when the days were fine in paradise lost.

## Litanie du sommeil

*J'ai scié le sommeil!*
MACBETH.

Vous qui ronflez au coin d'une épouse endormie,
RUMINANT! savez-vous ce soupir: L'INSOMNIE?
—Avez-vous vu la Nuit, et le Sommeil ailé,
Papillon de minuit dans la nuit envolé,
Sans un coup d'aile ami, vous laissant sur le seuil,
Seul, dans le pot-au-noir au couvercle sans oeil?
—Avez-vous navigué?...La pensée est la houle
Ressassant le galet: ma tête...votre boule.
—Vous êtes-vous laissé voyager en ballon?
—Non?—bien, c'est l'insomnie.—Un grand coup de talon
Là—Vous voyez cligner des chandelles étranges:
Une femme, une Gloire en soleil, des archanges...
Et, la nuit s'éteignant dans le jour à demi,
Vous vous réveillez coi, sans vous être endormi.

*

SOMMEIL! écoute-moi: je parlerai bien bas:
Sommeil.—Ciel-de-lit de ceux qui n'en ont pas!

Toi qui planes avec l'Albatros des tempêtes,
Et qui t'assieds sur les casques-à-mèche honnêtes!
SOMMEIL!—Oreiller blanc des vierges assez bêtes!
Et Soupape à secret des vierges assez faites!
—Moelleux Matelas de l'échine en arête!
Sac noir où les chassés s'en vont cacher leur tête!
Rôdeur de boulevard extérieur! Proxénète!
Pays où le muet se réveille prophète!
Césure du vers long, et Rime du poète!

SOMMEIL—Loup-Garou gris! Sommeil Noir de fumée!
SOMMEIL!—Loup de velours, de dentelle embaumée!
Baiser de l'Inconnue, et Baiser de l'Aimée!
—SOMMEIL! Voleur de nuit! Folle-brise pâmée!
Parfum qui monte au ciel des tombes parfumées!
*Carrosse à Cendrillon* ramassant *les Traînées!*
Obscène Confesseur des dévotes mort-nées!

Toi qui viens, comme un chien, lécher la vieille plaie
Du martyr que la mort tiraille sur sa claie!

O sourire forcé de la crise tuée!
SOMMEIL! Brise alizée! Aurorale buée!

TROP-PLEIN de l'existence, et Torchon neuf qu'on passe
Au CAFÉ DE LA VIE, à chaque assiette grasse!
Grain d'ennui qui nous pleut de l'ennui des espaces!
Chose qui court encor, sans sillage et sans traces!
Pont-levis des fossés! Passage des impasses!

SOMMEIL!—Caméléon tout pailleté d'étoiles!
Vaisseau-fantôme errant tout seul à pleines voiles!
Femme du rendez-vous, s'enveloppant d'un voile!
SOMMEIL!—Triste Araignée, étends sur moi ta toile!

SOMMEIL auréolé! féerique Apothéose,
Exaltant le grabat du déclassé qui pose!
Patient Auditeur de l'incompris qui cause!
Refuge du pêcheur, de l'innocent qui n'ose!
Domino! Diables-bleus! Ange-gardien rose!

VOIX mortelle qui vibre aux immortelles ondes!
Réveil des échos morts et des choses profondes,
—Journal du soir: TEMPS, SIECLE et REVUE
    DES DEUX MONDES!

FONTAINE de Jouvence et Borne de l'envie!
—Toi qui viens assouvir la faim inassouvie!
Toi qui viens délier la pauvre âme ravie,
Pour la noyer d'air pur au large de la vie!

TOI qui, le rideau bas, viens lâcher la ficelle
Du Chat, du Commissaire, et de Polichinelle,
Du violoncelliste et de son violoncelle,
Et la lyre de ceux dont la Muse est pucelle!

GRAND Dieu, Maître de tout! Maître de ma Maîtresse
Qui me trompe avec toi—l'amoureuse Paresse—
O Bain de voluptés! Eventail de caresse!

SOMMEIL! Honnêteté des voleurs! Clair de lune
Des yeux crevés!—SOMMEIL! Roulette de fortune
De tout infortuné! Balayeur de rancune!

O corde-de-pendu de la Planète lourde!
Accord éolien hantant l'oreille sourde!
—Beau Conteur à dormir debout: conte ta bourde?...
SOMMEIL!—Foyer de ceux dont morte est la falourde!

SOMMEIL—Foyer de ceux dont la falourde est morte!
Passe-partout de ceux qui sont mis à la porte!
Face-de-bois pour les créanciers et leur sorte!
Paravent du mari contre la femme-forte!

SURFACE des profonds! Profondeur des jocrisses!
Nourrice du soldat et Soldat des nourrices!
Paix des juges-de-paix! Police des polices!
SOMMEIL!—Belle-de-nuit entr'ouvrant son calice!
Larve, Ver-luisant et nocturne Cilice!
Puits de vérité de monsieur La Palisse!

SOUPIRAIL d'en haut! Rais de poussière impalpable,
Qui viens rayer du jour la lanterne implacable!

*

SOMMEIL—Ecoute-moi, je parlerai bien bas:
Crépuscule flottant de *l'Etre ou n'Etre pas!*...

SOMBRE lucidité! Clair-obscur! Souvenir
De l'Inouï! Marée! Horizon! Avenir!
Conte des *Mille-et-une-nuits* doux à ouïr!
Lampiste d'*Aladin* qui sais nous éblouir!
Eunuque noir! muet blanc! Derviche! Djinn! Fakir!
Conte de Fée où *le Roi* se laisse assoupir!
Forêt-vierge où *Peau-d'Ane* en pleurs va s'accroupir!
Garde-manger où *l'Ogre* encor va s'assouvir!
Tourelle où *ma soeur Anne* allait voir rien venir!
Tour où *dame Malbrouck* voyait page courir...
Où *Femme Barbe-Bleue* oyait l'heure mourir!...
Où *Belle-au-Bois-Dormant* dormait dans un soupir!

CUIRASSE du petit! Camisole du fort!
Lampion des éteints! Eteignoir du remord!
Conscience du juste, et du pochard qui dort!
Contre-poids des poids faux de l'épicier de Sort!
Portrait enluminé de la livide Mort!

GRAND fleuve où Cupidon va retremper ses dards
SOMMEIL!—Corne de Diane, et corne du cornard!
Couveur de magistrats et Couveur de lézards!
Marmite d'*Arlequin*!—bout de cuir, lard, homard—
SOMMEIL!—Noce de ceux qui sont dans les beaux-arts.

BOULET des forcenés, Liberté des captifs!
Sabbat du somnambule et Relais des poussifs!—
SOMME! Actif du passif et Passif de l'actif!
Pavillon de *la Folle* et *Folle* du poncif!...
—O viens changer de patte au cormoran pensif!

O brun Amant de l'Ombre! Amant honteux du jour!
Bal de nuit où Psyché veut démasquer l'Amour!
Grosse Nudité du chanoine en jupon court!
Panier-à-salade idéal! Banal four!
Omnibus où, dans l'Orbe, on fait pour rien un tour!

SOMMEIL! Drame hagard! Sommeil, molle Langueur!
Bouche d'or du silence et Bâillon du blagueur!
Berceuse des vaincus! Perchoir des coqs vainqueurs!
Alinéa du livre où dorment les longueurs!

Du jeune homme rêveur Singulier Féminin!
De la femme rêvant pluriel masculin!

SOMMEIL!—Râtelier du Pégase fringant!
SOMMEIL!—Petite pluie abattant l'ouragan!
SOMMEIL!—Dédale vague où vient le revenant!
SOMMEIL!—Long corridor où plangore le vent!

Néant du fainéant! Lazzarone infini!
Aurore boréale au sein du jour terni!

SOMMEIL!—Autant de pris sur notre éternité!
Tour du cadran *à blanc*! Clou du Mont-de-Piété!
Héritage en Espagne à tout déshérité!
Coup de rapière dans l'eau du fleuve Léthé!
Génie au nimbe d'or des grands hallucinés!
Nid des petits hiboux! Aile des déplumés!

IMMENSE Vache à lait dont nous sommes les veaux!
Arche où le hère et le boa changent de peaux!
Arc-en-ciel miroitant! Faux du vrai! Vrai du faux!
Ivresse que la brute appelle le repos!
Sorcière de Bohême à sayon d'oripeaux!
Tityre sous l'ombrage essayant des pipeaux!
Temps qui porte un chibouck à la place de faux!
Parque qui met un peu d'huile à ses ciseaux!
Parque qui met un peu de chanvre à ses fuseaux!
Chat qui joue avec le peloton d'Atropos!

SOMMEIL!—Manne de grâce au coeur disgracié!

. . . . . . . . . . . . . . . . . . . . . . . . . . . .

LE SOMMEIL S'EVEILLANT ME DIT: TU M'A SCIE.

. . . . . . . . . . . . . . . . . . . . . . . . . . . . . .

*

TOI qui souffles dessus une épouse enrayée,
RUMINANT! dilatant ta pupille éraillée;
Sais-tu?...Ne sais-tu pas ce soupir—LE REVEIL!—
Qui bâille au ciel, parmi les crins d'or du soleil
Et les crins fous de ta Déesse ardente et blonde?...
—Non?...—Sais-tu le réveil du philosophe immonde
—Le Porc—rognonnant sa prière du matin;
Ou le réveil, extrait-d'âge de la catin?...
As-tu jamais sonné le reveil de la meute;
As-tu jamais senti l'éveil sourd de l'émeute,
Ou le réveil de plomb du malade fini?...
As-tu vu s'étirer l'oeil des Lazzaroni?...
Sais-tu?...ne sais-tu pas le chant de l'alouette?
—Non—Gluants sont tes cils, pâteuse est ta luette,
Ruminant! Tu n'as pas l'INSOMNIE, éveillé;
Tu n'as pas LE SOMMEIL, ô Sac ensommeillé!

(Lits divers—Une nuit de jour)

Les Amours jaunes

## Litany of Sleep

*Macbeth does murther Sleep.*

You who snore by a sleeping spouse, cud-chewer, do you know the sigh "Insomnia"? Have you seen night and winged sleep, a midnight moth gone in the dark without a friendly flap of the wing, leave you on the threshold, alone, in the doldrums with no eye overhead? Have you gone to sea? Thought is the swell beating the pebble. My head is your high-tide signal. Have you gone up in a balloon? No? Well, that's insomnia. A big kick in the behind. You see strange tapers flickering: a woman, a halo like a sun, archangels. And, when night is turning into day, you wake up quietly without even having gone to sleep. O sleep! Hear me, I'll speak quite softly. Sleep! Bed canopy of those who have none! You who soar with the albatross in storms and who sit on honest nightcaps, o sleep! White pillow of silly virgins and secret safety valve of ripe virgins! Soft mattress for bony spines! Black sack the pursued hide their heads in! Prowler of the peripheral boulevard! Pimp! Land where the mute become prophets! Caesura in long lines and rhyme of the poet! O sleep! Grey werewolf! Sleep black with smoke! Sleep! Black velvet mask perfumed with lace! Kiss of the Unknown Woman and kiss of the loved one! Sleep! Night thief! Faint, changing breeze! Scent rising to heaven from scented tombs! Cinderella's coach picking up tarts! Obscene confessor of pious stillborn ladies! You who come, like a dog, to lick the old wound of the martyr tormented by death! O forced smile after an aborted attack! O sleep! Trade-winds! Dawn mist! Excess of vitality and new dish-cloth with which, in the Cafe of Life, they wipe each dirty plate! Boredom's squall raining on us from the boredom of space! Something still running with no wake or footprint. Drawbridge of moats! Exit from dead-ends! Sleep! Chameleon sequined with stars! Ghost ship drifting empty with full sails! Woman at the rendez-vous covered with a veil! Sleep! Gloomy spider, spread your web over me! Haloed sleep! Supernatural apotheosis raising the pallet of social climbers come down in the world! Patient listener of the misunderstood explaining themselves! Refuge of the fisherman! Of timid innocents! Disguise! Gone to the devil! Pink guardian angel! Mortal voice vibrating on immortal wave lengths! Awakening of dead news items and deep buried things! Evening paper! *Times*! *Century*! *Revue des deux Mondes*! Corner fountain of youth and milestone of envy! You who come to satisfy inappeasable hunger! You who come to free the poor delighted soul, only to drown it in pure air in the depths of life! You who, behind closed curtains, drop the strings of Puss-in-Boots, the Policeman, and Pulcinella! Of the cello and the cellist! Of the lyre of poets whose muse is virgin! Great God! Master of all! Master of my mistress who deceives me with you! Amorous idleness, sea of voluptuousness! Caress like a fan! Sleep! Honesty of thieves! Moonlight of the blinded! Sleep! Fortune's roulette for the unfortunate! Streetsweeper of rancor! Lucky hangman's noose for the heavy planet! Aeolian harmony ringing in a deaf ear! Beautiful teller of wild tales! Tell your wild tale! Sleep! Hearth of those whose faggot is dead! Sleep! Hearth of those whose faggot dead is! Skeleton key of the outcast! Impassive face for creditors and the like! Shield of the husband against a strong wife! Surface of the deep! Depth of the shallows! Nurse of soldiers and soldier courting nursemaids! Peace of the Justice of the Peace! Policer of the police! Sleep! Nightshade opening its bloom! Ghost, glow-worm, and noctural hairshirt! Truth of truisms! Ceiling vent! Impalpable motes of dust which bar the day's implacable lantern! O sleep! Hear me, I shall speak softly. Shifting twilight of To Be or Not To Be! Dark clarity! Chiaroscuro! Recollection of what never was heard of! Tide! Horizon! Future! Sweet sounding tale from the *Thousand and One Nights*! Stage-lighting crew dazzling us with Aladdin's lamp! Black eunuch! White mute! Dervish! Jinn! Fakir! Fairytale where the princess's father falls asleep! Virgin forest where Peau-d'Ane goes to crouch in tears! Buffet where the Ogre will eat some more! Tower from which Sister Ann sees no one coming! Tower where Marlborough's lady sees the page arrive! Where Bluebeard's wife hears the hour die! Where Sleeping Beauty slept in a quarter-rest! Armor of the little! Straitjacket for the strong! Lantern for those whose life is snuffed out! Snuffer of remorse! Conscience of the just and of the sleeping drunkard! Counterweight of the false scales of Fate's grocer! Colored portrait of pale death! Great river in which Cupid retempers his darts! Sleep! Diana's horn and cuckhold's horn! Fosterer of magistrates and hatcher of lizards! Pot of mixed second-hand stew, bits of leather, lard, lobster. Sleep! Debauchery of those in the fine arts! Shackle of the frantic and freedom of the captive! Sleepwalker's orgy and relay of the winded! Sleep! Assets of liabilities and liabilities of assets! Flag of the Madwoman and stereotyped madness! Oh, come make the pensive cormorant stand on the other leg! O suntanned lover of the shade, lover ashamed of day! Nighttime ball where Psyche tries to unmask Eros! Great nakedness of the canon in his short nightskirt! Ideal Black Maria! Common oven! Omnibus where, in the Sphere, you ride for nothing! Sleep! Haggard drama! Sleep! Soft languor! Golden mouth of silence and gag for the joker! Lullaby of the vanquished! Perch of conquering cocks! Paragraph in the book where the long dull passage sleeps! Feminine singular of the dreaming young man! Masculine plural of the dreaming woman! Sleep! Frisky Pegasus's food-trough! Sleep! Soft rain settling the storm! Sleep! Winding labyrinth where the ghost walks! Sleep! Long corridor of the plangent wind! Nothing of the do-nothing! Infinite riffraff! Aurora borealis in the midst of the dimming day! Sleep! A head start on eternity! Tower of the clock-face gone blank! Pawn of the pawnshop! Spanish inheritance for all the have-nots! Rapier slash in the water of the river Lethe! Gold-haloed genius of the great hallucinators! Nest of the little owls! Wing of the featherless! Immense milk cow whose calves we are! Ark in which the young stag and the boa change skins! Glittering rainbow! False side of truth and truth of what's false! Drunkenness the brute calls

rest! Bohemian witch in a tinsel tunic! Tityrus in the shade trying out
his pipes! Time bearing a chibouk instead of a scythe! Fate oiling her
scissors! Fate putting hemp on her spindle! Cat playing with Atropos's
ball of yarn! Sleep! Manna of grace for the disgraced heart! Sleep, wak-
ing up, said, "You murdered me!" You who puff over a spouse in sus-
pended motion, cud-chewer! dilating your reddened pupil, do you
know? Don't you know the sigh—awakening!—yawning at the sky
amid the sun's golden mane and the wild mane of your ardent blond
goddess? No? Do you know the awakening of the filthy philosopher,
the pig, grunting his morning prayer? Or the awakening, like a birth-
certificate, of the whore? Have you ever sounded the reveille of the
hunting pack? Have you ever felt the stealthy beginning of a riot? Or
the leaden awakening of the terminally ill? Have you seen the Neapoli-
tan riffraff roll open their eyes? Do you know, do you know the lark's
song? No, sticky are your eyes, coated is your uvula, cud-chewer! You
don't have insomnia, you awake one! You are not dying for sleep, O
dozing sack! (*various beds—a daytime night*)

# Paria

Qu'ils se payent des républiques,
Hommes libres!—carcan au cou—
Qu'ils peuplent leurs nids domestiques!...
—Moi je suis le maigre coucou.

—Moi,—coeur eunuque, dératé
De ce qui mouille et ce qui vibre...
Que me chante leur Liberté,
A moi? toujours seul. Toujours libre.

—Ma Patrie...elle est par le monde;
Et, puisque la planète est ronde,
Je ne crains pas d'en voir le bout...
Ma patrie est où je la plante:
Terre ou mer, elle est sous la plante
De mes pieds—quand je suis debout.

—Quand je suis couché: ma patrie
C'est la couche seule et meurtrie
Où je vais forcer dans mes bras
Ma moitié, comme moi sans âme;

Et ma moitié: c'est une femme...
Une femme que je n'ai pas.

—L'idéal à moi: c'est un songe
Creux; mon horizon—l'imprévu—
Et le mal du pays me ronge...
Du pays que je n'ai pas vu.

Que les moutons suivent leur route,
De Carcassonne à Tombouctou...
—Moi, ma route me suit. Sans doute
Elle me suivra n'importe où.

Mon pavillon sur moi frissonne,
Il a le ciel pour couronne:
C'est la brise dans mes cheveux...
Et, dans n'importe quelle langue;
Je puis subir une harangue;
Je puis me taire si je veux.

Ma pensée est un souffle aride:
C'est l'air. L'air est à moi partout.
Et ma parole est l'écho vide
Qui ne dit rien—et c'est tout.

Mon passé: c'est ce que j'oublie.
La seule chose qui me lie
C'est ma main dans mon autre main.
Mon souvenir—Rien—C'est ma trace.
Mon présent, c'est tout ce qui passe
Mon avenir—Demain...demain

Je ne connais pas mon semblable;
Moi, je suis ce que je me fais.
—*Le Moi humain est haïssable...*
—Je ne m'aime ni ne me hais.

—Allons! la vie est une fille
Qui m'a pris à son bon plaisir...
Le mien, c'est: la mettre en guenille,
La prostituer sans désir.

—Des dieux?...—Par hasard j'ai pu naître;
Peut-être en est-il—par hasard...
Ceux-là, s'ils veulent me connaître,
Me trouveront bien quelque part.

—Où que je meure: ma patrie
S'ouvrira bien, sans qu'on l'en prie,
Assez grande pour mon linceul...
Un linceul encor: pour que faire?...
Puisque ma patrie est en terre
Mon os ira bien là tout seul...

*Les Amours jaunes*

# Pariah

Let them treat themselves to republics—free men! with an iron collar
around the neck. Let them people their domestic nests—I am the thin
cuckoo. To me, a eunuch heart, amputated of whatever dampens and
quivers, what does their freedom mean? What does it mean to me, who
am always alone, always free? My country—is somewhere in the
world. And since the planet is round, I'm not worried about coming to
the end of it. My country is wherever I put it; on land or sea, it is under
the soles of my feet—when I am standing. When I am stretched out,
my country is the hard and lonely bed where in my arms I rape my
other half, soulless like me, my other half, a woman, a wife I don't
have. My idea of the ideal is an empty dream, my horizon the unex-
pected, and homesickness gnaws at me, for a home I've never seen. Let
sheep follow their road from Carcassonne to Timbuktu; *my* road fol-
lows me, and probably will follow me anywhere. My flag waves over
me and is crowned by the sky: it is the breeze in my hair. And in any
language I can listen to a harangue and be silent if I wish. My thought is
a dry gust, the air. The air belongs to me everywhere. And my speech
is the empty echo saying nothing, and that's all. My past is what I have
forgotten. The only connection I make is my one hand in the other. My
memory: nothing. It's my tracks. My present is whatever happens; my
future: tomorrow, tomorrow. I don't know my fellow man. I am what
I make of myself. *The human ego is detestable.* I neither love nor hate
myself. Oh well, life is a whore that took me for her pleasure; my
pleasure is to leave her in rags and copulate without desire. Gods? I was
perhaps born by chance. Perhaps there are gods—by chance. If they
want to know me, they can certainly find me somewhere. Wherever I
die, my country will be there and open up, unasked, wide enough for
my shroud. But why a shroud? Since my country is in the earth, my
bones can certainly get there by themselves.

## Male-Fleurette

Ici reviendra la fleurette blême
Dont les renouveaux sont toujours passés...
Dans les coeurs ouverts, sur les os tassés,
Une folle brise, un beau jour, la sème...

On crache dessus; on l'imite même,
Pour en effrayer les gens très-sensés...
Ici reviendra la fleurette blême.

—Oh! ne craignez pas son humble anathème
Pour vos ventres mûrs, Cucurbitacés!
Elle connaît bien tous ses trépassés!
Et, quand elle tue, elle sait qu'on l'aime...
—C'est la male-fleur, la fleur de bohème.—

Ici reviendra la fleurette blême.

*Les Amours jaunes*

## The Ill-starred Flower

The pale flowerlet will grow back here over the grave, the flowerlet whose return is always part of the past. In open hearts, over the heaped bones, a wild breeze sows it one fine day. People spit on it; some imitate it even, to horrify sensible people. The pale flowerlet will grow back here. Oh, don't fear its humble anathema will be cast on your ripe bellies, squash; it knows its own dead. And when it kills, it knows its victim loves it: it's the ill-starred flower, the bohemian flower. The pale flowerlet will grow back here.

# ARTHUR RIMBAUD

## Le Bateau ivre

Comme je descendais des Fleuves impassibles,
Je ne me sentis plus guidé par les haleurs:
Des Peaux-Rouges criards les avaient pris pour cibles
Les ayant cloués nus aux poteaux de couleurs.

J'étais insoucieux de tous les équipages,
Porteur de blés flamands ou de cotons anglais.
Quand avec mes haleurs ont fini ces tapages
Les Fleuves m'ont laissé descendre où je voulais.

Dans les clapotements furieux des marées,
Moi, l'autre hiver, plus sourd que les cerveaux d'enfants,
Je courus! Et les Péninsules démarrées
N'ont pas subi tohu-bohus plus triomphants.

La tempête a béni mes éveils maritimes.
Plus léger qu'un bouchon j'ai dansé sur les flots
Qu'on appelle rouleurs éternels de victimes,
Dix nuits, sans regretter l'oeil niais des falots!

Plus douce qu'aux enfants la chair des pommes sûres,
L'eau verte pénétra ma coque de sapin
Et des taches de vins bleus et des vomissures
Me lava, dispersant gouvernail et grappin.

Et dès lors, je me suis baigné dans le Poème
De la Mer, infusé d'astres, et lactescent
Dévorant les azurs verts; où, flottaison blême
Et ravie, un noyé pensif parfois descend;

Où, teignant tout à coup les bleuités, délires
Et rhythmes lents sous les rutilements du jour,
Plus fortes que l'alcool, plus vastes que nos lyres,
Fermentent les rousseurs amères de l'amour!

Je sais les cieux crevant en éclairs, et les trombes
Et les ressacs et les courants: je sais le soir,
L'Aube exaltée ainsi qu'un peuple de colombes,
Et j'ai vu quelquefois ce que l'homme a cru voir!

J'ai vu le soleil bas, taché d'horreurs mystiques,
Illuminant de longs figements violets,
Pareils à des acteurs de drames très-antiques
Les flots roulant au loin leurs frissons de volets!

J'ai rêvé la nuit verte aux neiges éblouies,
Baiser montant aux yeux des mers avec lenteurs,
La circulation des sèves inouïes,
Et l'éveil jaune et bleu des phosphores chanteurs!

J'ai suivi, des mois pleins, pareille aux vacheries
Hystériques, la houle à l'assaut des récifs,
Sans songer que les pieds lumineux des Maries
Pussent forcer le mufle aux Océans poussifs!

J'ai heurté, savez-vous, d'incroyables Florides
Mêlant aux fleurs des yeux de panthères à peaux
D'hommes! Des arcs-en-ciel tendus comme des brides
Sous l'horizon des mers, à de glauques troupeaux!

J'ai vu fermenter les marais énormes, nasses
Où pourrit dans les joncs tout un Léviathan!
Des écroulements d'eaux au milieu des bonaces,
Et les lointains vers les gouffres cataractant!

Glaciers, soleils d'argent, flots nacreux, cieux de braises!
Échouages hideux au fond des golfes bruns
Où les serpents géants dévorés des punaises
Choient, des arbres tordus, avec de noirs parfums!

J'aurais voulu montrer aux enfants ces dorades
Du flot bleu, ces poissons d'or, ces poissons chantants.
—Des écumes de fleurs ont bercé mes dérades
Et d'ineffables vents m'ont ailé par instants.

Parfois, martyr lassé des pôles et des zones,
La mer dont le sanglot faisait mon roulis doux
Montait vers moi ses fleurs d'ombre aux ventouses jaunes
Et je restais, ainsi qu'une femme à genoux...

Presque île, ballottant sur mes bords les querelles
Et les fientes d'oiseaux clabaudeurs aux yeux blonds.
Et je voguais, lorsqu'à travers mes liens frêles
Des noyés descendaient dormir, à reculons!

Or moi, bateau perdu sous les cheveux des anses,
Jeté par l'ouragan dans l'éther sans oiseau,
Moi dont les Monitors et les voiliers des Hanses
N'auraient pas repêché la carcasse ivre d'eau;

Libre, fumant, monté de brumes violettes,
Moi qui trouais le ciel rougeoyant comme un mur
Qui porte, confiture exquise aux bons poètes,
Des lichens de soleil et des morves d'azur,

Qui courais, taché de lunules électriques,
Planche folle, escorté des hippocampes noirs,
Quand les juillets faisaient crouler à coups de triques
Les cieux ultramarins aux ardents entonnoirs;

Moi qui tremblais, sentant geindre à cinquante lieues
Le rut des Béhémots et les Maelstroms épais,
Fileur éternel des immobilités bleues,
Je regrette l'Europe aux anciens parapets!

J'ai vu des archipels sidéraux! et des îles
Dont les cieux délirants sont ouverts au vogueur:
—Est-ce en ces nuits sans fond que tu dors et t'exiles,
Million d'oiseaux d'or, ô future Vigueur?—

Mais, vrai, j'ai trop pleuré! Les Aubes sont navrantes.
Toute lune est atroce et tout soleil amer:
L'âcre amour m'a gonflé de torpeurs enivrantes.
O que ma quille éclate! O que j'aille à la mer!

Si je désire une eau d'Europe, c'est la flache
Noire et froide où vers le crépuscule embaumé
Un enfant accroupi plein de tristesses, lâche
Un bateau frêle comme un papillon de mai.

Je ne puis plus, baigné de vos langueurs, ô lames,
Enlever leur sillage aux porteurs de cotons,
Ni traverser l'orgueil des drapeaux et des flammes,
Ni nager sous les yeux horribles des pontons.

*Poésies*

## The Drunken Boat

As I was going down impassive rivers, I suddenly felt I was no
longer guided by my haulers: screaming redskins had taken them for

targets, nailing them naked to colored poles. A carrier of Flemish grain or English cottons, I cared not at all about crews. When the screeching vanished with my haulers, the rivers let me go where I wanted. In the furious splash of tides, the other winter, I ran free, more headstrong than children. And the loosened peninsulas have not undergone a more triumphant uproar. Storms blessed my sea vigil. Lighter than a cork I danced on the waves, said to roll their victims eternally—ten nights, and I did not miss the idiotic eye of the lighthouses. Sweeter to me than the flesh of unripe apples to children, the green water penetrated my fir hull and washed off stains of vomit and cheap wine, scattering rudder and grappling hook. And from that moment on I bathed in the Poem of the Sea infused with stars and milky; I devoured the green azure surfaces where, like a bit of pale and ecstatic flotsam, a dead body occasionally sinks, where, dyeing the blue, like a delirium of slow rhythms under the dawn's ruddiness, stronger than alcohol and vaster than our lyres, the bitter russet shades of love ferment. I know skies bursting with flashes of lightning and waterspouts and clashing tides and streams; I know evening, dawn rising like a people of doves, and I have sometimes seen what man only thinks he has seen! I have seen the low sun spotted with mystic horrors, illuminating with long purple clots, like the actors of some ancient drama, the waves rolling in the distance like quivering slats. I have dreamed away the green night with shining snow like a kiss slowly rising to the sea's eyes, unheard-of saps in circulation, and the yellow and blue phosphorous awakening and singing. For whole months I followed the swell, like some hysterical cowbarn attacking the reefs, and never thought that the Saintes-Maries' shining foot could force back the puffing Ocean's snout. I encountered, can you believe it, incredible Floridas, where the flowers mingle with the eyes of panthers with human skins. Rainbows stretched out under the sea's horizon like reins to reach green flocks. I have seen great Sargasso Seas, traps in which a whole Leviathan rots in the reeds, water caving in amid the calms, and the distant reaches falling like a cataract into chasms. Glaciers, silver suns, pearly waves, skies glowing like embers! Hideous runnings aground in dark gulfs, where giant snakes devoured by bedbugs tumble from twisted trees with a black odor! I should like to have shown children the dorados in the blue wave, the golden fish, the singing fish—foams of flowers have rocked my harborless wanderings and indescribable winds winged me at moments. Sometimes, when I felt like the weary martyr of poles and zones, the sea, whose sob was my gentle roll, sent up toward me its shadow flowers with yellow suckers, and I paused like a kneeling woman, an islet almost, bearing in my turnings and tossings the screechings and droppings of quarrelsome blond-eyed birds. And I sailed on, when through my loosening planks dead men drifted down backwards to sleep. Yet now I—a boat lost in the hairy foliage of coves, tossed by hurricanes into the birdless ether—I, whose water-drunken body the Monitors and sailing ships of the Hanseatic League would not have salvaged, I, free, smoking, fitted out with purple mists, I, who pierced the reddening sky like a wall, who bear, like some jam loved of good poets, lichens of sunlight and azure mucus, who shot through the water like some wild stray board, covered with electric glowing spots and escorted by black seahorses, when July beat down with its cudgel the ultramarine skies and their burning funnels, I, who trembled, hearing groan fifty leagues away the copulating Behemoths and the thick Maelstroms, I, who skim along eternally in the immobile blue, I miss Europe and its ancient parapets! I have seen archipelagoes of stars! and islands whose wild skies are open to the passing ship: is it in these infinite nights that you sleep in exile, O golden birds by the millions, O future strength? But true, I have wept too much! Dawns are heart-breaking. All moons are horrible, and every sun bitter: acrid love has swollen me with intoxicating torpor. O let my keel burst, let me go out and into the sea! If I desire European water, it is the black, cold puddle into which, in the odoriferous twilight, a child, squatting and sad, sends a boat fragile as a May butterfly. I can no longer, bathed in your languid motion, O waves, follow hard on the merchant ships bearing cotton or cross in front of the haughty flags and flames of battleships or swim under the horrible eyes of prison ships.

## Mémoire

### I

L'eau claire; comme le sel des larmes d'enfance,
L'assaut au soleil des blancheurs des corps de femmes;
la soie, en foule et de lys pur, des oriflammes
sous les murs dont quelque pucelle eut la défense;

l'ébat des anges;—Non...le courant d'or en marche,
meut ses bras, noirs, et lourds, et frais surtout, d'herbe. Elle
sombre, ayant le Ciel bleu pour ciel-de-lit, appelle
pour rideaux l'ombre de la colline et de l'arche.

## II

Eh! l'humide carreau tend ses bouillons limpides!
L'eau meuble d'or pâle et sans fond les couches prêtes.
Les robes vertes et déteintes des fillettes
font les saules, d'où sautent les oiseaux sans brides.

Plus pure qu'un louis, jaune et chaude paupière
le souci d'eau—ta foi conjugale, ô l'Epouse!—
au midi prompt, de son terne miroir, jalouse
au ciel gris de chaleur la Sphère rose et chère.

## III

Madame se tient trop debout dans la prairie
prochaine où neigent les fils du travail; l'ombrelle
aux doigts; foulant l'ombelle; trop fière pour elle;
des enfants lisant dans la verdure fleurie

leur livre de maroquin rouge! Hélas, Lui, comme
mille anges blancs qui se séparent sur la route,
s'éloigne par delà la montagne! Elle, toute
froide, et noire, court! après le départ de l'homme!

## IV

Regret des bras épais et jeunes d'herbe pure!
Or des lunes d'avril au coeur du saint lit! Joie
des chantiers riverains à l'abandon, en proie
aux soirs d'août qui faisaient germer ces pourritures!

Qu'elle pleure à présent sous les remparts! l'haleine
des peupliers d'en haut est pour la seule brise.
Puis, c'est la nappe, sans reflets, sans source, grise:
un vieux, dragueur, dans sa barque immobile, peine.

## V

Jouet de cet oeil d'eau morne, je n'y puis prendre,
ô canot immobile! oh! bras trop courts! ni l'une
ni l'autre fleur: ni la jaune qui m'importune,
là; ni la bleue, amie à l'eau couleur de cendre.

Ah! la poudre des saules qu'une aile secoue!
Les roses des roseaux dès longtemps dévorées!

Mon canot, toujours fixe; et sa chaîne tirée
Au fond de cet oeil d'eau sans bords,—à quelle boue?

*Illuminations*
(first edition)

## Memory

I. Bright water; like the salt of childhood's tears; the women's white bodies defying the sun in their brilliance; the abundant silk banners with pure lilies and oriflammes under the walls some virgin defended; an angels' frolic—no, the golden current, as it advances, moves its arms, black, heavy, and cool with grass. It sinks and spreads, having the blue sky for a bed canopy, summoning for curtains the shadow of the hill and the bridge's arch. II. Ah, the wet surface spreads out its limpid bubbles! The water furnishes the waiting bed with pale bottomless gold. Willows, from which unbridled birds spring, look like little girls' green, faded dresses. Purer than a gold louis, a yellow warm eyelid, the marsh marigold—symbol of your fidelity, O spouse—turned to the south, closely follows, like some dim mirror, the dear, pink sphere in the sky grey with heat. III. Madam stands too straight in the nearby meadow on which snow down the sons of work; her parasol in her fingers, crushing the umbel, too proud for her; children reading in the flowering verdure their book bound in red leather. Alas, He, like a thousand white angels, taking leave on the road, goes off behind the mountain. She, quite cold and black, runs! after the man's departure! IV. Regret for the thick young arms of pure grass! April moon gold in the depths of the holy bed! Joy of abandoned river dockyards, in the grip of August evenings which made their rot germinate. Let her now weep under the ramparts! Her only breeze is the breath of the poplars above. Then comes the grey sheet of water without reflections or movement from the springs: an old man, a dredger, labors in his motionless boat. V. I am the plaything of this dreary eye of water. O, my motionless boat! Oh! my arms too short! I can pluck neither flower, the yellow, troubling one nor the friendly blue one, in the ashen grey water. Ah, the willows' dust disturbed by a wing! The reed roses long ago consumed; my boat, still immobile, and its chain pulled from what mud at the bottom of this limitless eye of water?

## Bonne Pensée du matin

A quatre heures du matin, l'été,
Le sommeil d'amour dure encore.
Sous les bosquets l'aube évapore
    L'odeur du soir fêté.

Mais là-bas dans l'immense chantier
Vers le soleil des Hespérides,
En bras de chemise, les charpentiers
    Déjà s'agitent.

Dans leur désert de mousse, tranquilles,
Ils préparent les lambris précieux
Où la richesse de la ville
    Rira sous de faux cieux.

Ah! pour ces Ouvriers charmants
Sujets d'un roi de Babylone,
Vénus! laisse un peu les Amants,
    Dont l'âme est en couronne.

    O Reine des Bergers!
    Porte aux travailleurs l'eau-de-vie,
    Pour que leurs forces soient en paix
En attendant le bain dans la mer, à midi.

*Illuminations*
(first edition)

## Kindly Morning Thought

At four in the morning in summer, love's sleep still lasts. In the groves, dawn evaporates the scent of the evening's festivities. But in the distance, in the immense shipyard, in the direction of the Hesperides' sun, the carpenters in shirtsleeves are already busy. Quiet in their expanses of moss, they are preparing the precious panels on which the city's wealth will laugh under false skies. Ah, for these charming workmen, subjects of a king of Babylon, Venus! leave for a moment the lovers whose souls' desires are crowned. O Queen of Shepherds, bring brandy to the workmen, so that their strength will be at peace, until their swim in the sea at noon.

Entends comme brame
près des acacias
en avril la rame
viride du pois!

Dans sa vapeur nette,
vers Phoebé! tu vois
s'agiter la tête
de saints d'autrefois...

Loin des claires meules
des caps, des beaux toits,
ces chers Anciens veulent
ce philtre sournois...

Or ni fériale
ni astrale! n'est
la brume qu'exhale
ce nocturne effet.

Néanmoins ils restent,
—Sicile, Allemagne,
dans ce brouillard triste
et blêmi, justement!

*Illuminations* (first edition)

Hear how in April, near the acacias, the peas' green stake bays. In its
sharp haze, toward the moon! you see the heads of old saints moving.
Far from the bright haystacks, the headlands, the fine roofs, these dear
Ancients want this sly magic potion. Now the mist emanating from
this nocturnal effect is neither from festivities nor stars. Nevertheless,
they remain, Sicily, Germany, in this sad and wan fog, rightly!

## Jeune Ménage

La chambre est ouverte au ciel bleu-turquin;
Pas de place: des coffrets et des huches!
Dehors le mur est plein d'aristoloches
Où vibrent les gencives des lutins.

Que ce sont bien intrigues de génies
Cette dépense et ces désordres vains!

C'est la fée africaine qui fournit
La mûre, et les résilles dans les coins.

Plusieurs entrent, marraines mécontentes,
En pans de lumière dans les buffets,
Puis y restent! le ménage s'absente
Peu sérieusement, et rien ne se fait.

Le marié a le vent qui le floue
Pendant son absence, ici, tout le temps.
Même des esprits des eaux, malfaisants
Entrent vaguer aux sphères de l'alcôve.

La nuit, l'amie oh! la lune de miel
Cueillera leur sourire et remplira
De mille bandeaux de cuivre le ciel.
Puis ils auront affaire au malin rat.

—S'il n'arrive pas un feu follet blême,
Comme un coup de fusil, après des vêpres.
—O spectres saints et blancs de Bethléem,
Charmez plutôt le bleu de leur fenêtre!

*Illuminations* (first edition)

## Newlyweds

The Chamber is open to the turquoise sky. There is no room: trunks and chests! Outside the wall is covered with birthwort vibrating with sprites' gums. It certainly looks like jinns have been at work: so much money spent and such pointless disorder! The African fairy provides the mulberries and spiderwebs in corners. Several none-too-pleased godmothers enter the sideboards on beams of light, then stay. The couple has gone out rather frivolously, and nothing gets done. The husband is being cheated here by the wind, all the time during his absence. Even evil water sprites come in and wander in the circles of the bed niche. At night, their friend, oh the honeymoon, will pluck their smile and fill the sky with a thousand copper bands. Then they will have to deal with the sly rat. Unless a pale *ignis fatuus* appears, like a gunshot, after vespers. O holy white ghosts of Bethlehem, enchant, rather, their blue window!

# Bruxelles

*Juillet.*        Boulevart du Régent,

Plates-bandes d'amarantes jusqu'à
L'agréable palais de Jupiter.
—Je sais que c'est Toi, qui, dans ces lieux,
Mêles ton Bleu presque de Sahara!

Puis, comme rose et sapin du soleil
Et liane ont ici leurs jeux enclos,
Cage de la petite veuve!...

                                                    Quelles
Troupes d'oiseaux! ô iaio, iaio!...

—Calmes maisons, anciennes passions!
Kiosque de la Folle par affection.
Après les fesses des rosiers, balcon
Ombreux et très-bas de la Juliette.

—La Juliette, ça rappelle l'Henriette,
Charmante station du chemin de fer
Au coeur d'un mont comme au fond d'un verger
Où mille diables bleus dansent dans l'air!

Banc vert où chante au paradis d'orage,
Sur la guitare, la blanche Irlandaise.
Puis de la salle à manger guyanaise
Bavardage des enfants et des cages.

Fenêtre du duc qui fais que je pense
Au poison des escargots et du buis
Qui dort ici-bas au soleil. Et puis
C'est trop beau! Gardons notre silence.

—Boulevart sans mouvement ni commerce,
Muet, tout drame et toute comédie,
Réunion des scènes infinie,
Je te connais et t'admire en silence.

*Illuminations* (first edition)

# Brussels

July. Regent's Boulevard. Beds of amaranthus as far as Jupiter's
pleasant palace. You are the one, I know, who mingles your almost

Saharan blue in these skies! Then, since the interplay of rose and sun fir
and vines is enclosed here, the little widow's cage! What flocks of birds!
O yaio, yaio! Calm houses, old passions! Summerhouse of the woman
mad from love. After the rose branches, Juliet's very low shadowy bal-
cony. Juliet brings to mind Henrietta, a charming train station located
in the heart of a mountain, as if in an orchard, where a thousand blue
devils dance in the air! A green bench where in the storm paradise the
white Irish lady sings with her guitar. Then from the Guianan dining
room, the chatter of children and cages. The duke's window reminding
me of poisonous snails and boxwood sleeping here in the sun. And
then—but it's too lovely, too lovely; let us remain silent. Boulevard
void of business and movement, silent, nothing but melodrama and
theater, the meeting place of a thousand scenes, I know you and admire
you without speaking.

> Est-elle almée?... aux premières heures bleues
> Se détruira-t-elle comme les fleurs feues...
> Devant la splendide étendue où l'on sente
> Souffler la ville énormément florissante!
>
> C'est trop beau! c'est trop beau! mais c'est nécessaire
> —Pour la Pêcheuse et la chanson du Corsaire,
> Et aussi puisque les derniers masques crurent
> Encore aux fêtes de nuit sur la mer pure!
>
> *Illuminations* (first edition)

Is it an Oriental dancer? In the first blue hours will she disintegrate
like dead flowers—before the splendid vastness in which you feel the
breath of the enormously flourishing city! It's too beautiful, too beauti-
ful to last, and must necessarily yield before the fisherwoman and the
pirate's song, and also because the last masks actually still believed in
nighttime festivities on the pure sea.

## Larme

> Loin des oiseaux, des troupeaux, des villageoises,
> Je buvais, accroupi dans quelque bruyère
> Entourée de tendres bois de noisetiers,
> Par un brouillard d'après-midi tiède et vert.

Que pouvais-je boire dans cette jeune Oise,
Ormeaux sans voix, gazon sans fleurs, ciel couvert.
Que tirais-je à la gourde de colocase?
Quelque liqueur d'or, fade et qui fait suer.

Tel, j'eusse été mauvaise enseigne d'auberge.
Puis l'orage changea le ciel, jusqu'au soir.
Ce furent des pays noirs, des lacs, des perches,
Des colonnades sous la nuit bleue, des gares.

L'eau des bois se perdait sur des sables vierges.
Le vent, du ciel, jetait des glaçons aux mares...
Or! tel qu'un pêcheur d'or ou de coquillages,
Dire que je n'ai pas eu souci de boire!

*Illuminations* (first edition)

## Tear

Far from birds, flocks, and village girls, I was drinking, squatting in the heather, surrounded by tender hazelnut groves, in a warm, green afternoon fog. What could I be drinking in this affluent of the Oise, voiceless elms, flowerless turf, cloudy sky! What was I drinking from the colocasia gourd? Insipid golden beer that makes you sweat. Looking the way I did, I would not have made an appealing picture for an inn sign. Then a storm changed the sky until evening. There were black lands, lakes, poles, colonnades in the blue night, stations. The water from the woods ran off into virgin sand. The wind from the sky threw hailstones into the ponds. Now! looking like a fisherman of gold or shells in the sunset, just imagine, I didn't care to drink!

## Fêtes de la patience

## 1. Bannières de mai

Aux branches claires des tilleuls
Meurt un maladif hallali.
Mais des chansons spirituelles
Voltigent parmi les groseilles.
Que notre sang rie en nos veines,
Voici s'enchevêtrer les vignes.
Le ciel est joli comme un ange.

L'azur et l'onde communient.
Je sors. Si un rayon me blesse
Je succomberai sur la mousse.

Qu'on patiente et qu'on s'ennuie
C'est trop simple. Fi de mes peines.
Je veux que l'été dramatique
Me lie à son char de fortune.
Que par toi beaucoup, ô Nature,
—Ah moins seul et moins nul!—je meure.
Au lieu que les Bergers, c'est drôle,
Meurent à peu près par le monde.

Je veux bien que les saisons m'usent.
A toi, Nature, je me rends;
Et ma faim et toute ma soif.
Et, s'il te plaît, nourris, abreuve.
Rien de rien ne m'illusionne;
C'est rire aux parents, qu'au soleil,
Mais moi je ne veux rire à rien;
Et libre soit cette infortune.

## Rejoicings in Misfortune

## 1. Banners of May

In the bright branches of the linden trees, a sickly death cry grows faint. But spiritual canticles bound through the gooseberries. Let our blood rejoice in our veins, for now the vines are entwining thickly. The sky is pretty as an angel. The blue sky and blue sea receive the sacrament. I go out. If a sunbeam wounds me, I shall succumb on the moss. It is too simple for me merely to suffer and be wretched. Enough of my troubles! I want dramatic summer to bind me to her chariot of fortune. O Nature, let me die immensely through you—less alone and null! Whereas shepherds, it's funny, die more or less throughout the world. I am ready for the seasons to wear me thin. To you, Nature, I give myself, and my hunger and all my thirst. And, if you please, give food, give drink. I am no longer deceived about anything. Laughing to the sun is laughing to parents. But I want to laugh at nothing. And let my misfortune be free.

## 2. Chanson de la plus haute tour

Oisive jeunesse
A tout asservie,
Par délicatesse
J'ai perdu ma vie.
Ah! Que le temps vienne
Où les coeurs s'éprennent.

Je me suis dit: laisse,
Et qu'on ne te voie:
Et sans la promesse
De plus hautes joies.
Que rien ne t'arrête
Auguste retraite.

J'ai tant fait patience
Qu'à jamais j'oublie;
Craintes et souffrances
Aux cieux sont parties.
Et la soif malsaine
Obscurcit mes veines.

Ainsi la Prairie
A l'oubli livrée,
Grandie, et fleurie
D'encens et d'ivraies
Au bourdon farouche
De cent sales mouches.

Ah! Mille veuvages
De la si pauvre âme
Qui n'a que l'image
De la Notre-Dame!
Est-ce que l'on prie
La Vierge Marie?

Oisive jeunesse
A tout asservie
Par délicatesse
J'ai perdu ma vie.
Ah! Que le temps vienne
Où les coeurs s'éprennent!

## 2. Song of the Highest Tower

In my useless youth, a slave to every concern, by thoughtfulness for others, I lost my life. Ah! Let the time come, when hearts are in love. I told myself stop! have nothing to do with others, and until you are certain of the highest joys, let nothing put an end to your august retreat. I have been patient in misfortune for so long that by now I can't remember the causes or beginnings. Fears and sufferings have risen to heaven, and unwholesome thirst darkens my veins. Thus the meadow given over to oblivion, growing wild and rank with incense and tares, under the fearful drone of a hundred filthy flies. Ah! The thousand widowhoods of my poor soul, which has only a cheap image of Our Lady. Should I pray to the Virgin Mary? In my useless youth, a slave to every concern, by thoughtfulness for others I lost my life. Ah! Let the time come, when hearts are in love.

## 3. L'Eternité

Elle est retrouvée.
Quoi?—L'Eternité.
C'est la mer allée
Avec le soleil.

Ame sentinelle,
Murmurons l'aveu
De la nuit si nulle
Et du jour en feu.

Des humains suffrages,
Des communs élans
Là tu te dégages
Et voles selon.

Puisque de vous seules,
Braises de satin,
Le Devoir s'exhale
Sans qu'on dise: enfin.

Là pas d'espérance,
Nul orietur.
Science avec patience,
Le supplice est sûr.

Elle est retrouvée.
Quoi?—L'Eternité.
C'est la mer allée
Avec le soleil.

### 3. Eternity

It has been found. What? Eternity. It is the sea stretching out under the sun. My soul on watch, let us murmur our recognition of night's nullity and the fiery day. From human approbation, from common aspirations, you now free yourself and soar as you wish. Since from you alone, satin embers of the sky, breathes spiritual duty, to which one never says: enough. There is no hope there, no new sunrise; knowledge with suffering, the torment is certain. It has been found. What? Eternity. It is the sea stretching out under the sun.

### 4. Age d'or

Quelqu'une des voix
Toujours angélique
—Il s'agit de moi,—
Vertement s'explique:

Ces mille questions
Qui se ramifient
N'amènent, au fond,
Qu'ivresse et folie;

Reconnais ce tour
Si gai, si facile:
Ce n'est qu'onde, flore,
Et c'est ta famille!

Puis elle chante. O
Si gai, si facile,
Et visible à l'oeil nu...
—Je chante avec elle,—

Reconnais ce tour
Si gai, si facile,
Ce n'est qu'onde, flore,
Et c'est ta famille!...etc...

Et puis une voix
—Est-elle angélique!—

Il s'agit de moi,
Vertement s'explique;

Et chante à l'instant
En soeur des haleines:
D'un ton Allemand,
Mais ardente et pleine:

Le monde est vicieux;
Si cela t'étonne!
Vis et laisse au feu
L'obscure infortune.

O! joli château!
Que ta vie est claire!
De quel Age es-tu,
Nature princière
De notre grand frère! etc...

Je chante aussi, moi:
Multiples soeurs! voix
Pas du tout publiques!
Environnez-moi
De gloire pudique...etc...

*Illuminations* (first edition)


# 4. Golden Age

    One of the ever angelic voices, talking about me, sharply expresses
its opinion: "Trying to answer these thousand questions and their ram-
ifications simply brings on self-intoxication and madness. Learn this
turn of thought, so gay, so simple: The world is only wave and flora,
your family!" Then the voice sings, oh, so gay, so simple, and visible
to the naked eye; I sing with it: "Learn this turn of thought, so gay, so
simple: the world is only wave and flora, your family! etc." And then a
voice—how angelic!—talking about me, sharply expresses its opinion
and sings immediately, like a sister of the breezes, in a German tone,
but ardent and full: "The world is vitiated, as if that surprised you! Live
and cast your dark misfortune into the fire." O pretty castle! How
bright your life is! What age do you belong to, princely nature of our
big brother! etc. I sing also: Multiple sisters! Private voices! Surround
me with chaste glory, etc.

O saisons, ô châteaux
Quelle âme est sans défauts?

O saisons, ô châteaux,

J'ai fait la magique étude
Du Bonheur, que nul n'élude.

O vive lui, chaque fois
Que chante son coq gaulois.

Mais! je n'aurai plus d'envie,
Il s'est chargé de ma vie.

Ce Charme! il prit âme et corps,
Et dispersa tous efforts.

Que comprendre à ma parole?
Il fait qu'elle fuie et vole!

O saisons, ô châteaux!

(Et, si le malheur m'entraîne,
Sa disgrâce m'est certaine.

Il faut que son dédain, las!
Me livre au plus prompt trépas!

—O Saisons, ô Châteaux!)

*Illuminations* (first edition)

O seasons, O castles, what soul is without faults? O seasons, O cas-
tles, I have made the magic study of happiness which no one can avoid
making. O praise to him each time his Gallic cock sings. Why, I shall
have no more desires; he has taken on the care of my life. This spell! It
took body and soul and relieved me of any further effort. What can my
words mean? They must flee and fly! O seasons, O castles. [And if
misfortune leads me into its error, I shall be in his certain disgrace. His
disdain for me must, alas, give me over to death directly! O seasons, O
castles!— *Lines added on the manuscript and crossed out.*]

# GEORGES RODENBACH

## La Vie des chambres IV

Mon âme, tout ce long et triste après-midi,
A souffert de la mort d'un bouquet, imminente!
Il était, loin de moi, dans la chambre attenante
Où ma peur l'éloigna, déjà presque engourdi,
Bouquet dépérissant de fleurs qu'on croyait sauves
Encor pour tout un jour dans la pitié de l'eau,
Gloxinias de neige avec des galons mauves,
Bouquet qui dans la chambre éteignait son halo
Et se désargentait en ce soir de dimanche!
Mon âme, tu souffris et tu t'ingénias
A voir ta vie, aussi fanée et qui se penche,
Agoniser avec ces deux gloxinias.
Or me cherchant moi-même en cette analogie
J'ai passé cette fin de journée à m'aigrir
Par le spectacle vain et la psychologie
Douloureuse des fleurs pâles qui vont mourir.
Triste vase: hôpital, froide alcôve de verre
Qu'un peu de vent, par la fenêtre ouverte, aère,
Mais qui les fait mourir plus vite, en spasmes doux,
Les pauvres fleurs, dans l'eau vaine, qui sont phtisiques,
Répandant, comme en de brusques accès de toux,
Leurs corolles sur les tapis mélancoliques.
Douceur! mourir ainsi sans heurts, comme on s'endort,
Car les fleurs ne sont pas tristes devant la mort,
Et disparaître avec ce calme crépuscule
Qui d'un jaune rayon à peine s'acidule.

*Le Règne du silence*

## The Life of Rooms IV

My soul has, this whole long sad afternoon, suffered from the fast
approaching death of a bouquet! It was far from me, in the next room,
to which I had banished it through cowardice when it was almost
numb, a bouquet of perishing flowers I had thought were saved for yet
another whole day by pitying water, snow-white gloxinias, with

mauve stripes, a bouquet whose halo was growing faint in the room and losing all its silvery quality on this Sunday evening. My soul, you suffered, and cleverly managed to see your life, as withered and as drooping, dying with these two gloxinias. Seeking myself in this analogy I spent the end of the day growing bitter at the hopeless spectacle and the sorrowful frame of mind of pale flowers about to die. A sad vase: like a hospital, this cold glass alcove aired by a bit of wind from the open window, which makes them die faster with delicate spasms, these poor flowers, in the useless water, tubercular flowers, casting, as if in sudden coughing fits, their petals on the melancholy rugs. What sweetness to die thus peacefully, the way one falls asleep, for flowers are not sad confronted with death. To disappear with this calm twilight but faintly harshened by a yellow sunbeam!

## La Vie des chambres VII

Les vitrages de tulle en fleur et de guipures
Pendent sur les carreaux en un blanc nonchaloir;
On y voit des bouquets comme des découpures
Adhérant sur la vitre au verre déjà noir.
Mais le tulle est si loin, encor qu'il les effleure,
Et ne s'y mêle pas, en vivant à côté;
Les blancheurs des rideaux n'étant au fond qu'un leurre
Qui laisse aux carreaux froids toute leur nudité!
Et leurs frimas figés, flore artificielle,
Ne font pas oublier aux vitres d'autres soirs
Où de réelles fleurs naissent des carreaux noirs,
Des fleurs que la gelée élabore et nielle,
—Au lieu de ce grésil de linge mensonger—
Songe de fleurs qui ne leur est plus étranger,
Blancheurs où leur cristal se sent brusquement vivre,
Ramages incrustés dans le verre, et brodés
Sur les carreaux qui s'en sont tout enguirlandés,
Rideaux incorporés en dentelles de givre!

*Le Règne du silence*

## The Life of Rooms VII

The glass curtains of flowered tulle and lace hang in the windows, white and indifferent. You see in them bouquets like cut-outs adhering to the window on the already black glass. But the tulle is so far away, even though it grazes them, and lives apart, not mingling with them, since the curtains' whiteness is really only a deception, leaving the cold panes their perfect bareness. And their rigid frost, artificial flora, does not make the windows forget other evenings when real flowers are born out of the black panes: flowers drawn by the ice and nielloed by it, instead of this deceptive linen frost. A dream of flowers is not alien to the windowpanes, a whiteness in which their crystal comes suddenly to life, a floral pattern incrusted in the glass and embroidered on panes completely garlanded with its branches: curtains incorporated into lace of hoarfrost.

## La Vie des chambres XVII

Les chambres, dans le soir, meurent réellement:
Les persiennes sont des paupières se fermant
Sur les yeux des carreaux pâles où tout se brouille;
Chaque fauteuil est un prêtre qui s'agenouille
Pour l'entrée en surplis d'une Extrême-Onction;
La pendule dévide avec monotonie
Les instants brefs de son rosaire d'agonie;
Et la glace encor claire offre une Assomption
Où l'on devine, au fond de l'ombre, un envol d'âme!
Quotidienne détresse! Ame blanche du jour
Qui nous quitte et nous laisse orphelins de sa flamme!
Car chaque soir cette douleur est de retour
De la mort du soleil en adieu sur nos tempes
Et de l'obscurité de crêpe sur nos mains.
O chambres en grand deuil où jusqu'aux lendemains
Nous consolons nos yeux avec du clair de lampes!

*Le Règne du silence*

## The Life of Rooms XVII

Rooms in the evening really die: the blinds are eyelids closing over the eyes of the pale panes, where everything grows dim. Each armchair is a priest kneeling and putting on his surplice for the last rites. The clock ticks off, one by one, the brief moments of its rosary of death. And the still bright mirror looks like an assumption, where you sense that a soul is rising from the depths of the shadow. A daily agony! The

white soul of the day leaving us, orphaned of his flame. For each eve-
ning this sorrow recurs, from the death of the sun and its farewell on
our temples and from the crepe-like darkness on our hands. O rooms in
deep mourning, where until the next day, we console our eyes with the
brightness of lamps!

## Aquarium mental V

Ah! mon âme sous verre, et si bien à l'abri!
Toute elle s'appartient dans l'atmosphère enclose;
Ce qu'elle avait de lie ou de vase dépose;
Le cristal contigu n'en est plus assombri.
Transparence de l'âme et du verre complice,
Que nul désir n'atteint, qu'aucun émoi ne plisse!
Mon âme s'est fermée et limitée à soi;
Et, n'ayant pas voulu se mêler à la vie,
S'en épure et de plus en plus se clarifie.
Ame déjà fluide où cesse tout émoi;
Mon âme est devenue aquatique et lunaire;
Elle est toute fraîcheur, elle est toute clarté
Et je vis comme si mon âme avait été
De la lune et de l'eau qu'on aurait mis sous verre.

*Les Vies encloses*

## Mental Aquarium V

Ah! my soul under glass and so sheltered! Shut up in this atmosphere
it belongs solely to itself, discharges any dregs or mud it had, but the
contiguous crystal is none the darker for it. Transparency of the soul
and its accomplice the glass, touched by no desire, furrowed by no
emotion! My soul has closed and is limited to itself, and, having refused
to mingle with life, purifies itself of any mundane traces and grows
clearer and clearer. My soul, already emotionless and fluid, has become
aquatic and lunar; it is all coolness and brightness, and I live as if my
soul were moon and water put under glass.

## Les Malades aux fenêtres II

Le malade souvent examine ses mains,
Si pâles, n'ayant plus que des gestes bénins

De sacerdoce et d'offices, à peine humaines;
Il consulte ses mains, ses doigts trop délicats
Qui, plus que le visage, élucident son cas
Avec leur maigre ivoire et leurs débiles veines.

Surtout le soir, il les considère en songeant
Parmi le crépuscule, automne des journées,
Et dans elles, qui sont longues d'être affinées,
Voit son mal comme hors de lui se prolongeant,
Mains pâles d'autant plus que l'obscurité tombe!
Elles semblent s'aimer et semblent s'appeler;
Elles ont des blancheurs frileuses de colombe
Et, sveltes, on dirait qu'elles vont s'envoler.
Elles font sur l'air des taches surnaturelles
Comme si du nouveau clair de lune en chemin
Entrait par la fenêtre et se posait sur elles.
Or la pâleur est la même sur chaque main,
Et le malade songe à ses mains anciennes;
Il ne reconnaît plus ces mains pâles pour siennes;
Tel un petit enfant qui voit ses mains dans l'eau.

Puis le malade mire au miroir sans mémoire
—Le miroir qui concentre un moment son eau noire—
Ses mains qu'il voit sombrer comme un couple jumeau;
O vorace fontaine, obstinée et maigrie,
Où le malade suit ses mains, dans quel recul!
Couple blanc qui s'enfonce et de plus en plus nul
Jusqu'à ce que l'eau du miroir se soit tarie.
Il songe alors qu'il va bientôt ne plus pouvoir
Les suivre, quand sera total l'afflux du soir
Dans cette eau du profond miroir toute réduite:
Et n'est-ce pas les voir mourir, que cette fuite?

*Les Vies encloses*

## Invalids at the Window II

The invalid often looks at his hands, so pale, with their scarcely human, their benign priestly and liturgical gestures. He examines his hands with their too delicate fingers, which, more than his face, make clear his case, by their thin and weakly veined ivory. Above all in the evening he looks at them, as he dreams in the twilight, autumn of the

day, and in his hands, longer seeming because of their thinness, he sees
his sickness projected outside himself, in his hands all the more pale
because darkness is falling. They seem to love and summon one an-
other; with their dovelike white shivers, and, slim as they are, they
appear about to take wing. They seem like unreal things in the air, as if
rising new moonlight had come through the window and lit upon
them. The hands are equal in pallor, and the invalid thinks of his former
hands; he does not recognize these pale hands as his, like a small child
seeing his hands in water. Then he holds up to the memoryless mirror
his hands, which he sees sink like a twin pair in the black, concentrated
water of the mirror. Oh devouring, persistent, dwindling spring, in
which the invalid follows his hands—at what distance! The white pair
plunge and will vanish to nothingness when the mirror's water is dried
up. He thinks then that soon he will no longer be able to follow them,
when the flood of evening will be complete in this condensed water of
the deep mirror. And is their flight not their death?


## Les Malades aux fenêtres XII

L'eau des anciens canaux est débile et malade,
Si morne, parmi les villes mortes, aux quais
Parés d'arbres et de pignons en enfilade
Qui sont, dans cette eau pauvre, à peine décalqués.
Eau vieillie et sans force; eau malingre et déprise
De tout élan pour se raidir contre la brise
Qui lui creuse trop de rides... Oh! la triste eau
Qui va pleurer sous les ponts noirs et qui s'afflige
Des reflets qu'elle doit porter, eau vraiment lige,
Et qui lui sont comme un immobile fardeau.
Mais, trop âgée, à la surface qui se moire,
Elle perd ses reflets, comme on perd la mémoire,
Et les délaie en de confus mirages gris.
Eau si dolente, au point qu'elle en semble mortelle,
Pourquoi si nue et si déjà nulle? Et qu'a-t-elle,
Toute à sa somnolence, à ses songes aigris,
Pour n'être ainsi plus qu'un traître miroir de givre
Où la lune elle-même a de la peine à vivre?

*Les Vies encloses*

## Invalids at the Window XII

Water in the old canals is weak and sickly, so dreary in dead cities, where the canal-side streets are lined with trees and gables whose shapes are barely reproduced in this poor water. Aged and feeble water, sickly, devoid of any strength to stiffen against the breeze which furrows it with too many wrinkles. Oh! sad water going to weep under black bridges and dismayed at the reflections it must bear, this serf water, and which are like a motionless burden. But, being too old, on the surface now like watered silk, it is losing its reflections, the way one's memory goes, and diluting them into confused grey mirages. Such aching water it almost seems fatal, why is it so bare and already so null? And what is wrong with it, absorbed in sleep and bitter dreams, that it is hardly anything more than a treacherous frost mirror where the moon itself can barely survive?

## Le Soir dans les vitres XI

Les vitres tout à l'heure étaient pâles et nues.
Mais peu à peu le soir entra dans la maison;
On y sent à présent le péril d'un poison.
C'est que les vitres, pour le soir, sont des cornues
Où se distille on ne sait quoi dans leur cristal;
Le couchant y répand un or qui les colore;
Et pour qu'enfin le crépuscule s'élabore,
L'ombre, comme pour un apprêt médicinal,
Semble y verser ses ténèbres, d'une fiole.
Dans les verres, teintés de ce qui souffre en eux,
Un nuage s'achève, un reflet s'étiole;
Il est en germe quelque chose de vénéneux,
Menaçant la maison déjà presque endormie;
Et c'est de plus en plus le nocturne élixir...
Ah! les vitres et leur délétère chimie
Qui chaque soir ainsi me font un peu mourir!

*Les Vies encloses*

## Evening in the Windowpanes XI

The windowpanes just now were pale and bare. But gradually evening entered the house. You now feel yourself endangered by poison, for windowpanes in the evening are retorts distilling some essence in their crystal; the setting sun spreads and colors them with gold. And to carry out the alchemy of evening, shadow, as if it were part of a medical procedure, seems to pour out its darkness from a vial. In the panes colored with their suffering state, a cloud dims, a reflection grows faint. There is the germ of some poison threatening the already dozing house, and it turns more and more into elixir of night. Ah, the panes and their destructive chemistry each evening make me die a little!

# EMILE VERHAEREN

## Londres

Et ce Londres de fonte et de bronze, mon âme,
Où des plaques de fer claquent sous des hangars,
    Où des voiles s'en vont, sans Notre-Dame
Pour étoile, s'en vont, là-bas, vers les hasards.

Gares de suie et de fumée, où du gaz pleure
Ses spleens d'argent lointain vers des chemins d'éclair,
    Où des bêtes d'ennui bâillent à l'heure
Dolente immensément, qui tinte à Westminster.

Et ces quais infinis de lanternes fatales,
Parques dont les fuseaux plongent aux profondeurs,
    Et ces marins noyés, sous les pétales
Des fleurs de boue où la flamme met des lueurs.

Et ces châles et ces gestes de femmes soûles,
Et ces alcools de lettres d'or jusques aux toits,
    Et tout à coup la mort, parmi ces foules;
O mon âme du soir, ce Londres noir qui traîne en toi!

*Les Soirs*

## London

And this London of cast-iron and bronze, my soul, with iron sheets clattering on warehouses, with sails going off, without Our Lady for star, going off on the horizon toward chance; soot and smoke train stations, with gas weeping its distant silver spleen toward flashing rails, with beasts of ennui yawning as the immensely sorrowful hour rings at Westminster; and these infinite riverbanks lined by fatal streetlamps—Fates whose spindles plunge into the depths—and these drowned sailors, beneath the mudflower petals, where the reflection of the flame glistens; and these shawls and drunken women's gestures and gold letters advertising liquor up to the rooftops; and, suddenly, death amid the crowds; Oh my evening soul, this black London lurking in you!

# La Dame en noir

—Dans la ville d'ébène et d'or,
La dame en noir des carrefours,
Qu'attendre, après autant de jours,
Qu'attendre encor?

—Les chiens du noir espoir ont aboyé, ce soir,
Vers les lunes de mes deux yeux,
Si longuement, vers les lunes en noir
De mes deux yeux silencieux,
Si longuement et si lointainement, ce soir,
Vers les lunes de mes deux yeux en noir.
Quel deuil superbe agitent-ils mes crins,
Pour affoler ainsi ces chiens,
Et quel bondissement et quel orgueil mes reins
Et tout mon corps toisonné d'or?

—La dame en noir des carrefours,
Qu'attendre, après de si longs jours,
Qu'attendre?

—Vers quel paradis noir font-ils voile mes seins,
Et vers quels horizons ameutés de tocsins?
Dites, quel Walhalla tumultueux de fièvres
Ou quels chevaux cabrés vers l'amour sont mes lèvres?

Dites, quel incendie et quel effroi
Suis-je? pour ces grands chiens, qui me lèchent ma rage
Et quel naufrage espèrent-ils en mon orage
Pour tant chercher leur mort en moi?

—La dame en noir des carrefours
Qu'attendre après de si longs jours?

—Je suis la mordeuse, entre mes bras,
De toute force exaspérée
Vers les toujours mêmes pourchas;
Ou dévorante—ou dévorée

Mes dents, comme des pierres d'or,
Mettent en moi leurs étincelles:
Je suis belle comme la mort
Et suis publique aussi comme elle.

Aux douloureux traceurs d'éclairs
Et de désirs sur mes murailles,
J'offre le catafalque de mes chairs
Et les cierges des funérailles.

Je leur donne tout mon remords
Pour les soûler au seuil du porche
Et le blasphème de mon corps
Brandi vers Dieu comme une torche.

Ils me savent comme une tour
De fer et de siècles vêtue,
Et s'exècrent en mon amour
Qui les affole et qui les tue.

Ce qu'ils aiment—coeur naufragé,
Esprit dément ou rage vaine—
C'est le dégoût surtout que j'ai
De leurs baisers ou de leur haine.

C'est de trouver encore en moi
Leur pourpre et noire parélie
Et mon drapeau de rouge effroi
Échevelé dans leur folie.

—La dame en noir des carrefours
Qu'attendre, après de si longs jours,
Qu'attendre?

—A cette heure de vieux soleil, chargé de soir,
Qui se projette en morceaux d'or sur le trottoir,
Quand la ville s'allonge en un serpentement
De feux et de lueurs, vers cet aimant
Toujours debout à l'horizon: la femme,
Les chiens du désespoir
Ont aboyé vers les yeux de mon âme,
Si longuement vers mes deux yeux,
Si longuement et si lointainement, ce soir,
Vers les lunes de mes deux yeux en noir!

Dites, quel brûlement et quelle ardeur mes reins
Font-ils courir, au long de mon corps d'or?
Et de quelle clarté s'éclairent-ils mes seins
Devant les yeux hallucinés des chiens?

Et moi aussi, dites, quel Walhalla de fièvres
Vient me tenter les lèvres
Et vers quels horizons ameutés de tocsins
Et quels paradis noirs, font-ils voile mes crins?

Dites quel incendie et quel effroi
Viennent le soir, me chasser hors de moi,
Sur les places, dans les villes,
Reine foudroyante et servile?

—La dame en noir des carrefours
Qu'attendre, après de si longs jours,
Qu'attendre?

—Hélas! quand viendra-t-il, celui
Qui doit venir—peut-être aujourd'hui—
Qui doit venir vers mon attente,
Fatalement, et qui viendra?

La démence incurable et tourmentante
Qui donc en lui la sentira
Monter jusqu'a mes seins qui hallucinent.
Vers les deux mains de ceux qui assassinent
Mon corps se dresse ardent et blême;
Je suis celle qui ne crains rien
Et dont personne ne s'abstient:
Je suis tentatrice suprême.

Dites? Qui donc doit me vouloir, ce soir, au fond
    d'un bouge?

—La dame en noir des carrefours
Qu'attendre après de si longs jours
        Qu'attendre?

—J'attends tel homme au couteau rouge.

                                *Les Flambeaux noirs*

## The Lady in Black

In the city of ebony and gold, the lady in black of the street
corners—what is she waiting for after so many days, what is she still
waiting for? "The dogs of black hope barked this evening, toward the
moons of my two eyes, for so long, toward the black moons of my
two silent eyes. For so long and from so far, toward the black moons of

my two eyes. What proud mourning ripples through my hair, to excite so these dogs, and what saltation and pride runs through my loins and my whole body fleeced with gold?" The lady in black of the street corners—what is she waiting for after such long days, what is she waiting for? "Toward what black paradise do my breasts seem to set sail, and toward what horizons filled with throngs by the ringing alarm? Listen, what Valhalla tumultuous with fevers or what horses rearing up toward love are my lips? Listen, what conflagration and what terror am I—for these great dogs who lick at my rabidness, and what shipwreck do they hope for in my storm, that they so seek their death in me?" The lady in black of the street corners—what is she waiting for after such long days? "I bite, between my arms, any force exacerbated by the pursuit of ever the same ends; I devour or am devoured. My teeth like golden stones illuminate me with their sparks: I am beautiful as death and serve all men like her. To the sorrowful tracers of lightning bolts and desires on my walls, I offer the bier of my flesh and funereal tapers. I give them all my remorse to intoxicate them at the threshold of my church, and the blasphemy of my body elevated and shaken at God like a torch. They know me to be a tower clothed in iron and past ages and abominate themselves in my love, which excites them to frenzy and kills them. What they love—whether they are shipwrecked hearts, demented minds, or victims of vain fury—is my disgust at their kisses or at their hatred. They further love to find in me their crimson and black mock sun and my banner of red fear blowing in their madness." The lady in black of the street corners—what is she waiting for, after such long days, what is she waiting for? "At this hour, when the aged sun, laden with evening, projects golden shapes on the sidewalk, when the city unwinds its coils of lights and glimmerings toward the magnet of Woman always silhouetted on the horizon, the dogs of despair barked at my soul's eyes, so lengthily at my two eyes, so lengthily and so distantly this evening, toward the moons of my two eyes in black! Listen, what burning sensation and what ardor do my loins send along my golden body? And what glimmer illuminates my breasts, before the dogs' hallucinated eyes? And as for me, listen, what Valhalla of fevers tempts my lips, and toward what horizons filled with throngs by the alarm ringing and toward what black paradises does my mane seem to set sail? Listen, what conflagration and what fear come at evening to drive me out of myself, on squares, in cities, me, the terrifying and servile queen?" The lady in black of the street corners—what is she waiting for after such long days, what is she waiting for? "Alas, when will he come, the one who is to come—perhaps today—who is to come in response to my waiting, fatefully, and who will come? Who will feel in himself incurable and tormenting madness rise toward my hallucinatory breasts? Toward the assassins' two hands my body stiffens, burning and pale; I am the one who fears nothing and from whom no one abstains. I am the final temptress. Listen, who is to want me tonight, in a hovel?" The lady in black of the street corners—what is she waiting for after such long days? What is she waiting for? "I am waiting for a certain man with a red knife."

## Au bord de l'eau

Chairs de vulves ou de gencives,
Les pétales des fleurs nocives
Bougent au vent,
Torpide et lent,
Qui les pourrit d'automne monotone
Et les emporte sur l'étang.

On croirait voir de grands morceaux
De coeurs brisés,
On croirait voir de grands lambeaux
De vie ardente et dispersée,
On croirait voir de gros caillots
De sang tomber, parmi les flots,
A moins qu'on ne se voie enfin soi-même
Défini là, par un emblème.

Les fleurs charnelles et nocives,
Et flasques comme des gencives,
Abandonnent au vent dolent
Leurs pétales et leurs couleurs;
Les fleurs mornes abandonnent
Au vent d'automne
Leur sang et leurs douleurs
Monotones.

Le soir a beau filtrer ses ombres,
Par le treillis des taillis sombres,
Et le soleil, comme un cri rouge,
Se perdre et s'étouffer dans l'eau qui bouge,

Elles réapparaissent sous la lune,
Les fleurs mornes et importunes,
Grappes de pleurs, bouquets de sang,
Qui se mirent et se déchirent
Dans la pâleur de l'étang blanc.

*Poèmes*

## By the Water

Like the flesh of vulvas or gums, the poisonous flower petals move in
the wind, lazy and slow, which rots them with unchanging autumn and
blows them off over the pond. They look like big hunks of broken
hearts; they look like big shreds of burning, scattered life. They look
like big clots of blood falling in the ripples, unless, of course, one sees
oneself defined by them as by an emblem. The fleshy poisonous flow-
ers, soft like gums, cast off in the sorrowful wind their petals and
colors; the dreary flowers exude in the autumn wind their blood and
monotonous sorrows. Even though evening shadows filter through the
trellislike thicket and the sun, like a red cry, sinks and smothers in
the rippling water, the dismal, importunate flowers appear again in the
moonlight, like bunches of tears, bouquets of blood, reflecting and dis-
integrating in the pale white pond.

## Chanson de fou

Le crapaud noir sur le sol blanc
Me fixe indubitablement
Avec des yeux plus grands que n'est grande sa tête;
Ce sont les yeux qu'on m'a volés
Quand mes regards s'en sont allés,
Un soir, que je tournai la tête.

Mon frère?—il est quelqu'un qui ment,
Avec de la farine entre ses dents;
C'est lui, jambes et bras en croix,
Qui tourne au loin, là-bas,
Qui tourne au vent,
Sur ce moulin de bois.

Et celui-ci, c'est mon cousin
Qui fut curé et but si fort du vin

Que le soleil en devint rouge;
J'ai su qu'il habitait un bouge,
Avec des morts, dans ses armoires.

Car nous avons pour génitoires
Deux cailloux
Et pour monnaie un sac de poux
Nous, les trois fous,
Qui épousons, au clair de lune,
Trois folles dames sur la dune.

*Les Campagnes hallucinées*

## Mad Song

The black toad on the white ground indubitably stares at me with
eyes bigger than his head. They are the eyes stolen from me when I
gazed off, one evening, when I turned my head. My brother? He is
someone who lies, with flour in his mouth. There he is, with his arms
and legs making a cross, turning in the distance, turning in the wind,
on that wooden mill. And the closer one is my cousin, a priest, who
drank so much wine that the sun turned red. I heard that he lived in a
hovel, with corpses in his wardrobes. For our testicles are two stones,
and our coins a sack of lice, ours, the three madmen marrying three
madwomen on the dune in the moonlight.

## Le Péché

Sur sa butte que le vent gifle,
Il tourne et fauche et ronfle et siffle
Le vieux moulin des péchés vieux
Et des forfaits astucieux.

Il geint des pieds jusqu'à la tête,
Sur fond d'orage et de tempête,
Lorsque l'automne et les nuages
Frôlent son toit de leurs voyages.

L'hiver, quand la campagne est éborgnée,
Il apparaît une araignée
Colossale, tissant ses toiles
Jusqu'aux étoiles.

C'est le moulin des vieux péchés.

Qui l'écoute, parmi les routes,
Entend battre le coeur du diable,
Dans sa carcasse insatiable.

Un travail d'ombre et de ténèbres
S'y fait, pendant les nuits funèbres,
Quand la lune fendue
Gît-là, sur le carreau de l'eau,
Comme une hostie atrocement mordue.

C'est le moulin de la ruine
Qui moud le mal et le répand aux champs,
Infini, comme une bruine.

Ceux qui sournoisement écornent
Le champ voisin en deplaçant les bornes;
Ceux qui, valets d'autrui, sèment l'ivraie
Au lieu de l'orge vraie;
Ceux qui jettent les poisons clairs dans l'eau
Où l'on amène le troupeau:
Ceux qui, par les nuits seules,
En brasiers d'or font éclater les meules,
Tous passèrent par le moulin,

Encore:

Les conjureurs de sorts et les sorcières
Que vont trouver les filles-mères;
Ceux qui cachent dans les fourrés
Leurs ruts et leurs spasmes vociférés;
Ceux qui n'aiment la chair que si le sang
Gicle aux yeux, frais et luisant;
Ceux qui s'entre'égorgent, à couteaux rouges,
Volets fermés, au fond des bouges;
Ceux qui flairent l'espace
Avec, entre leurs poings, la mort pour tel qui passe,
Tous passèrent par le moulin.

Aussi
Les vagabonds qui habitent des fosses
Avec leurs filles qu'ils engrossent;
Les fous qui choisissent des bêtes
Pour assouvir leur rut et ses tempêtes;

Les mendiants qui déterrent les mortes
Rageusement et les emportent;
Les couples noirs, pervers et vieux,
Qui instruisent l'enfant à coucher entre eux deux
Tous passèrent par le moulin.

Enfin:

Ceux qui font de leur coeur l'usine,
Où fermente l'envie et cuve la lésine;
Ceux qui dorment, sans autre voeu,
Avec leurs sous, comme avec Dieu;
Ceux qui projettent leurs prières,
Croix à rebours et paroles contraires;
Ceux qui cherchent un tel blasphème
Que descendrait vers eux Satan lui-même;
Tous passèrent par le moulin.
Ils sont venus sournoisement,
Choisissant l'heure et le moment,
Les uns lents et chenus
Et les autres mâles et fermes,
Avec le sac au dos.
Ils sont venus des bourgs perdus
Gagnant les bois, tournant les fermes,
Les vieux, carcasses d'os,
Mais les jeunes, drapeaux de force.
Par des chemins rugueux comme une écorce,
Ils sont montés—et quand ils sont redescendus,
Avec leurs chiens et leurs brouettes
Et leurs ânes et leurs charrettes,
Chargés de farine ou de grain,
Par groupes noirs de pèlerins,
Les grand'routes charriaient toutes,
Infiniment, comme des veines,
Le sang du mal parmi les plaines.

Et le moulin tournait au fond des soirs,
La croix grande de ses bras noirs,
Avec des feux, comme des yeux,
Dans l'orbite de ses lucarnes
Dont les rayons gagnaient les loins.

Parfois, s'illuminaient des coins,
Là-bas, dans la campagne morne
Et l'on voyait les porteurs gourds,
Ployant au faix des péchés lourds,
Hagards et las, buter de borne en borne.

Et le moulin ardent,
Sur sa butte, comme une dent,
Alors, mêlait et accordait
Son giroiement de voiles
Au rythme même des étoiles
Qui tournoyaient, par les nuits seules,
Fatalement, comme ses meules.

*Les Campagnes hallucinées*

## Sin

On its wind-slapped hill, the old mill of old sins and sly crimes turns and reaps and snores and whistles. It moans from top to bottom against the rain and wind storms, when autumn with its clouds grazes its roof as it passes. In winter when the landscape is maimed, it looks like a colossal spider, spinning its web right up to the stars. It's the mill of old sins. When you listen to it from the roads, you hear the devil's heartbeat in his insatiable body. A dark and shadowy task is done there, on funereal nights, when the slashed moon lies there, on the pane of water, like a frightfully bitten communion wafer. It's the mill of ruin grinding evil and spreading it over the fields, infinite like a drizzly day. Those who stealthily take a nick out of their neighbor's field by moving markers; those who, as hired hands, sow tares in place of true barley; those who throw bright poisons into the water where the sheep are brought to drink; those who on lonely nights make the haystacks burst into golden brasiers; all these pass through the mill. And further: conjurers of spells and the witches who find out unwed mothers; those who hide their copulations and screaming spasms in thickets; those who love flesh only when fresh, gleaming blood spurts into their eyes; those who knife each other to death in hovels behind closed shutters; those who sniff the air and bear between their fists death for the passerby; all those pass through the mill. Also: the tramps who live in ditches with their daughters whom they make pregnant; madmen who choose beasts to satisfy their storms of lust; beggars who furiously dig up female corpses and bear them off; black old perverse couples who instruct the child to lie between them; all pass through the mill. Finally: those who make of their heart a factory fermenting envy and avarice; those who, with no other wish, sleep with their pennies as with God; those who project their prayers with reversed signs of the cross and words backwards; those who seek such a blasphemy that Satan himself would come down to them; all pass through the mill. They came stealthily, choosing the hour and moment, some slow and white haired and others vigorous and firm with their sack on their back. They came from remote villages, passing through forests, going around farms, the old ones like bony carcasses, but the young like emblems of strength. By roads rough as tree bark they went up, and when they came down, with their dogs and wheelbarrows, their donkey and carts, loaded with flour or grain, all the highways, stretching out infinitely like veins, bore groups of black pilgrims and carried the blood of evil into the plains. And the mill turned, in the distance of evening, the great cross of its black arms, with fires like eyes in the sockets of its windows, from which the beams reached far. Sometimes certain spots were lit up in the dreary plains, and you could see the numb bearers bent under the weight of heavy sins, tired and haggard, and stumbling from milestone to milestone. And the burning mill on its hill, like a tooth, then mingled and harmonized its turning sails to the very rhythm of the stars, which, on deserted nights, turned fatally like millstones.

## Celui de l'horizon

J'ai regardé, par la lucarne ouverte, au flanc
D'un phare abandonné que flagellait la pluie:
Des trains tumultueux, sous des tunnels de suie,
Sifflaient, fixés, au loin, par des fanaux en sang.

Le port immensément enchevêtré de mâts,
Dormait, huileux et lourd, en ses bassins d'asphalte;
Un seul levier, debout sur un bloc de basalte,
Serrait, en son poing noir, un énorme acomas

Et sous l'envoûtement de ce soir de portor,
Une à une, là-bas, s'éloignaient les lanternes,
Vers des quartiers de bruit, de joie et de tavernes,
Où bondissent les ruts, parmi des miroirs d'or.

Quand plaie énorme et rouge, une voile, soudain,
Tuméfiée au vent, cingla vers les débarcadères,
Quelqu'un qui s'en venait des pays légendaires,
Parut, le front compact d'orgueil et de dédain.

Comme des glaives d'or en des fourreaux de fer,
Il enserrait sa rage et ses désirs sauvages
Et ses cris grands cassaient les échos des rivages
Et traversaient, de part en part, l'ombre et la mer.

Il était d'Océan. Il était vieux d'avoir
Mordu chaque horizon saccagé de tempête
Et de sentir, encore et quand même, sa tête
Crier, vers la souffrance et les affres du soir.

Il se voulait supplicié. Il se savait
Le prisonnier de son désir. Sur sa croix d'âme,
Il se saignait, avec de rouges clous de flamme,
Et dégustait toute la mort, qu'il en buvait.

Sa vie?—Elle s'était dardée en cette foi
De n'être rien, sinon celui qui s'épouvante
Et des sabrants éclairs de son âme savante
Flagelle, obstinément, les orages du soi.

Effrayant effrayé. Il cherchait le chemin
Vers une autre existence éclatée en miracles,
En un désert de rocs illuminés d'oracles,
Où le chêne vivrait, où parlerait l'airain;

Où tout l'orgueil serait: se vivre, en déploiements
D'effroi sauvage, avec, sur soi, la voix profonde
Et tonnante des Dieux, qui ont tordu le monde
Grand de terreur, sous le froid d'or des firmaments.

Et depuis des mille ans, il luttait, sur la mer,
Bombant à l'horizon les torses de ses voiles,
Toujours, vers les lointains, des plus rouges étoiles
Dont les cristaux sanglants se cassaient dans la mer.

*Les Apparus dans mes chemins*

## The One from the Horizon

Through the open skylight I looked toward the sides of an abandoned lighthouse whipped by rain. Roaring trains in sooty tunnels whistled, caught in the stare of blood-red signals. The enormous port, with its intertwined masts, slept, oily and heavy, in its asphalt wet docks. A single crane, erect like a lever on a block of basalt, grasped in its black fist an enormous acoma tree, and under the vault of the black and green marbled sky, the lanterns, one by one, vanished in the distance toward the noisy, joyous tavern district with its copulatory convulsions amid golden mirrors. When a sail, like an enormous red wound, swollen in the wind, sped toward the wharves, someone coming from legendary countries appeared, his brow marked by pride and disdain. Like golden swords in iron scabbards, he shut in his rage and savage desires, and his loud roars shattered the waterfront's echo and pierced through shadow and sea. He was an ocean creature. He had grown old defying each storm-torn horizon and feeling still, despite it, his head scream toward suffering and the terror of evening. He let himself be tormented. He knew he was the prisoner of his desire. On the cross of his soul he bled, with red nails of fire, and had so savored death he felt it as liquid in his throat. His life? It had stung itself like an insect, in his belief that he was nothing, only someone in terror of himself. He stubbornly whipped his inner torments with the sharp flashes of his cunning soul. Terrifying and terrified. He sought the path toward another existence, bursting with miracles, in a desert of rocks lit up like oracles, where the oak would live and bronze would speak, where all pride would consist in living to the fullest, with unfurlings of savage fear, with, over one, the deep, thundering voice of the gods who twisted the world, great in its terror, under the golden cold of the heavens. And for a thousand years he had been struggling on the sea, swelling his twisted sails on the horizon, always toward the farthest distances with their stars redder than others, whose bloody crystals shatter in the sea.

# JEAN LORRAIN

Modernité, Modernité!
A travers les cris, les huées,
L'impudeur des prostituées
Resplendit dans l'éternité.

Auprès de vos amants en blouse,
Dont les copailles sont jalouses,
De Saint-Lazare aux abattoirs
Fleurissez, roses de trottoir,
Et, filles de luxe, ou faunesses,
Marchandant ferme vos jeunesses
Aux vieux, qu'a grisés votre odeur,
Enthousiasmez Paris rôdeur.

Modernité, Modernité!

*Modernités*

Modern times! Modern times! Through the shouts and yelling the prostitutes' shamelessness shines in all eternity. Flower beside your proletarian lovers the queers are jealous of, sidewalk roses, flower from Saint-Lazare to the slaughterhouses, and, whether you are de luxe tarts or wild creatures, drive a hard bargain for your young bodies with the old men intoxicated by your odor. Delight the Paris of prowlers! Modern times! Modern times!

## Effeuillement

Dans un vieux ciboire d'étain
S'effeuille, morne et douloureuse,
Une rose d'automne ocreuse,
D'un jaune de soleil éteint.

Près d'un grand verre de Venise,
Sur un tapis d'ancien lampas
La rose malade agonise
D'un lent et somptueux trépas

Parmi les étoffes brochées,
Dont les vieux ors appesantis
Semblent réfléchir amortis
Les tons de ses feuilles séchées.

Au fond dans l'ombre des tentures
Un grand vitrail limpide et clair
Laisse apparaître les mâtures
D'un port de pêche, un ciel d'hiver,

Un ciel tiède et doux de décembre,
Dont les gris de cendre attendris
Font de la rose aux tons pourris
Une transparente fleur d'ambre;

Et cette hautaine agonie
De fleur parmi ce luxe ancien
Est bien dans l'âme et l'harmonie
De ce logis patricien,

Ce logis, où sous de longs voiles
De grands archiluths attristés
Font de leurs manches incrustés
De nacre et d'or autant d'étoiles.

Un doux relent de frangipane,
A force de douceur malsain,
Discrètement monte et s'émane
D'un angle, où dort un clavecin,

Et cette chose pauvre et laide
Qu'est l'effeuillement d'une fleur,
Devient une exquise douleur
Dans cette chambre haute et tiède.

Dans un vieux ciboire d'étain
S'effeuille, morne et douloureuse,
Une rose d'automne ocreuse
D'un jaune de soleil éteint.

*Les Griseries*

# Dropping Petals

In an old pewter ciborium, an earth-yellow autumn rose, the color of
a sun grown dim, dismally, sorrowfully loses its petals. Near a huge

Venetian glass, on an old lampas rug, the sickly rose is dying a slow and rich death, among the brocaded fabrics whose heavy old gold seems dimly to reflect the tones of its dry petals. In the recesses of the chamber, in the shadow of the hangings, through a great stained-glass window, clear and bright, there appear the masts and riggings of a fishing port, a winter sky, a soft warmish December sky whose tender ash grey makes of the rose with its rotting shades a transparent flower of amber. And the haughty death of a flower amidst old-fashioned luxury suits completely the soul and harmony of this patrician dwelling, where under long veils great melancholy theorbos make so many stars of their necks incrusted with gold and mother-of-pearl. A gentle whiff of frangipani, unwholesome it is so sweet, gently rises and breathes forth from a corner with a sleeping harpsichord. And the poor, ugly thing which is a flower losing its petals becomes an exquisite sorrow in the high and warmish chamber. In an old pewter ciborium, an earth-yellow autumn rose, the color of a sun grown dim, dismally, sorrowfully loses its petals.

## A la fange

"Sportsmen, voyous, banquiers, potaches, à la fange!
"Entrez."
   Là le succès est immense, on se tord.
Debout dans un landau, d'un fabuleux décor,
Peint de cupidons bleus sur un fond rose orange,
Ricane, raide et blême, une vendeuse étrange.
Dans un baiser savant et long contre un louis
Elle vend la Folie et le Spasme et la Mort;
Et son nom stigmatise une époque. Elle est d'Ange.

Le public arrêté, dans la stupeur farouche
D'un bétail, a l'horreur du rouge de sa bouche,
Gouffre ignoble où le sang luit et perle en corail.

Tous ont peur et pourtant chacun d'un regard louche,
Epris de cette lèvre au sûr et lent travail
Couve cette artisane habile en fausse couche.

         *Modernités*

## Filth

"Sportsmen, hoodlums, bankers, schoolboys, come in and have a look at filth!" The show is a great success; they're laughing themselves sick. Standing in a baby carriage fantastically decorated, with blue cupids painted on a pale vermilion background, a strange saleslady sneers, stiff and sallow. For a louis, she sells a long, studied kiss which brings madness and spasms and death. And her name stigmatizes our whole age. She is Madam Abortion. The audience, still, like cows dumbfounded and nervous, is horrified by her red mouth, a vile chasm where blood gleams in drops like coral beads. They are all afraid and yet each one, with a suspicious air, thrilled with this mouth careful and accurate in its task, covets this skillful specialist in miscarriages.

## Narcissus

Ni les douces langueurs des flûtes et des lyres,
Ni les parfums mourants des vagues encensoirs
En cadence envolés dans le calme des soirs,
Ni les bras frais et nus ni les savants sourires

Ne peuvent rallumer le feu des vains espoirs
En mon coeur et, lassé d'amours et de délires
Factices, blond éphèbe effroi des hétaïres
Jalouses, j'ai posé mon front dans les lys noirs.

Et les lys vénéneux, fleurs d'ombre et de ténèbres,
Sur ma tempe entr'ouvrant leurs calices funèbres,
M'ont appris mon infâme et chaste déshonneur;

Et, descendu vivant dans l'horreur de mon être,
J'ai savouré l'étrange et suave bonheur
De pouvoir me haïr, ayant pu me connaître.

*L'Ombre ardente*

## Narcissus

Not the sweet languors of flutes and lyres, not dying perfumes from dim censers swinging in cadence in the evening calm, nor fresh and bare arms, nor artful smiles can rekindle the flame of empty hopes in my heart; and, weary of artificial loves and raptures, I, a blond youth terrifying jealous courtesans, I laid my head amid the black lilies. And the poisonous lilies, flowers of shadow and darkness, opening their funereal blossoms at my brow, taught me my unspeakable and virgin dishonor. And, sunk living into the horror of my being, I have savored the strange and delicate happiness of being able to hate myself, because I have been able to know myself.

# JEAN MOREAS

## Chimaera

J'allumai la clarté mortuaire des lustres
Au fond de la crypte où se révulse ton oeil,
Et mon rêve cueillit les fleuraisons palustres
Pour ennoblir ta chair de pâleur et de deuil.

Je proférai les sons d'étranges palatales,
Selon les rites des trépassés nécromants,
Et sur ta lèvre teinte au sang des digitales
Fermentèrent soudain des philtres endormants.

Ainsi je t'ai créé de la suprême essence,
Fantôme immarcescible au front d'astres nimbé,
Pour me purifier de la concupiscence,
Pour consoler mon coeur dans l'opprobe tombé.

*Les Syrtes*

## Chimaera

I lit the mortuary brightness of crystal lamps in the depths of the
crypt where you lie, eyes rolled back; and my dream gathers swamp
flowers to ennoble your pale mourning flesh. I spoke strange palatal
sounds after the necromancer's rite for the dead, and on your lips of
bloody foxglove red, sleeping potions suddenly fermented. Thus I
created you from the ultimate essence, an unwitherable ghost haloed
with stars, to purify myself of lust, to console my heart sunken into
infamy.

## Agnès

Il y avait des arcs où passaient des escortes
Avec des bannières de deuil et du fer
Lacé, des potentats de toutes sortes
—Il y avait—dans la cité au bord de la mer.
Les places étaient noires et bien pavées, et les portes,
Du côté de l'est et de l'ouest, hautes; et comme en hiver

La forêt, dépérissaient les salles de palais, et les porches,
Et les colonnades de belvéder.

> C'était (tu dois bien t'en souvenir) c'était aux plus
> beaux jours de ton adolescence.

Dans la cité au bord de la mer, la cape et la dague lourdes
De pierres jaunes, et sur ton chapeau des plumes de perroquets,
Tu t'en venais, devisant telles bourdes,
Tu t'en venais entre tes deux laquais
Si bouffis et tant sots—en vérité, des happelourdes!—
Dans la cité au bord de la mer tu t'en venais et tu vaguais
Parmi de grands vieillards qui travaillaient aux felouques,
Le long des môles et des quais.

> C'était (tu dois bien t'en souvenir) c'était aux plus
> beaux jours de ton adolescence.

Devant ta tante Madame la Prieure,
Que tu sentisses quelque effroi
Lorsque parlait d'Excommunication Majeure
Le vieux évêque en robe d'orfroi,—
Tu partais, même à l'encontre du temps et de l'heure,
Avec Hans, Gull, Salluste et Godefroy,
Courir la bague, pour amuser la veuve
Aux yeux couleur de roy.

> C'était (tu dois bien t'en souvenir) c'était aux plus
> beaux jours de ton adolescence.

Bien assise était la demeure, et certe
Il pendait des filigranes du perron;
Et le verger fut grand où hantait la calandre diserte.
Et quant à la Dame, elle avait ce geste prompt,
Ce "ce me plaît" qui déconcerte;
Et quant à la Dame, elle avait environ
Septante et sept saphirs avec un cercle
De couronne à son front.

> C'était (tu dois bien t'en souvenir) c'était la plus noble
> Dame de la cité.

Certes les fleurs florirent, et le dictame
Florit au verger qui fut grand, en effet.
Toute fleur florit au verger; et quant à la Dame,

Son penal d'arroi fut fait
De ces riches draps que rien n'entame,
Et ses cavales étaient de Frise, et l'on pouvait
En compter cent, et nulle bête qui soit en mer ni en bocage
Qui ne fût à fin or portraite sur son chevet.

    C'était (tu dois bien t'en souvenir) c'était la plus
           noble Dame de la cité.

Claire était la face de la Dame, telle la fine pointe
Du jour, et ses yeux étaient cieux marins;
Claire était la face de la Dame et de parfums ointe.
Claire était la face de la Dame, et plus que purpurins
Fruits, fraîche était la bouche jointe
De la Dame. Et pour ses crins
Recercelés, ne fussent les entraves d'ivoire,
Eussent encourtiné ses reins.

    C'était (tu dois bien t'en souvenir) c'était la plus
           belle Dame de la cité.

Cieux marins étaient les yeux de la Dame et lacs que rehausse
La sertissure des neiges, et calice ce pendant
Qu'il éclôt, était sa bouche; et ni la blonde Isex, ni la fausse
Cressida, ni Hélène pour qui tant
De barons descendirent dans la fosse;
Ni Florimel la fée, et ni l'ondine armée de son trident
Ni aucune mortelle ou déesse, telle beauté en sa force
Ne montrèrent, de l'aurore à l'occident.

    C'était (tu dois bien t'en souvenir) c'était la plus
           belle Dame de la cité.

"Soeur douce amie" lui disais-tu "douce amie,
Les étoiles peuvent s'obscurcir et les amarantes avoir été
Que ma raison ne cessera mie
De radoter de votre beauté;
Car Cupidon ravive sa torche endormie
A vos yeux, à leur clarté,
Et votre regarder" lui disais-tu "est seul mire
De mon coeur atramenté."

    C'était (tu dois bien t'en souvenir) c'était par un
           soir de la mi-automne.

"Vos cheveux traînent jusqu'en bas et nimbent votre face,
Et vos sourires sont les duègnes de votre vertu;
Ah, prenons garde que notre âme ne se fasse
Putain, Madame" lui disais-tu.
"Vos cheveux traînent, et vos yeux portent d'azur à la fasce
D'or, et votre corps est de lys vêtu;
Ah, prenons garde que notre désir ne se farde
Pareil à quelque gnome tortu."

> C'était (tu dois bien t'en souvenir) c'était par un
>      soir de la mi-automne.

"Soeur douce amie" lui disais-tu "mon coeur est moire
D'eaux claires sous les midis.
Madame" lui disais-tu "mon coeur est grimoire
Tout couvert de signes maudits;
Et je vous eusse cédée pour mille besants et voire
Pour quelques maravédis.
Soeur douce amie" lui disais-tu "pieux cloître
Est mon coeur, et sainte fleur en paradis."

> C'était (tu dois bien t'en souvenir) c'était par un
>      soir de la mi-automne.

*Le Pèlerin passionné*

## Agnes

There were arches through which passed escorts with mourning banners and laced in armor; potentates of all sorts there were in the city beside the sea. The squares were black and well paved, and the gates high, to the east and west, and, like a forest in winter, the palace halls were deserted and the porticoes and colonnades along the high walk. It was (you must remember) in the finest days of your youth. In the city beside the sea, with a cape and a dagger heavy with yellow gems and with parakeet feathers on your hat, you went along telling fantastic stories with lackeys on either side of you, such puffed up and stupid ones, specious idiots really. In the city beside the sea, you went along and wandered among the tall old men who worked in the feluccas along the breakwaters and wharves. It was (you must remember) in the finest days of your youth. If you felt some terror when, before your aunt the Prioress, the old bishop in his gold-bordered vestments spoke of Major Excommunication, you went off despite the weather and the hour with

Hans, Gull, Sallustius, and Godfrey to tilt at the ring, to amuse the
widow with the royal-colored eyes. It was (you must remember) in the
finest days of your youth. Grandly placed was her dwelling, and, to be
sure, metal filigree decorated the stairs, and the grove was vast where
the lark chattered at length. And as for the Lady, she had a brusque
manner, a "This I like," that was disconcerting. And as for the Lady,
she had some seventy-seven sapphires on a crown circle on her
forehead. She was (you must remember) the noblest lady of the city.
Certainly the flowers flowered, and balm-giving dittany flowered in the
grove, which was, indeed, vast. All flowers flowered in the grove. And
as for the Lady, her ceremonial saddle-cushion was made of those rich
stuffs that nothing unravels, and her mares were from Friesland, and
you could count a hundred of them. And there was no beast in sea or
wood that was not depicted in fine gold embroidery on her pillow. She
was (you must remember) the noblest Lady of the city. Bright was the
Lady's face like the delicate dawn, and her eyes were the blue of skies at
sea. Bright was the Lady's face and anointed with perfumes. Bright was
the Lady's face, and fresher than crimson fruit were the Lady's joined
lips. And as for her bound hair, it would have covered her body had it
not been for the ivory hoops. She was (you must remember) the most
beauteous Lady in the city. Sea-sky blue were the Lady's eyes, and like
lakes set off by surrounding snow, and an opening flower was her
mouth; and not blond Iseult, nor false Cressida, not Helen for whom so
many nobles went to the grave, not Florimel the fairy, nor the undine
armed with her trident, nor any mortal nor goddess showed such
power of beauty, from east to west. She was (you must remember) the
most beauteous Lady in the city. "Sweet sister friend," you said to her,
"the stars can darken and the amaranths die before my mind will cease
raving about your beauty. For Cupid rekindles his burnt-out torch in
your eyes, in their brightness, and to look at you," you said to her, "is
the sole healer of my gloomy heart." It was (you must remember) an
evening in mid-autumn. "Your hair falls to the ground and haloes your
face, and your smiles are the duennas of your virtue. Ah, we must keep
our soul from becoming a whore, Madam," you said to her. "Your hair
falls, and your eyes are azure with a band of gold, and your body is clad
in lilies. Ah, let us beware lest our desire disguise itself like some
twisted gnome." It was (you must remember) an evening in mid-
autumn. "Sweet sister friend," you said to her, "my heart is like
watered silk under the noonday sun. Madam," you said to her, "my
heart is a book of magic covered with infernal signs, and I would have

sold you for a thousand besants or even a Spanish maravedis. Sweet sister friend," you said to her, "a pious cloister is my heart, and a holy flower in Paradise." It was (you must remember) on an evening in mid-autumn.

## Chanson

On a marché sur les fleurs au bord de la route,
Et le vent d'automne les secoue si fort, en outre.

La malle-poste a renversé la vieille croix au bord de la route,
Elle était vraiment si pourrie, en outre.

L'idiot (tu sais) est mort au bord de la route,
Et personne ne le pleurera, en outre.

*Le Pèlerin passionné*

## Song

Feet have stepped on the flowers on the side of the road, and the autumn wind blows them so hard, besides. The stagecoach has knocked down the old cross on the side of the road. It was really so rotted, anyway. The idiot (you know the one) died on the side of the road. And no one will weep for him in any case.

# REMY DE GOURMONT

## Oraisons mauvaises

Que tes mains soient bénies, car elles sont impures!
Elles ont des péchés secrets à toutes les jointures;
Lys d'épouvante, leurs ongles blancs font penser sous
   la lampe,
A des hosties volées dans l'ombre blanche, sous la lampe,
Et l'opale prisonnière qui se meurt à ton doigt,
C'est le dernier soupir de Jésus sur la croix.

### II

Que tes yeux soient bénis, car ils sont homicides!
Ils sont pleins de fantômes et pleins de chrysalides,
Comme dans l'eau fanée, bleue au fond des grottes vertes,
On voit dormir des fleurs qui sont des bêtes vertes,
Et ce douloureux saphir d'amertume et d'effroi,
C'est le dernier regard de Jésus sur la croix.

### III

Que tes seins soient bénis, car ils sont sacrilèges!
Ils se sont mis tout nus, comme un printanier florilège,
Fleuri pour la caresse et la moisson des lèvres et des
   mains,
Fleurs du bord de la route, bonnes à toutes les mains,
Et l'hyacinthe qui rêve là, avec un air triste de roi,
C'est le dernier amour de Jésus sur la croix.

### IV

Que ton ventre soit béni, car il est infertile!
Il est beau comme une terre de désolation; le style
De la herse n'y hersa qu'une glèbe rouge et rebelle,

La fleur mûre n'y sema qu'une graine rebelle,
Et la topaze ardente qui frissonne sur ce palais de joie,
C'est le dernier désir de Jésus sur la croix.


V

Que ta bouche soit bénie, car elle est adultère!
Elle a le goût des roses nouvelles et le goût de la vieille
    terre,
Elle a sucé les sucs obscurs des fleurs et des roseaux;
Quand elle parle on entend comme un bruit perfide de
    roseaux,
Et ce rubis cruel tout sanglant et tout froid,
C'est la dernière blessure de Jésus sur la croix.


VI

Que tes pieds soient bénis, car ils sont déshonnêtes!
Ils ont chaussé les mules des lupanars et des temples
    en fête,
Ils ont mis leurs talons sourds sur l'épaule des pauvres,
Ils ont marché sur les plus purs, sur les plus doux, sur
    les plus pauvres,
Et la boucle améthyste qui tend ta jarretière de soie,
C'est le dernier frisson de Jésus sur la croix.


VII

Que ton âme soit bénie, car elle est corrompue!
Fière émeraude tombée sur le pavé des rues,
Son orgueil s'est mêlé aux odeurs de la boue,
Et je viens d'écraser dans la glorieuse boue,
Sur le pavé des rues, qui est un chemin de croix,
La dernière pensée de Jésus sur la croix.

*Divertissements*

# Evil Prayers

Blessed be thy hands for they are unchaste! They have secret sins at
every joint; like lilies of horror, their white nails under the lamp recall
hosts stolen in the white shadow under the lamp, and the captive opal

expiring on thy finger is Jesus' last sigh on the cross. Blessed be thy eyes for they are murderous! They are full of ghosts and chrysalides, as one sees sleeping flowers which are green creatures in lifeless water, blue in the depth of green grottoes. And this sorrowful sapphire of bitterness and fright is Jesus' last glance on the cross. Blessed be thy breasts for they are sacrilegious! They have bared themselves like a spring bouquet, flowering for caresses and the harvest of lips and hands, wayside flowers, fit for all hands, and the jacinth dreaming there like a sad king is Jesus' last love on the cross. Blessed be thy womb for it is infertile! It is fair as a land of desolation; in it the blade of the harrow turned over nothing but red and tough clods; the ripe flower sowed in it only sterile seeds, and the burning topaz quivering on this palate of joy is Jesus' last desire on the cross. Blessed be thy mouth for it is adulterous! It has the taste of new roses and old soil; it has sucked the dark sap of flowers and reeds. When it speaks, you hear, as it were, a treacherous sound of reeds, and this cruel ruby, bloody and cold, is Jesus' last wound on the cross. Blessed be thy feet for they are depraved. They have worn slippers in the brothel and at temple festivities; they have put their unfeeling heels on the shoulder of the poor; they have trodden on the purest, the gentlest, the poorest; and the amethyst buckle of thy silk garter is Jesus' last shudder on the cross. Blessed be thy soul for it is corrupt! A proud emerald fallen on the street pavement, its pride has mingled with the smell of mud; and I have now, in the glorious mud, on the street pavement, itself a way of the cross, crushed Jesus' last thought on the cross.

## Agathe

Joyau trouvé parmi les pierres de la Sicile,
Agathe, vierge vendue aux revendeuses d'amour,
Agathe, victorieuse des colliers et des bagues,
Des sept rubis magiques et des trois pierres de lune,
Agathe, réjouie par le feu des fers rouges,
Comme un amandier par les douces pluies d'automne,
Agathe, embaumée par un jeune ange vêtu de pourpre,
Agathe, pierre et fer, Agathe, or et argent,
Agathe, chevalière de Malte,
Sainte Agathe, mettez du feu dans notre sang.

*Les Saintes du paradis*

## Agatha

Gem found among the stones of Sicily, Agatha, virgin sold to the secondhand dealers in love, Agatha, victorious over necklaces and rings, over the seven magic rubies and the three moonstones, Agatha, rejoicing in the red-hot irons, like an almond tree in the sweet autumn rains, Agatha, perfumed by a young angel clad in purple, Agatha, stone and iron, Agatha, gold and silver, Agatha, knight of Malta, Saint Agatha, put fire in our blood.

## Ursule

Griffon du Nord, bête sacrée venue
Dans la lumière bleue d'un rêve boréal,
Ursule, flocon de neige bu par les lèvres de Jésus,
Ursule, étoile rouge vers la tulipe de pourpre,
Ursule, soeur de tant de coeurs innocents,
Et dont la tête sanglante dort comme une escarboucle
Dans la bague des arceaux,
Ursule, nef, voile, rame et tempête,
Ursule, envolée sur le dos de l'oiseau blanc,
Sainte Ursule emportez nos âmes vers les neiges.

*Les Saintes du paradis*

## Ursula

Griffin from the North, sacred animal descending in the blue light of a boreal dream, Ursula, snowflake drunk by Jesus' lips, Ursula, red star over the crimson tulip, Ursula, sister of so many innocent hearts, whose bloody head sleeps like a carbuncle in the keystone of arches, Ursula, ship, sail, oar, and storm, Ursula, soaring on the white bird's back, Saint Ursula, carry off our souls toward the snow.

# ALBERT SAMAIN

Je rêve de vers doux et d'intimes ramages,
De vers à frôler l'âme ainsi que des plumages,

De vers blonds où le sens fluide se délie,
Comme sous l'eau la chevelure d'Ophélie,

De vers silencieux, et sans rythme et sans trame,
Où la rime sans bruit glisse comme une rame,

De vers d'une ancienne étoffe, exténuée,
Impalpable comme le son et la nuée,

De vers de soirs d'automne ensorcelant les heures
Au rite féminin des syllabes mineures,

De vers de soirs d'amour énervés de verveine,
Où l'âme sente, exquise, une caresse à peine,

Et qui au long des nerfs baignés d'ondes câlines
Meurent à l'infini en pâmoisons félines,
Comme un parfum dissous parmi des tiédeurs closes,

Violes d'or, et *pianissim' amorose* . . .

Je rêve de vers doux mourant comme des roses.

*Au jardin de l'infante*

I dream of gentle verse and intimate song; verse to graze the soul like
wings; blond verse in which the fluid sense spreads out tenuously, like
Ophelia's hair in the water; silent verse, without rhythm or consistency,
in which the noiseless rhyme slips like an oar; verse cut of an ancient
cloth, worn thin, impalpable like sounds and clouds; autumn evening
verse, enchanting the hours with the feminine rite of minor syllables;
verse of an evening of love enervated with verbena, when the soul
scarcely feels an exquisite caress; verse which, along nerves bathed in
soothing waves, dies infinitely in feline swoons, like a perfume dis-
solved in a warm, closed room, golden viols, *pianissimo amoroso* — I
dream of gentle verse dying like roses.

## Dilection

J'adore l'indécis, les sons, les couleurs frêles,
Tout ce qui tremble, ondule, et frissonne, et chatoie,
Les cheveux et les yeux, l'eau, les feuilles, la soie,
Et la spiritualité des formes grêles;

Les rimes se frôlant comme des tourterelles,
La fumée où le songe en spirales tournoie,
La chambre au crépuscule, où Son profil se noie,
Et la caresse de Ses mains surnaturelles;

L'heure de ciel au long des lèvres câlinée,
L'âme comme d'un poids de délice inclinée,
L'âme qui meurt ainsi qu'une rose fanée,

Et tel coeur d'ombre chaste, embaumé de mystère,
Où veille, comme le rubis d'un lampadaire,
Nuit et jour, un amour mystique et solitaire.

*Au jardin de l'infante*

## Spiritual Love

I love the evanescent, fragile sounds and colors, everything that trembles, undulates, quivers, and shimmers, hair and eyes, water, leaves, silk, and the spiritual quality of indefinite forms; rhymes brushing against one another like turtle doves, smoke with dreams spiraling in it, the bedroom at dusk with Her profile growing dim, and the caress of Her unearthly hands; the daylight hour drifting along lips, the soul bent as it were under a burden of delight, the soul dying like a withered rose, and a certain heart of chaste shadow, redolent of mystery, where night and day a mystic solitary love keeps its vigil like a ruby holy lamp.

Des soirs fiévreux et forts comme une venaison,
Mon âme traîne en soi l'ennui d'un vieil Hérode;
Et prostrée aux coussins, où son mal la taraude,
Trouve à toute pensée un goût de trahison.

Pour fuir le désespoir qui souffle à l'horizon,
Elle appelle la sombre danseuse qui rôde,

Et Salomé vient dans la salle basse et chaude
Secouer le péché touffu de sa toison.

Elle danse!... Oh! pendant qu'avec l'éclat des pierres
Au soleil, ses deux yeux brûlent dans leurs paupières,
Mon âme, entends-tu pas bêler dans le verger?

Tu le sais bien pourtant quel enfer te l'amène,
Et qu'elle va, ce soir, réclamer pour sa peine
L'Agneau blanc de ton pauvre coeur pour l'égorger.

*Au jardin de l'infante*

On evenings feverish and gamy like venison, my soul is burdened with some old Herod's ennui, and prostrate on pillows, penetrated by its drilling hurt, it finds a hint of betrayal in every passing thought. To escape despair gusting on the horizon, my soul summons the shadowy, roving dancer, and Salome enters the hot, low room, shaking the tangle of sin in her mane. She dances. Oh, while with the brightness of gems in the sun, her two eyes burn in their lids, my soul, can you not hear the bleating in the grove? You certainly know what hell comes with her and that this evening she is going, for her reward, to ask for the white Lamb of your heart to slaughter it.

Le Bouc noir passe au fond des ténèbres malsaines.
C'est un soir rouge et nu! Tes dernières pudeurs
Râlent dans une mare énervante d'odeurs;
Et minuit sonne au coeur des sorcières obscènes.

Le simoun du désir a balayé la plaine!...
Plongée en tes cheveux pleins d'une âcre vapeur,
Ma chair couvre ta chair, et rumine en torpeur
L'amour qui doit demain engendrer de la haine.

Face à face nos Sens, encore inapaisés,
Se dévorent avec des yeux stigmatisés;
Et nos coeurs desséchés sont pareils à des pierres.

La Bête Ardente a fait litière de nos corps;
Et, comme il est prescrit quand on veille des morts,
Nos âmes à genoux—là-haut—sont en prières.

*Au jardin de l'infante*

In the distance the black goat moves through the unwholesome darkness. It is a red and naked evening. Your last remnants of modesty expire in a nerve-wracking pool of odors. And midnight rings in the heart of obscene witches. The desert wind of desire has swept the plain. Bathed in your hair with its acrid exhalations, my flesh covers your flesh, and torpidly ruminates the love which tomorrow must engender hatred. Face to face our senses, still unsatisfied, devour each other with eyes bearing a stigma. And our desiccated hearts are like stones. The burning beast has befouled our bodies, and, as it is prescribed when one keeps vigil over the dead, our kneeling souls, above, are occupied in prayer.

## Luxure

Luxure, fruit de mort à l'arbre de la vie,
Fruit défendu qui fait claquer les dents d'envie.

Chimère d'or assise au désert de l'Ennui.
Fille infâme du vieux Désir et de la Nuit.

Diamant du Péché scellé sous les sept voiles.
Feu du feu, Sang du sang et Moelle de nos moelles.

Sorcière de Bohême aux philtres souterrains.
Suceuse des cerveaux, et Dompteuse des reins.

Je te salue, ô très occulte, ô très profonde,
Luxure, Pavillon de ténèbres du monde.

\*

Luxure, avènement des sens à la splendeur.
Diadème de stupre et manteau d'impudeur.

Nudité. Jardin rose et divin de la femme.
Paradis de la chair qui fait sangloter l'âme.

Longs cheveux balayant l'air enivré des soirs.
Sombre incantation des odeurs, Parfums noirs.

Grandes ondes du sang qui chante. Pleurs d'ivresse,
Frissons, vagues toujours plus lentes des caresses.

Caresse au long des nerfs...Caresse infiniment!
Caresse au long des yeux...Évanouissement...

Musique dans les fleurs trop douces...Défaillance.
Languide archet d'extase aux cordes du Silence.

Lèvres! lèvres! Baiser qui meurt, baiser qui mord.
Lèvres, lit de l'amour profond comme la mort!

Je te salue, ô très occulte, ô très profonde,
Luxure, Etoile pourpre au ciel triste du monde.

*

Luxure, aspic subtil endormi dans les os.
Désirs aigus comme des pointes de ciseaux.

Tocsin ivre qui tinte aux minutes néfastes.
Succube, soeur nocturne et jalouse des Chastes.

Broussailles d'insomnie exaspérant l'éveil.
Sabbat-fresque grouillant au grand mur du Sommeil.

Gaze entr'ouverte au rythme irrité des Crotales.
Coupe vive qui fait grelotter les Tantales.

Glace qui fait brûler, Flamme qui fait transir.
Etable grasse où dort la bête du plaisir.

Je te salue, ô très occulte, ô très profonde,
Luxure, Oeil dévorant qui regarde le monde!

*

Luxure, vision farouche des Tropiques.
Rois sauvages parmi les plumes et les piques.

Palais de jade au bord des Ganges inouïs,
Jardins géants, lacs de parfums, ors enfouis.

Germinal effrayant des Equateurs torrides.
Silences d'or cinglés de vols de cantharides.

Vertige des parfums âcres et des toisons.
Lune de sang sur les marais verts de poisons.

Je te salue, ô très occulte, ô très profonde,
Luxure, Idole noire et terrible du monde.

*

Luxure, Tiare des Césars pâles et fous.
Collier des grandes hétaïres aux crins roux.

Reine des Mimes, et des Rythmes, et des Danses,
Et Porte d'or triomphale des Décadences.

Rêve effrayant des Empereurs voluptueux
Parmi les marbres et les tigres somptueux.

Fleurs humides de sang. Délices et supplices.
Mort respirée au plus suave des calices.

Flûtes et luths et cymbales dans les flambeaux!
Mort épousée aux lampes vertes des tombeaux.

Couchants d'empire oriental. Apothéoses.
Religion des éréthismes grandioses.

Derniers festins...Derniers soupirs...Râle subtil
Aux feux de l'art phosphorescent et volatil.

Je te salue, ô très occulte, ô très profonde,
Luxure, Lèpre d'or rayonnante du Monde.

*

Luxure, haleine ardente au long des coeurs charnels,
Passion, mer de pourpre aux frissons solennels.

Vigne de volupté, grappe lourde, ambroisie.
Vin du sexe qui met le sexe en frénésie.

Baume du mal amour. Cordial de rancoeur.
Auberge de la route aux pèlerins du coeur.

Frissons d'éternité vibrés par l'éphemère.
Fontaine vive où boit en courant la Chimère.

Giron des Esseulés, Vaillance des Peureux.
Opium de l'esclave, et Chienne du lépreux.

Urne jamais tarie où s'acharne la lèvre,
Faiblesse du puissant, et puissance du mièvre.

Male herbe de minuit tueuse de remords.
Gourde qui fait encor ouvrir la bouche aux morts.

Vaisseau splendide et nef des grandes nostalgies,
Cinglant, haute la proue, au large des orgies.

Jument du cavalier qui va, naseau béant,
Les poils dressés, au grand galop, vers le néant.

Lacs de soufre où l'on voit—au fond—brûler encore
Les jardins de Sodome et les tours de Gomorrhe.

Ciel d'angoisse aux confins du sentir éperdu.
Martyre! Pleurs d'extase au long du coeur tordu!

Tour noire où l'Enchanteur, dans son cercle de flammes,
Adjure l'infini par les rites infâmes.

Appétit du péché mortel, et soif et faim.
Gouffre, soleil sans ombre et spirale sans fin.

*

Luxure, nerf des nerfs, acide de l'acide,
Luxure, ultime amour damné qui se suicide.

Spasme vers l'unité. Noces dans l'absolu.
Luxure, fin du monde et cycle révolu.

Vierge d'or et de sang, vierge consolatrice,
Vierge vierge à jamais, vierge dévoratrice.

Cité de feu—Philtre d'oubli—Vrille de fer.
Vierge damnée, et Notre-Dame de l'Enfer.

Je te salue, ô très occulte, ô très profonde,
Luxure, Impératrice Immortelle du monde.

*Au jardin de l'infante*

## Lust

Lust, fruit of death on the tree of life, forbidden fruit making our teeth ache with desire. Golden chimaera seated in a desert of ennui. Infamous daughter of night and old desire. Diamond of sin sealed under the seven veils. Fire of fire, blood of blood, marrow of our marrow. Gypsy witch with subterranean philters, sucking out brains and taming loins. I salute you, O most hidden, O most deep lust, tent of shadow cast over the world. Lust, advent of the senses to your splendor. Diadem of filth and mantle of immodesty. Nakedness. Pink and divine garden of woman. Paradise of flesh at which the soul sobs. Long hair sweeping through the evening's intoxicating air. Dark incantation of odors. Black scents. Great waves of singing blood. Drunken tears, shudders, ever slower waves of caresses. Caress of the nerves—infinite. Caress of the eye—swooning. Music in too sweet flowers. Fainting. Languid bow of ecstasy on the strings of silence. Lips! Lips! Dying kiss, biting kiss. Lips! Bed of love deep as death, I salute you, O most hidden, O most deep lust, red star in the dismal sky of the world. Lust, subtle asp dozing in our bones. Desire sharp as scissor points. Drunken alarm ringing in inauspicious midnight. Succuba, nocturnal and jealous sister of the chaste. Bramble of insomnia making waking an agony. Fresco of the Witches' Sabbath squirming on the great wall of sleep. Gauze robe half opened to the irritating sound of a rattlesnake. A living cup at which Tantalus shivers. Burning ice, flame that benumbs. Rank stable where the beast of pleasure sleeps. I salute you, O most hidden, O most deep lust, devouring eye gazing at the world. Lust, frightful vision of the tropics. Savage kings amid feathers and pikes. Undreamed-of jade palaces beside the Ganges, giant gardens, scented lakes, hidden gold. Terrifying April of torrid equators. Golden silences lashed by swarms of cantharides. Whirl of acrid scents and hair. Blood moon over swamps green with poison. I salute you, O most hidden, O most deep lust, black and terrible idol of the world. Lust, tiara of pale demented Caesars. Necklace of the great redhaired courtesans. Queen of mimes and rhythms and dances. Golden triumphal gate of decadence. Terrifying dream of voluptuous emperors amid marbles and costly tigers. Flowers damp with blood. Rapture and torture. Death inhaled in the most delicate of chalices. Flutes and lutes and cymbals in torchlight. Death espoused in the tomb's green lamps. Sunsets from the Eastern Empire. Apotheoses. Religion of grandiose stimuli. Last feasts, last sighs. Subtle death rattle illuminated by a phosphorescent and volatile art. I salute you, O most hidden, O most deep lust, golden leprosy gleaming on the world. Lust, burning breath the length of carnal hearts. Passion, purple sea with solemn undulations. Vine of voluptuousness, heavy grapes, ambrosia. Wine of sex organs putting them in a frenzy. Balm of evil love. Rancor's cordial. Wayside inn for the heart's pilgrims. Shudders of eternity emanating from the ephemeral. Flowing spring from which the hurrying chimaera drinks. Bosom gathering in the lonely, courage of the fearful. Opium of slaves and leper's bitch. Urn never empty sought eagerly by lips. Weakness of the powerful and power of the delicate. Evil midnight herb that kills remorse. Drinking gourd for which even the dead open their mouths. Splendid ship of profound nostalgia, sailing, high on the waves, off the coast of orgies. Horseman's mare galloping, with flaring nostrils and bristling coat, toward nothingness. Sulphur lake in whose depths you still see burning the gardens of Sodom and towers of Gomorrah. Sky of anguish frantic at the boundaries of sensation. Martyrdom! Tears of ecstasy along the twisted heart. Black tower where, with unspeakable rites, the sorcerer in his circle of fire constrains the infinite. Appetite for mortal sin, both hunger and thirst. Chasm, shadowless sun, and endless spiral. Lust, nerve of nerves, acid of acid, lust, final damned love committing suicide. Spasm toward unity, marriage in the absolute. Lust, end of the world and completed cycle. Golden and bloody virgin, consoling virgin. Virgin forever virgin, consuming virgin. City of fire—philter of oblivion—iron gimlet. Damned virgin and Our Lady of Hell. I salute you, O most hidden, O most deep lust, immortal empress of the world.

# GUSTAVE KAHN

Très loin, toujours plus loin, loin de la face humaine
    Près des fleuves, par-là,
    Près de la lune amène,
    Des mineurs que voilà
Le blanc chagrin qui va de son masque à la terre
    Et que la nuit scella
Près d'une eau qui s'endort au fond d'un vieux cratère.

Exil, lointain exil! Trouveras-tu jamais
Les palais tapissés de clair où veut ton rêve
Dans des fraîcheurs, des puretés, musiques brèves,
Revêtir un oubli profond du: Je t'aimais.

Inconnu, bel inconnu, naviguer sur tes rivières
    Entre tes quais de marbre noir,
    Toucher du doigt les vieux lierres
    De tes nostalgiques manoirs,
Revivre, blanc et dolent, renouvelé des lumières
    Mentales de tes renouveaux
Dans l'aise indicible et la chaste paix des purs cerveaux.

En avant! L'heure tarde et les cheveux sont gris;
Leurs pauvres corps loués au vague des tavernes,
Les trésors si gardés d'amour dans leurs cavernes,
Nous ne les verrons plus; suivons mon coeur épris.

*Les Palais nomades*

Far, still farther, far from the human visage, by the river, in the distance, by the lovely moon, the moon of those miners. Her white sorrow going from her mask to the earth and sealed by night, near water sleeping in an old crater. Exile, distant exile! Will you ever find the palaces with brightly hung walls where your dream, amidst coolness, purity, brief passages of music, wishes to don the deep oblivion of "I loved you." Stranger, beautiful stranger, if only I could sail on your rivers, between your black marble banks, and touch with my finger the old ivy of your nostalgic manors; if only I could come to life again, slow and suffering, renewed by the mental light of your springtimes, in

the unutterable joy and chaste peace of pure minds. Onward! The hour
is late, and heads are grey! We shall not see again their poor bodies
rented in the confusion of taverns, the closely guarded treasure of love
in their caves. Let us follow my burning heart.

Tant grande douleur vint des gestes pâles
du timbre du verbe illusoire aux soirs.
Tant cruelle étreinte vint de tes mains pâles,
l'âge du mirage des caresses des soirs.

Abandonnée dans ta foule
toute fléchissante en ta dureté,
La neige de l'immanent hiver, à ton coeur qui croule
émanait de langueur des roses-thé.

Ah si nous savons se déchirer demain
laisse le sommeil s'imposer de tes mains,
fuyons la peur de neige aux pupilles solaires
boucliers lucescents de ta face nécessaire.

*Les Palais nomades*

Such a great sorrow came from your pale gestures, from the timbre
of the word, illusory in the evening. Such a cruel embrace came from
your pale hands, the time of the miragelike evening caresses. Alone in
your throngs, weak in the midst of your hardness, the snow of the
inner winter, for your crumbling heart, emanated from the tearoses'
languor. Ah, if we know tomorrow will be rent and wasted, therefore
let your hands now impose slumber on us; let us not be afraid of the
solar eyes in the snow, the shining shields of your necessary facial
expression.

Parc du silence, opacité
Mortelle cécité du soi,
Vers les boudoirs tendus de soie
Volète sa sincérité.

Tout à l'heure, c'était sonorant le bal
Puis, large, la vague aux nappes liliales,
Et l'assourdissement de langueurs filiales,
Et les discrets appels déments du triomphal.

Parc du silence où tout est clos,
Un trille lent volète aux cimes,
S'enamourent les purs azymes
De l'âme: argentins discrets tintent des grelots,
Course somnambulique aux abymes.

*Les Palais nomades*

Park of silence, fatal opacity, blindness of one's inner self; toward silk-hung boudoirs its sincerity fluttered. Just minutes ago the dance was resonant, then broad, a wave with lily-white expanses of froth; and the muffling of filial languors, and brief, insane, and discreet calls toward triumph. Park of silence, completely enclosed; a slow trill flutters in the treetops; enamoured are the pure Passovers of the soul: bells tinkle, silvery and discreet; a somnambulic race to the abyss.

Vers le plein ciel qui se dérobe
tangue la barque évanescente,
la barque aux citrines voilures des vesprées désespérées
par les pleurs des vagues et l'ocellure de leurs robes.

    Les hâvres exilés de là la haute mer
    les hâvres désirés dès les matins éphémères:
    à quelle ancre fixés les repos de la haute mer.

    Et les chevaliers blancs fuyards du marécage
    les yeux vers l'infini du regret primordial
    si calmes d'épuiser dans la coupe éternelle
    le désespoir qui se fixe en perpétuelles ritournelles
    attendent le magique, le soudain cordial
        pour guérir le temps, des âges.

Vers le plein ciel qui se dérobe
les barques éployées sur la mer
multiplient les cadences des rames perpétuelles
vers les hâvres enfuis de là la haute mer.

*Les Palais nomades*

Toward the elusive open sky pitches the vanishing ship, the citron-sailed ship of desperate evenings, beyond the tears of the waves and the ocellated fabric of their surface. The exiled harbors beyond the high seas, the harbors longed for from ephemeral mornings onward. By what anchor are the resting places of the high sea stayed? And the white knights fleeing the swamp, with their eyes on the infinity of primordial regret, so calm as they drink up in the eternal cup the despair caught in perpetual romances, wait for the sudden magic cordial of the ages to heal time. Toward the elusive open sky the boats deployed on the sea multiply the rhythms of perpetual oars, moving toward the vanishing harbors beyond the high sea.

Les rondes, les raisins, les roses!
Les curieux sont venus aussi
Pour se trouver si bien ici,
Les rondes, les raisins, les roses.

La cité d'or et de lointains
Si fabuleuse d'astrologues
De médailles et d'analogues,
La cité d'or des temps éteints...

Et puis se soucier des choses
Des lointains, des teints, des pantins!

*Les Palais nomades*

Rounds, grapes, roses! The curious have also come to enjoy themselves here, rounds, grapes, roses. The golden city of distances, so fabulous in its astrologers, medals, and analogies, the golden city of vanished time. Why worry about things in the distance, hues, puppets!

Je suis rentré dans la demeure
Avec la taciturne ivresse qui pardonne
Les cloches de mémoires qui meurent
Grondaient l'instant qui s'abandonne.

Les cloches de mémoire redisaient les yeux morts.
Les chevelures redénouées
Et les langueurs tant douées
D'un mirage furtif et frêle de bonne mort.

Et dans la brève demeure où meurent
Cuirasses des seins vaincus, des fleurs
L'ombre s'est apaisée de l'âme qui pardonne
Aux bras tordus, qui vers d'autres pôles s'abandonnent.

*Les Palais nomades*

I came back to the dwelling with the silent intoxication that pardons. The bells of dying memories scolded the moment of yielding. The bells of memory told again of the dead eyes, the hair again undone, and the languors so skillful of a furtive, frail mirage of welcome death. And in the brief dwelling, where, like the armor of vanquished breasts, flowers die, the shade of the pardoning soul has become calm, with its twisted arms now yielding to other poles.

# ALBERT GIRAUD

## Coucher de soleil

Le Soleil s'est ouvert les veines
Sur un lit de nuages roux:
Son sang, par la bouche des trous,
S'éjacule en rouges fontaines.

Les rameaux convulsifs des chênes
Flagellent les horizons fous:
Le Soleil s'est ouvert les veines
Sur un lit de nuages roux.

Comme, après les hontes romaines,
Un débauché plein de dégoûts
Laissant jusqu'aux sales égouts
Saigner ses artères malsaines,
Le Soleil s'est ouvert les veines!

*Pierrot lunaire*

## Sunset

The sun has cut his wrists on a bed of reddish clouds: his blood,
through gaping holes, spurts in red fountains. The oaks' convulsive
branches whip the mad horizons. The sun has cut his wrists on a bed of
reddish clouds. Just like a delicate debauchee after the Roman shame, a
debauchee allowing his sickly arteries to bleed into filthy sewers, the
sun has cut his wrists!

## Rouge et Blanc

Une cruelle et rouge langue,
Aux chairs salivantes de sang,
Comme un éclair érubescent
Sillonne son visage exsangue.

Sa face pâle est une gangue
D'où sort ce rubis repoussant:

Une cruelle et rouge langue,
Aux chairs salivantes de sang.

Son corps vertigineux qui tangue
Est comme un blanc vaisseau hissant
A son grand mât éblouissant
Son pavillon couleur de mangue:
Une cruelle et rouge langue!

*Pierrot lunaire*

## Red and White

A cruel red fleshy tongue salivating blood like a ruddy flash of lightning furrows his bloodless face. His pale face is a matrix from which this repulsive ruby projects: a cruel red fleshy tongue salivating blood. His dizzying, pitching body is like a white ship hoisting on its dazzling topmast its mango-colored flag: a cruel red tongue.

## Automne

Comme ce soir d'octobre, anxieux et puissant,
Qu'empourpre de sa mort, splendeur désespérée,
Le plus royal soleil de la saison dorée,
Voluptueusement dans mon âme descend!

O fureur des baisers! Jets de flamme et de sang!
Rouges lèvres que mord une bouche égarée!
Derniers cris de la chair misérable et sacrée!
Votre ivresse est pareille au ciel éblouissant!

*La Guirlande des dieux*

## Autumn

How voluptuously this October evening, anguished and powerful, descends into my soul, an evening reddened by its own death, a desperate splendor, the most royal sun of the gilded season! Fury of kisses! Spurts of fire and blood! Red lips bitten by a wild mouth! Last screams of the wretched and sacred flesh! Your drunkenness is like the dazzling sky!

# JULES LAFORGUE

## Complainte
## A Notre-Dame des Soirs

L'Extase du soleil, peuh! La Nature, fade
Usine de sève aux lymphatiques parfums.
Mais les lacs éperdus des longs couchants défunts
Dorlotent mon voilier dans leurs plus riches rades,
    Comme un ange malade...
    O Notre-Dame des Soirs,
    Que Je vous aime sans espoir!

Lampes des mers! blancs bizarrants! mots à vertiges!
Axiomes *in articulo mortis* déduits!
Ciels vrais! Lune aux échos dont communient les puits!
Yeux des portraits! Soleil qui, saignant son quadrige,
    Cabré, s'y crucifige!
    O Notre-Dame des Soirs,
    Certes, ils vont haut vos encensoirs!

Eux sucent des plis dont le frou-frou les suffoque;
Pour un regard, ils battraient du front les pavés;
Puis s'affligent sur maint sein creux, mal abreuvés;
Puis retournent à ces vendanges sexciproques.
    Et moi, moi Je m'en moque!
    Oui, Notre-Dame des Soirs,
    J'en fais, paraît-il, peine à voir.

En voyage, sur les fugitives prairies,
Vous me fuyez; ou du ciel des eaux m'invitez;
Ou m'agacez au tournant d'une vérité;
Or vous ai-je encor dit votre fait, je vous prie?
    Ah! coquette Marie,
    Ah! Notre-Dame des Soirs,
    C'est trop pour vos seuls Reposoirs!

Vos Rites, jalonnés de sales bibliothèques,
Ont voûté mes vingt ans, m'ont tari de chers goûts.
Verrai-je l'oasis fondant au rendez-vous,

Où... vos lèvres (dit-on!) à jamais nous dissèquent?
O Lune sur la Mecque!
Notre-Dame, Notre-Dame des Soirs,
De *vrais* yeux m'ont dit: au revoir!

*Les Complaintes*

## Lament to Our Lady of the Evenings

The sun's ecstasy, ugh! Nature is an insipid sap factory giving off sluggish odors. But the passionate lakes of long, dead sunsets cuddle my sailing ship in their richest harbors like a sick angel. O Our Lady of the Evenings, how hopelessly I love you. Lamps of the sea! Whites growing steadily stranger! Dizzying words! Axioms deduced in the moment of death! True skies! Moon with whose echoes the wells take communion! Eyes of portraits! Sun bleeding its four-horse team and, rearing up, cruciclotting itself in the blood! O Our Lady of the Evenings, your censers certainly swing high! Some men suckle on folds of dresses and are suffocated by their frou-frou. In exchange for a glance, they would beat their heads against the ground. Then, ill satisfied, they moan over the hollowness of the breasts they have worshipped. And then they return to these sexciprocal harvests of desires. And I don't give a damn, no, Our Lady of the Evenings, and apparently I look rather pitiful. Traveling over evanescent meadows, you flee me, or your reflection invites me to come into the water. Or else you come annoy me just as I am about to think an important thought. Have I really told you what I think of you? Ah! coquettish Mary. Ah! Our Lady of the Evenings, you are too big for your altars! Your rites, leading me through dirty libraries, have left me stooping at the age of twenty and dulled many cherished tastes. Will I meet you in the candy oasis where, they say, your lips will dissect us forever? O Moon over Mecca! Our Lady, Our Lady of the Evenings. Real eyes have said goodby to me!

## Complainte
## De l'orgue de Barbarie

Orgue, orgue de Barbarie,
Don Quichotte, Souffre-Douleur,
Vidasse, vidasse ton coeur,
Ma pauvre rosse endolorie.

Hein, étés idiots,
Octobres malades,
Printemps, purges fades,
Hivers tout vieillots?

—"Quel silence, dans la forêt d'automne,
Quand le soleil en son sang s'abandonne!"

Gaz, haillons d'affiches,
Feu les casinos,
Cercueils des pianos,
Ah! mortels postiches.

—"Déjà la nuit, qu'on surveille à peine
Le frou-frou de sa titubante traîne."

Romans pour les quais,
Photos élégiaques,
Escarpins, vieux claques,
D'un coup de balai!

—"Oh! j'ai peur, nous avons perdu la route;
Paul, ce bois est mal famé! chut, écoute..."

Végétal fidèle,
Eve aime toujours
LUI! jamais pour
Nous, jamais pour elle.

—"O ballets corrosifs! réel, le crime?
La lune me pardonnait dans les cimes."

Vêpres, Ostensoirs,
Couchants! Sulamites
De province aux rites
Exilants des soirs!

—"Ils m'ont brûlée; et depuis, vagabonde
Au fond des bois frais, j'implore le monde."

Et les vents s'engueulent,
Tout le long des nuits!
Qu'est-c'que moi j'y puis,
Qu'est-ce donc qu'ils veulent?

—"Je vais guérir, voyez la cicatrice,
Oh! je ne veux pas aller à l'hospice!"

Des berceaux fienteux
Aux bières de même,
Bons couples sans gêne,
Tournez deux à deux.

Orgue, Orgue de Barbarie!
Scie autant que Souffre-Douleur,
Vidasse, vidasse ton coeur,
Ma pauvre rosse endolorie.

*Les Complaintes*

## Lament of the Hurdy-gurdy

Hurdy-gurdy, hurdy-gurdy, Don Quixote, scapegoat, pour out, pour out your heart, my poor old wretch. You mean stupid summers, sick Octobers, springs like a dreary purge, out-of-date winters?—"What silence in the autumn forest, when the sun sinks down in its own blood!"—Gas, tattered posters, closed casinos, pianos like coffins, fatal fake curls.—"Already night; why, we've scarcely paid attention to the frou-frou of her staggering train-dress."—Novels to be remaindered, sad photographs of days past, dancing slippers, old collapsible top hats, out with a whisk of the broom!—"Oh! I'm afraid we've lost our way, Paul. These woods are supposed to be dangerous! Ssh! Listen!"—Like a faithful plant, Eve still loves HIM! Never for us, never for herself.—"O corrosive ballets! Was it a real crime? The moon in the treetops pardoned me!"—Vespers, monstrances, sunsets! Provincial Shulamites in the exiling rites of evenings!—"They ruined my reputation, and, ever since, wandering in the cool woods, I implore passersby."—And the winds yell at each other all night long. What can I do about it? What do they expect of me?—"I am going to heal, look at the scar. Oh! I don't want to go to the poor-house."—From soiled cradles to soiled biers, good couples, unembarrassed, turn two by two. Hurdy-gurdy, hurdy-gurdy! Cliché as much as scapegoat. Pour out, pour out your heart, my poor old suffering wretch.

## Complainte des pianos
### Qu'on entend dans les quartiers aisés

Menez l'âme que les Lettres ont bien nourrie,
Les pianos, les pianos, dans les quartiers aisés!

Premiers soirs, sans pardessus, chaste flânerie,
Aux complaintes des nerfs incompris ou brisés.

    Ces enfants, à quoi rêvent-elles,
    Dans les ennuis des ritournelles?

        —"Préaux des soirs,
        Christs des dortoirs!

    "Tu t'en vas et tu nous laisses,
    Tu nous laiss's et tu t'en vas,
    Défaire et refaire ses tresses,
    Broder d'éternels canevas."

Jolie ou vague? triste ou sage? encore pure?
O jours, tout m'est égal? ou, monde, moi je veux?
Et si vierge, du moins, de la bonne blessure,
Sachant quels gras couchants ont les plus blancs aveux?

    Mon Dieu, à quoi donc rêvent-elles?
    A des Roland, à des dentelles?

        —"Coeurs en prison,
        Lentes saisons!

    "Tu t'en vas et tu nous quittes,
    Tu nous quitt's et tu t'en vas!
    Couvents gris, choeurs de Sulamites,
    Sur nos seins nuls croisons nos bras."

Fatales clés de l'être un beau jour apparues;
Psitt! aux hérédités en ponctuels ferments,
Dans le bal incessant de nos étranges rues;
Ah! pensionnats, théâtres, journaux, romans!

    Allez, stériles ritournelles,
    La vie est vraie et criminelle.

        —"Rideaux tirés,
        Peut-on entrer?

    "Tu t'en vas et tu nous laisses,
    Tu nous laiss's et tu t'en vas,
    La source des frais rosiers baisse,
    Vraiment! Et lui qui ne vient pas…"

Il viendra! Vous serez les pauvres coeurs en faute,
Fiancés au remords comme aux essais sans fond,

Et les suffisants coeurs cossus, n'ayant d'autre hôte
Qu'un train-train pavoisé d'estime et de chiffons.

Mourir? peut-être brodent-elles,
Pour un oncle à dot, des bretelles?

—"Jamais! Jamais!
Si tu savais!

"Tu t'en vas et tu nous quittes,
Tu nous quitt's et tu t'en vas,
Mais tu nous reviendras bien vite
Guérir mon beau mal, n'est-ce pas?"

Et c'est vrai! l'Idéal les fait divaguer toutes,
Vigne bohême, même en ces quartiers aisés.
La vie est là; le pur flacon des vives gouttes
Sera, *comme il convient,* d'eau propre baptisé.

Aussi, bientôt, se joueront-elles
De plus exactes ritournelles.

"—Seul oreiller!
Mur familier!

"Tu t'en vas et tu nous laisses,
Tu nous laiss's et tu t'en vas.
Que ne suis-je morte à la messe!
O mois, ô linges, ô repas!"

*Les Complaintes*

## Lament of the Pianos Heard
## in Rich Neighborhoods

Lead your soul well nourished on literature—the pianos, the pianos, in the expensive quarters! First spring evenings, without a coat, a chaste walk, with your lamenting, misunderstood, and jangled nerves. What are those girls dreaming of, as they sing their dreary songs?—"Convent garden in the evening, Christ in the dormitories! You are going and leaving us, you are leaving us and going, while we do and undo our hair and embroider on endless hoops."—Is she pretty or vapid? sad or good? Still pure? Is she satisfied with everything or always saying "Give me." And if she is virgin at least in body, does she know the voluptuousness of sunsets and of virginal confessions in the evening? My God, what are they thinking of, Rolands? Lace?—"Imprisoned hearts, interminable seasons! You are going and leaving us, you are leaving us and going. In our grey convents, like a chorus of Shulamites, let us cross our arms over our undeveloped breasts."—Inevitable genetic decay showing up one fine day! Sentimental outcome of fermenting heredity! Bad influences in the endless dance of our unheard-of streets: boarding-schools, theaters, newspapers, novels! Stop, empty songs! Life is real and criminal!—"Curtains drawn, can one enter? You are going and leaving us, you are leaving us and going. The spring under the cool rosebushes is drying up, really! And he hasn't come!"—He will come! But your poor hearts will be at fault in not recognizing him; they will be betrothed to remorse and to baseless attempts to escape their fate: you have smug, rich hearts occupied with nothing more than your routine enhanced with self-esteem and new clothes. Dying? Are they perhaps embroidering suspenders for the bachelor uncle who will supply the dowry?—"Never! Never! If you only knew! You are going and leaving us, you are leaving us and going. But you'll come back soon, won't you, and cure my exquisite ache?"—And it's true, the Ideal has them all gushing, like some wild bohemian weed, even in these bourgeois neighborhoods. But life is there. The pure flagon of their living essence will be *properly* baptized with clean water. Soon, therefore, they will be playing more knowledgeable songs.—"Single pillow, wall I know too well! You are going and leaving us, you are leaving us and going. Why didn't I drop dead at Mass? O time, O trousseaus, O meals!"

## Complainte des printemps

Permettez, ô sirène,
Voici que votre haleine
Embaume la verveine;
C'est l' printemps qui s'amène!

—Ce système, en effet, ramène le printemps,
Avec son impudent cortège d'excitants.

Otez donc ces mitaines;
Et n'ayez, inhumaine,
Que mes soupirs pour traîne:
Ous'qu'il y a de la gêne...

—Ah! yeux bleus méditant sur l'ennui de leur art!
Et vous, jeunes divins, aux soirs crus de hasard!

Du géant à la naine,
Vois, tout bon sire entraîne
Quelque contemporaine,
Prendre l'air, par hygiène...

—Mais vous saignez ainsi pour l'amour de l'exil!
Pour l'amour de l'Amour! D'ailleurs, ainsi soit-il...

T'ai-je fait de la peine?
Oh! viens vers les fontaines
Où tournent les phalènes
Des Nuits Elyséennes!

—Pimbèche aux yeux vaincus, bellâtre aux beaux jarrets,
Donnez votre fumier à la fleur du Regret.

Voilà que son haleine
N'embaum' plus la verveine!
Drôle de phénomène...
Hein, à l'année prochaine?

—Vierges d'hier, ce soir traîneuses de foetus,
A genoux! voici l'heure où se plaint l'Angélus.

Nous n'irons plus au bois,
Les pins sont éternels,
Les cors ont des appels!...

Neiges des pâles mois,
Vous serez mon missel!
—Jusqu'au jour de dégel.

*Les Complaintes*

## Lament of the Springtime

Let me take your arm, O siren; your breath now smells of verbena.
Springtime is here!—This system, indeed, brings back spring with its
unchaste accompaniment of stimulants.—Take off those mittens, cruel
one, and let my sighs be your train: wherever it is hard to walk...
—Ah, blue eyes meditating on the terrible demands of their art! And
you, divine young men, on what seemed like chance evenings!—From
the giant to the dwarf, see, every John Doe is taking out the female of
the species for a hygienic walk.—But you are bleeding for love of exile,
for love of love! So be it, moreover.—Did I upset you? Oh, come
toward the fountains with the moths of our Elysian nights!—Carmen
with conquered eyes, Don Juan with handsome calves, cast your drop-

pings on the Flower of Regret.—Now her breath no longer smells of
verbena. Funny phenomenon. Till next year, let's say?—Yesterday's
virgins, this evening loaded down with foetuses—on your knees! It's
time for the Angelus' lament.—We shall go to the woods no more; the
pine trees are eternal; the horns have such calls! Snows of the pale
months, you will be my Missal!—Until the day they melt.

## Complainte
### De l'automne monotone

Automne, automne, adieux de l'Adieu!
La tisane bout, noyant mon feu;
   Le vent s'époumonne
A reverdir la bûche où mon grand coeur tisonne.
   Est-il de vrais yeux?
Nulle ne songe à m'aimer un peu.

     Milieux aptères,
     Ou sans divans;
     Regards levants,
     Deuils solitaires,
     Vers des Sectaires!

Le vent, la pluie, oh! le vent, la pluie!
Antigone, écartez mon rideau;
   Cet ex-ciel tout suie,
Fond-il *decrescendo, statu quo, crescendo?*
   Le vent qui s'ennuie,
Retourne-t-il bien les parapluies?

     Amours, gibiers!
     Aux jours de givre,
     Rêver sans livre,
     Dans les terriers
     Chauds de fumiers!

Plages, chemins de fer, ciels, bois morts,
Bateaux croupis dans les feuilles d'or,
   Le quart aux étoiles,
Paris grasseyant par chic aux prises de voiles:
   De trop poignants cors
M'ont hallalisé ces chers décors.

Meurtres, alertes,
Rêves ingrats!
En croix, les bras;
Roses ouvertes,
Divines pertes!

Le soleil mort, tout nous abandonne.
Il se crut incompris. Qu'il est loin!
Vent pauvre, aiguillonne
Ces convois de martyrs se prenant à témoins!
La terre, si bonne
S'en va, pour sûr, passer cet automne.

Nuits sous-marines!
Pourpres forêts,
Torrents de frais,
Bancs en gésines,
Tout s'illumine!

—Allons, fumons une pipette de tabac,
En feuilletant un de ces si vieux almanachs,

En rêvant de la petite qui unirait
Aux charmes de l'oeillet ceux du chardonneret.

*Les Complaintes*

## Lament of Monotonous Autumn

Autumn, autumn, farewells of the definitive Farewell. My tea water boils over and puts out my fire. The wind grows hoarse trying to make the log unburnable that my great heart is stirring with the poker. Are there true eyes? No one thinks of loving me a bit. —Milieus without wings or divans of poetry. Rising eyes, solitary mourning, schismatic verse! —Wind, rain, oh! wind, rain! Antigone, open my curtains. This ex-sky, all soot, is it melting *decrescendo, statu quo, crescendo?* Is the bored wind really turning the umbrellas inside out? —Loves, prey! On days of frost, dreaming without a book, in burrows warm with dung!— Beaches, railroads, skies, dead woods, boats sunk in golden leaves, the watch under the stars, Paris thinking it clever to make crude remarks when virgins take the veil: too poignant horns have echoed with the death cry through these dear settings! —Murders, alarms, unrewarding dreams! Stretch your arms on a cross, open roses, divine losses! —Once the sun is dead, we are completely abandoned. It felt itself misunderstood. How far away it is! Poor wind, spur on these funereal processions of martyr clouds calling on each other to bear witness! The earth, so good to us, surely won't last out this autumn.—Submarine nights! Purple forests, cool water currents, fish schools spawning, everything lights up!—Come now, let's smoke a pipe and look through these ancient almanacs, while dreaming of the girl who would join the charms of the carnation to those of the finch.

## Complainte
## De pauvre chevalier-errant

Jupes des quinze ans, aurores de femmes,
Qui veut, enfin, des palais de mon âme?
Perrons d'oeillets blancs, escaliers de flamme,
    Labyrinthes alanguis,
      Edens qui
Sonneront, sous vos pas reconnus, des airs reconquis.

Instincts-levants souriant par les fentes,
Méditations un doigt à la tempe,
Souvenirs clignotant comme des lampes,
    Et, battant les corridors,
      Vains essors,
Les Dilettantismes chargés de colliers de remords.

Oui, sans bruit, vous écarterez mes branches,
Et verrez comme, à votre mine franche,
Viendront à vous mes biches les plus blanches,
    Mes ibis sacrés, mes chats,
      Et, rachats!
Ma Vipère de Lettre aux bien effaçables crachats.

Puis, frêle mise au monde! ô Toute Fine,
O ma Tout-universelle orpheline,
Au fond de chapelles de mousseline
    Pâle, ou jonquille à pois noirs,
      Dans les soirs,
Feu-d'artificeront envers vous mes sens encensoirs!

Nous organiserons de ces parties!
Mes caresses, naïvement serties,
Mourront, de ta gorge aux vierges hosties,

Aux amandes de tes seins!
        O tocsins,
Des coeurs dans le roulis des empilements de coussins.

Tu t'abandonnes au Bon, moi j'abdique;
Nous nous comblons de nos deux Esthétiques;
Tu condimentes mes piments mystiques,
        J'assaisonne tes saisons;
                Nous blasons,
A force d'étapes sur nos collines, l'Horizon!

Puis j'ai des tas d'éternelles histoires.
O mers, ô volières de ma Mémoire!
Sans compter les passes évocatoires!
        Et quand tu t'endormiras,
                Dans les draps
D'un somme, je t'éventerai de lointains opéras.

Orage en deux coeurs, ou jets d'eau des siestes,
Tout sera Bien, contre ou selon ton geste,
Afin qu'à peine un prétexte te reste
        De froncer tes chers sourcils,
                Ce souci:
"Ah! suis-je née, infiniment, pour vivre par ici?"

—Mais j'ai beau parader, toutes s'en fichent!
Et je repars avec ma folle affiche,
Boniment incompris, piteux *sandwiche:*
        Au Bon Chevalier-Errant,
                Restaurant,
Hôtel meublé, Cabinets de lecture, prix courants.

                        *Les Complaintes*

## Lament of the Poor Knight Errant

Skirts of girls fifteen, dawns of women, who, to be brief, is interested in the palace of my soul? Outer staircases of white carnations, inner ones of fire, languorous labyrinths, Edens which, recognizing your step, will play reconquered melodies. Rising instincts smiling through the look-out slits, meditations with one finger on your temple, memories blinking like signal lights, and, marching through the corridors in vain attempts to soar, dilettantisms burdened with collars of remorse. Yes, soundlessly, you will push aside my branches; and you will see how, at the sight of your candid face, my whitest does will come to you, my sacred ibises, my cats, and, for its redemption, my literary viper whose venom is quite easily wiped off. Then, like a fragile birth, O very subtle one, O my cosmic orphan, in the depths of pale muslin chapels—or yellow with black polka dots—in the evening, like fireworks, my censer-senses will rise toward you! We shall organize such fêtes! My caresses, naïvely presented, will die from your throat to the virgin eucharists, to the almonds of your breasts. O alarm bells of hearts rolling in stacks of pillows! You will give yourself over to a good man; I will abdicate. Our two esthetics will complement each other. You will put your spices in my mystic condiments; I shall season your seasons. We will linger so much on our hills that we will wear out the horizon. Then, I have a lot of eternal stories, O seas, O aviaries of my memory! To say nothing of summoning ghosts in seances. And when you fall asleep in sleeping sheets, I shall fan you with distant operas. A storm in two hearts, or siestas like fountains, everything will be perfect both at and against your bidding, so that scarcely a pretext will remain for you to frown, thinking, "Ah! was I born, according to the infinite verities, to live here?"—But it doesn't matter how long I walk up and down, none of them gives a damn. And I set off again with my crazy sign, my come-on misunderstood, a pitiful sandwich man: "At the Sign of the Good Knight Errant. Restaurant. Furnished Rooms. Lending Library. Competitive Prices."

## Complainte
## Du roi de Thulé

Il était un roi de Thulé,
    Immaculé,
Qui loin des jupes et des choses,
Pleurait sur la métempsychose
    Des lys en roses,
    Et quel palais!

Ses fleurs dormant, il s'en allait,
    Traînant des clés,
Broder aux seuls yeux des étoiles,
Sur une tour, un certain Voile.
    De vive toile,
    Aux nuits de lait!

Quand le voile fut bien ourlé,
　　　　Loin de Thulé,
Il rama fort sur les mers grises,
Vers le soleil qui s'agonise,
　　　　Féerique Eglise!
　　　　Il ululait:

"Soleil-crevant, encore un jour,
Vous avez tendu votre phare
Aux holocaustes vivipares,
Du culte qu'ils nomment l'Amour.

"Et comme, devant la nuit fauve,
Vous vous sentez défaillir,
D'un dernier flot d'un sang martyr
Vous lavez le seuil de l'Alcôve!

"Soleil! Soleil! moi je descends
Vers vos navrants palais polaires,
Dorloter dans ce Saint-Suaire
　　　　Votre coeur bien en sang,
　　　　En le berçant!"

Il dit, et, le Voile étendu,
　　　　Tout éperdu,
Vers les coraux et les naufrages,
Le roi raillé des doux corsages,
　　　　Beau comme un Mage
　　　　Est descendu!

Braves amants! aux nuits de lait,
　　　　Tournez vos clés!
Une ombre, d'amour pur transie,
Viendrait vous gémir cette scie:
"Il était un roi de Thulé
　　　　Immaculé . . ."

*Les Complaintes*

## Lament of the King of Thule

There once was a king in Thule, spotless, who, far from skirts and
material life, wept over the transformation of virgin lilies into voluptary
roses, and what a palace he had! While his flowers were sleeping, he

went, dragging his bunch of keys, to embroider a certain Veil in a
tower, under the eyes of the stars alone, a Veil of living fabric in milky
white nights. When the Veil had been properly hemmed, far from
Thule, he rowed hard on the grey seas toward the moribund sun,
which looked like a fairy church! He wailed, "Dying sun, for yet one
more day you have lent your light to the viviparous holocausts of the
cult called Love. And as, before darkening night, you feel yourself
growing weak, you wash the threshold of the Bedroom with a last
wave of martyr's blood. Sun! Sun! I am going down toward your sor-
rowful polar palaces to cuddle and rock your bleeding heart in this Holy
Shroud." He spoke, and, with the Veil stretched out, frantically, toward
corals and shipwrecks, the king mocked by gentle feminine breasts
went down, handsome as one of the Magi. Good lovers, on milky
nights lock your doors. A shade frozen with pure love might come
moan at you this refrain, "There once was a king in Thule, spotless..."

## L'Hiver qui vient

Blocus sentimental! Messageries du Levant!...
Oh, tombée de la pluie! Oh, tombée de la nuit!
Oh, le vent!...
La Toussaint, la Noël, et la Nouvelle Année,
Oh, dans les bruines, toutes mes cheminées!...
D'usines...

On ne peut plus s'asseoir, tous les bancs sont mouillés;
Crois-moi, c'est bien fini jusqu'à l'année prochaine,
Tant les bancs sont mouillés, tant les bois sont rouillés,
Et tant les cors ont fait ton ton, ont fait ton taine!...

Ah, nuées accourues des côtes de la Manche,
Vous nous avez gâté notre dernier dimanche.

Il bruine;
Dans la forêt mouillée, les toiles d'araignées
Ploient sous les gouttes d'eau, et c'est leur ruine.
Soleils plénipotentiaires des travaux en blonds Pactoles
Des spectacles agricoles,
Où êtes-vous ensevelis?
Ce soir un soleil fichu gît au haut du coteau
Gît sur le flanc, dans les genêts, sur son manteau,

Un soleil blanc comme un crachat d'estaminet
Sur une litière de jaunes genêts,
De jaunes genêts d'automne.
Et les cors lui sonnent!
Qu'il revienne...
Qu'il revienne à lui!
Taïaut! Taïaut! et hallali!
O triste antienne, as-tu fini!...
Et font les fous!...
Et il gît là, comme une glande arrachée dans un cou,
Et il frissonne, sans personne!...

Allons, allons, et hallali!
C'est l'Hiver bien connu qui s'amène;
Oh! les tournants des grandes routes,
Et sans petit Chaperon Rouge qui chemine!...
Oh! leurs ornières des chars de l'autre mois,
Montant en don quichottesques rails
Vers les patrouilles des nuées en déroute
Que le vent malmène vers les transatlantiques bercails!...
Accélérons, accélérons, c'est la saison bien connue, cette fois.
Et le vent, cette nuit, il en a fait de belles!
O dégâts, ô nids, ô modestes jardinets!
Mon coeur et mon sommeil: ô échos des cognées!...

Tous ces rameaux avaient encor leurs feuilles vertes,
Les sous-bois ne sont plus qu'un fumier de feuilles mortes,
Feuilles, folioles, qu'un bon vent vous emporte
Vers les étangs par ribambelles,
Ou pour le feu du garde-chasse,
Ou les sommiers des ambulances
Pour les soldats loin de la France.

C'est la saison, c'est la saison, la rouille envahit les masses,
La rouille ronge en leurs spleens kilométriques
Les fils télégraphiques des grandes routes où nul ne passe.

Les cors, les cors, les cors—mélancoliques!...
Mélancoliques!...
S'en vont, changeant de ton,
Changeant de ton et de musique,
Ton ton, ton taine, ton ton!...

Les cors, les cors, les cors!...
S'en sont allés au vent du Nord.

Je ne puis quitter ce ton: que d'échos!...
C'est la saison, c'est la saison, adieu vendanges!...
Voici venir les pluies d'une patience d'ange,
Adieu vendanges, et adieu tous les paniers,
Tous les paniers Watteau des bourrées sous les marronniers,
C'est la toux dans les dortoirs du lycée qui rentre,
C'est la tisane sans le foyer,
La phtisie pulmonaire attristant le quartier,
Et toute la misère des grands centres.

Mais, lainages, caoutchoucs, pharmacie, rêve,
Rideaux écartés du haut des balcons des grèves
Devant l'océan de toitures des faubourgs,
Lampes, estampes, thé, petits-fours,
Serez-vous pas mes seules amours!...
(Oh! et puis, est-ce que tu connais, outre les pianos,
Le sobre et vespéral mystère hebdomadaire
Des statistiques sanitaires
Dans les journaux?)

Non, non! C'est la saison et la planète falote!
Que l'autan, que l'autan
Effiloche les savates que le Temps se tricote!
C'est la saison, Oh déchirements! c'est la saison!
Tous les ans, tous les ans,
J'essaierai en choeur d'en donner la note.

*Derniers Vers*

## Coming Winter

Sentimental blockade! Wind deliveries from the East! Oh, the falling rain! Oh, the falling night! Oh, the wind! All Saints' Day, Christmas, and the New Year, oh, in the drizzle, all my factory chimneys! You can't sit down anymore, all the benches are wet. Believe me, everything is finished until next year. The benches are so wet, the woods so rusted, and the hunting horns have blown so much. Ah, storm clouds gathered from the Channel coast, you have spoiled our last Sunday. It is drizzling. In the wet forest the spiderwebs collapse under the water drops and it's the end of them. Fully empowered suns presiding over the farming display of rivers of gold, where are you buried? This evening a done-for sun lies on top of the hill, lies on his side, in the broom, on his coat, a sun white as spittle in taverns, on a litter of yellow broom, of yellow autumn broom. And the horns blow for him! Let him come back, come back to his senses! Tallyho! Tallyho! The death cry! O sad anthem, are you ended? And go crazy. And he lies there like a gland ripped out of a throat, and shivers all alone! Come now, the death cry! It's the winter we know so well settling in. Oh! the curves in the high-way! and no Little Red Riding Hood walking along! Oh, the cart ruts from last month, rising like crazy rails toward the fleeing patrols of dark clouds, which the wind is beating along toward the transatlantic sheepfolds! Let's get along faster, let's get along faster, it's the well-known season this time. And the wind last night really made a mess! O wreckage, O nests, O neat little gardens! My heart and my sleep! O sound of the axes! All the branches still had their green leaves; now the underbrush is just a heap of dead leaves. Leaves, leaflets, may a good wind carry you in long streams toward the ponds, or for the game warden's fire, or for the mattresses in ambulances for soldiers far from France. It's the season, it's the season; the rusty color is penetrating the great masses of trees; rust gnaws at the kilometric ennui of telegraph wires along the abandoned highways. The horns, the horns — melancholy ones! They are heading off changing their note, changing their note and call, toot toot, toot toot; the horns, the horns, the horns have gone off in the north wind. I cannot leave off this note: what echoes! It's the season, it's the season, farewell grape harvest! Here are the rains patient as angels. Farewell grape harvest and farewell hoop skirts, Watteauesque hoop skirts dancing bourrées under the chestnut trees. It's the cough returning to the lycée dormitories, it's medicinal tea with no home to drink it in, tuberculosis making the neighborhood dismal, and all the wretchedness of urban life. But woolens, rubbers, medicines, daydreaming, curtains open on balconies, as if over strands, giving onto the ocean of roofs in the poor districts, lamps, prints, tea, cookies, you will be my only love! (Oh, and furthermore, do you know, besides the pianos, the sober, weekly evening mystery of death and epidemic statistics in the newspapers?) No, no, it's the season and the foolish planet. Let the spring breeze unravel the slippers Time knits for herself. It's the season, oh heartbreak! It's the season! Every year, every year, I shall try to convey its tone in my chorus.

# Dimanches

C'est l'automne, l'automne, l'automne,
Le grand vent et toute sa séquelle
De représailles! et de musiques!...
Rideaux tirés, clôture annuelle,
Chute des feuilles, des Antigones, des Philomèles:
Mon fossoyeur, *Alas poor Yorick!*
Les remue à la pelle!...

Vivent l'Amour et les feux de paille!...

Les Jeunes Filles inviolables et frêles
Descendent vers la petite chapelle
Dont les chimériques cloches
Du joli joli dimanche
Hygiéniquement et élégamment les appellent.

Comme tout se fait propre autour d'elles!
Comme tout en est dimanche!

Comme on se fait dur et boudeur à leur approche!...

Ah! moi, je demeure l'Ours Blanc!
Je suis venu par ces banquises
Plus pures que les communiantes en blanc...
Moi, je ne vais pas à l'église,
Moi je suis le Grand Chancelier de l'Analyse,
Qu'on se le dise.

Pourtant! pourtant! Qu'est-ce que c'est que cette anémie?
Voyons, confiez vos chagrins à votre vieil ami...

Vraiment! Vraiment!
Ah! Je me tourne vers la mer, les éléments
Et tout ce qui n'a plus que les noirs grognements!

Oh, que c'est sacré!
Et qu'il y faut de grandes veillées!

Pauvre, pauvre, sous couleur d'attraits!...

Et nous, et nous,
Ivres, ivres, avant qu'émerveillés...
Qu'émerveillés et à genoux!...

Et voyez comme on tremble,
Au premier grand soir
Que tout pousse au désespoir
D'en mourir ensemble!

O merveille qu'on n'a su que cacher!
Si pauvre et si brûlante et si martyre!
Et qu'on n'ose toucher
Qu'à l'aveugle, en divin délire!

O merveille,
Reste cachée, idéale violette,
L'Univers te veille,
Les générations de planètes te tettent,
De funérailles en relevailles!...

Oh, que c'est plus haut
Que ce Dieu et que la Pensée!
Et rien qu'avec ces chers yeux en haut,
Tout inconscients et couleurs de pensée!...
Si frêle, si frêle!
Et tout le mortel foyer
Tout, tout ce foyer en elle!...

Oh, pardonnez-lui si, malgré elle,
Et cela tant lui sied,
Parfois ses prunelles clignent un peu
Pour vous demander un peu
De vous apitoyer un peu!

O frêle, frêle, et toujours prête
Pour ces messes dont on a fait un jeu
Penche, penche ta chère tête, va,
Regarde les grappes des premiers lilas,
Il ne s'agit pas de conquêtes, avec moi,
Mais d'au-delà!

Oh! puissions-nous quitter la vie
Ensemble dès cette Grand'Messe,
Écoeurés de notre espèce
Qui bâille assouvie
Dès le parvis!...

*Derniers Vers*

## Sundays

It's autumn, autumn, autumn, the great winds and their whole sequel of reprisals and music! Curtains drawn, annual closing, falling leaves, Antigones, Philomelas: my gravedigger, *Alas poor Yorick!*, stirs these memories with his shovel. Long live love and straw fires! Untouchable, frail girls walk down to the little chapel, whose fanciful bells on a pretty, pretty Sunday elegantly call them to a hygienic service. How clean everything is around them! How Sundayish everything is. How hard and crabby I get when I see them coming! I remain the White Bear from ice floes purer than girls dressed in white for First Communion. I don't go to church; I am the Bismarck of Philosophical Analysis, just remember. At the same time, still—What's that I hear about your being anemic? Come tell your troubles to your old friend. Really, really! Ah, I'll confide in the sea, the elements, the rumbling black inhuman cosmos. Oh, my thought is sacred, and it has cost much midnight oil! How poor and fragile she is, despite her outward appearance. And with her, we are intoxicated even before being dazzled and falling on our knees. And see how she trembles in the first magnificent autumn evening that fills one with despair and the desire to die together. O marvel that could only be hidden, so fragile and burning and martyred! And whom one dares touch only without looking, in a divine delirium! O marvel, remain hidden like an ideal violet. The universal life process is looking out for you. Generations of planets are suckling you in a round of births and deaths. How much higher she is than her God and my thought. Just with her dear eyes looking up, unawares and pansy colored. So fragile, so fragile, and containing in herself the whole mortal womb of being. Oh, pardon her if, despite herself—and it so becomes her—her eyes sometimes blink a little, and she asks you to take pity on her instincts. O frail one, frail yet always ready for those erotic Masses people make a game of, lean your dear head over, come, and look at the racemes of the first lilacs. I am not interested in conquests but in the Higher Life. Oh! would that we could die together at this very High Mass we are celebrating, revolted by the human race, which is yawning, sated, at the very doors!

## Légende

Armorial d'anémie!
Psautier d'automne!
Offertoire de tout mon ciboire de bonheur et de génie,
A cette hostie si féminine,
Et si petite toux sèche maligne,
Qu'on voit aux jours déserts, en inconnue,
Sertie en de cendreuses toilettes qui sentent déjà l'hiver,
Se fuir le long des cris surhumains de la Mer.

Grandes amours, oh: qu'est-ce encor!...

En tout cas, des lèvres sans façon,
Des lèvres déflorées,
Et quoique mortes aux chansons,
Apres encore à la curée.
Mais les yeux d'une âme qui s'est bel et bien cloîtrée
Enfin; voici qu'elle m'honore de ses confidences,
J'en souffre plus qu'elle ne pense.

—"Mais, chère perdue, comment votre esprit éclairé
"Et le stylet d'acier de vos yeux infaillibles,
"N'ont-ils pas su percer à jour la mise en frais
"De cet économique et passager bellâtre?"

—"Il vint le premier; j'étais seule près de l'âtre;
"Son cheval attaché à la grille
"Hennissait en désespéré..."

—"C'est touchant (pauvre fille)
"Et puis après?
"Oh! regardez, là-bas, cet épilogue sous couleur de couchant!
"Et puis, vrai,
"Remarquez que dès l'automne, l'automne!
"Les casinos,
"Qu'on abandonne
"Remisent leur piano;
"Hier l'orchestre attaqua
"Sa dernière polka,
"Hier, la dernière fanfare
"Sanglotait vers les gares..."

(Oh! comme elle est maigrie!
Que va-t-elle devenir?
Durcissez, durcissez,
Vous, caillots de souvenirs!)

—"Allons, les poteaux télégraphiques
"Dans les grisailles de l'exil
"Vous serviront de pleureuses de funérailles;
"Moi, c'est la saison qui veut que je m'en aille,
"Voici l'hiver qui vient.
"Ainsi soit-il.
"Ah! soignez-vous! Portez-vous bien.

"Assez! assez!
"C'est toi qui as commencé!

"Tais-toi! Vos moindres clins d'yeux sont des parjures.
"Laisse! Avec vous autres rien ne dure.
"Va, je te l'assure,
"Si je t'aimais, ce serait par gageure.

"Tais-toi! tais-toi!
"On n'aime qu'une fois!"

Ah! voici que l'on compte enfin avec Moi!

Ah! ce n'est plus l'automne, alors
Ce n'est plus l'exil.
C'est la douceur des légendes, de l'âge d'or,
Des légendes des Antigones,
Douceur qui fait qu'on se demande:
"Quand donc cela se passait-il?"

C'est des légendes, c'est des gammes perlées,
Qu'on m'a tout enfant enseignées,
Oh! rien, vous dis-je, des estampes,
Les bêtes de la terre et les oiseaux du ciel
Enguirlandant les majuscules d'un Missel,
Il n'y a pas là tant de quoi saigner?

Saigner! moi pétri du plus pur limon de Cybèle!
Moi qui lui eusse été dans tout l'art des Adams
Des Edens aussi hyperboliquement fidèle
Que l'est le soleil chaque soir envers l'Occident...

*Derniers Vers*

# Legend

Blazonry of anemia! Autumnal psalter! Offertory of all my ciborium of happiness and genius to this so feminine eucharist (and her sly little dry cough) whom you see on deserted days, completely unknown to you and set like a stone in ashen-colored dresses smelling already of winter, whom you see fleeing from herself along the edge of the sea with its superhuman cries. Great love stories—and what else? Well, in any case, lips of no particular character, lips with no bloom, and while dead to lyricism, still avid. But her eyes are those of a soul who has buried herself in a cloister. Briefly, she now does me the honor of confiding in me. It bothers me more than she thinks. "But, dear lost lady, how could your enlightened mind and the steel stiletto of your infallible eyes fail to pierce the imposture of that budget Apollo passing through town?" "He was the first to come, I was alone by the hearth. His horse, tied to the gate, whinnied desperately." "That's touching (poor girl), and then what?" "Oh! look at that epilogue disguised as a sunset. And then, haven't you noticed, as soon as autumn comes, the deserted casinos put their pianos in storage; yesterday the orchestra struck up its last polka; yesterday the last band salute sobbed toward the railway stations." (Oh, how thin she has become! What is going to happen to her? Harden, harden, clots of memory!) "It doesn't matter; the telegraph poles in the grey tones of their exile will serve as your professional mourners. As for me, this is the season I must leave; winter is coming. So be it. Take care of yourself! Keep well! Enough! Enough! You're the one who started it. Silence! Your least blinks are lies. Stop! With women nothing lasts. I assure you, really, that if I loved you, it would be on a bet. Don't say any more. One loves only once." Ah! now she's taking me into account finally! Ah! it's no longer autumn; in that case, it's no longer exile. It's the sweetness of legends, the golden age, legends of Antigones, sweetness that makes one ask, "Just when did that take place?" It's legends, perfectly played scales, taught to me as a child. Oh, nothing, really, pictures, the beasts of the earth and the birds of the sky interwoven with the capitals in a Missal. That's not enough to make you suffer so? Me! Suffer! I am molded of Cybele's purest clay, I, who would have been, with the whole of Adam's art in Eden, as faithful as the sun is to the west in the evening, when it describes its hyperbola as it descends.

O géraniums diaphanes, guerroyeurs sortilèges,
Sacrilèges monomanes!
Emballages, dévergondages, douches! O pressoirs
Des vendanges des grands soirs!
Layettes aux abois,
Thyrses au fond des bois!
Transfusions, représailles,
Relevailles, compresses et l'éternelle potion,
*Angelus!* n'en pouvoir plus
De débâcles nuptiales! de débâcles nuptiales!...

Et puis, ô mes amours
A moi son tous les jours,
O ma petite mienne, ô ma quotidienne,
Dans mon petit intérieur,
C'est-à-dire plus jamais ailleurs!

O ma petite quotidienne!...

Et quoi encore? Oh du génie,
Improvisations aux insomnies!

Et puis? L'observer dans le monde,
Et songer dans les coins:
"Oh, qu'elle est loin! Oh, qu'elle est belle!
"Oh, qui est-elle? A qui est-elle?
"Oh, quelle inconnue? Oh, lui parler! Oh, l'emmener!"
(Et, en effet, à la fin du bal,
Elle me suivrait d'un air tout simplement fatal.)

Et puis, l'éviter des semaines
Après lui avoir fait de la peine,
Et lui donner des rendez-vous,
Et nous refaire un chez nous.

Et puis, la perdre des mois et des mois,
A ne plus reconnaître sa voix!...

Oui, le Temps salit tout,
Mais, hélas! sans en venir à bout.

Hélas, hélas! et plus la faculté d'errer,
Hypocondrie et pluie,
Et seul sous les vieux cieux,
De me faire le fou!

Le fou sans feux ni lieux
(Le pauvre, pauvre fou sans amours!)

Pour, alors, tomber bien bas
A me purifier la chair,
Et exulter au petit jour
En me fuyant en chemin de fer,
O Belles-Lettres, ô Beaux-Arts
Ainsi qu'un Ange à part!

J'aurai passé ma vie le long des quais
A faillir m'embarquer
Dans de bien funestes histoires,
Tout cela pour l'amour
De mon coeur fou de la gloire d'amour.

Oh, qu'ils sont pittoresques les trains manqués!...

Oh, qu'ils sont "A bientôt! à bientôt!"
Les bateaux
Du bout de la jetée!...

De la jetée bien charpentée
Contre la mer,
Comme ma chair
Contre l'amour.

*Derniers Vers*

O diaphanous geraniums, magic warriors, monomaniac sacrileges! Excitement, depravity, showers! O winepresses of the evenings' great grape harvests, pursuit of layettes! Thyrsi in the depths of the woods! Transfusions, reprisals, churching, compresses, and the eternal potion, Angelus! Exhaustion from nuptial routs! Nuptial routs! And then, O my love, her everyday routine is mine, O my little mine, O my daily one, in my little dwelling, that is, never anywhere else! O my little daily one! And what else? Oh, genius, improvisations during insomnia. And then? I'll watch her with others and sit in the corner thinking, "How far away she is. How beautiful she is. Oh, who is she? Whose is she? Oh, what a stunning stranger! Oh, I must speak to her, leave with her!" (And, indeed, at the end of the ball, she would follow me with an absolutely destined air.) And then, I would avoid her for weeks, after hurting her, and make appointments with her, and we would reinvent our domestic arrangements. And then, I wouldn't see her for months and months, to the point of not recognizing her voice! Yes, time spoils everything, without, unfortunately, disposing of it. Alas, alas, and no more possibility of wandering, hypochondria and rain, and no more, alone under the ancient skies, the possibility of acting crazy! Poor demented madman without hearth or home (a poor, poor unloved madman)! And then, falling very low to purify my flesh and exult in the dawn by fleeing from myself in a train. O Literature, O Fine Arts, I am like some special angel completely unlike anyone else. I will have spent my life in the train station, almost setting off on deplorable adventures. All that for the love of my heart crazy for the glory of love. How picturesque, the trains we miss! How "goodby for now" the boats at the end of the pier! The well-built pier protecting me from the sea, from my flesh, from love.

> Get thee to a nunnery: why wouldst
> thou be a breeder of sinners? I
> am myself indifferent honest; but
> yet I could accuse me of such
> things, that it were better my
> mother had not borne me. We are
> arrant knaves, all; believe none
> of us. Go thy ways to a nunnery.
>
> HAMLET.

Noire bise, averse glapissante,
Et fleuve noir, et maisons closes,
Et quartiers sinistres comme des Morgues,
Et l'Attardé qui à la remorque traîne
Toute la misère du coeur et des choses,
Et la souillure des innocentes qui traînent,
Et crie à l'averse. "Oh, arrose, arrose
"Mon coeur si brûlant, ma chair si intéressante!"

Oh, elle, mon coeur et ma chair, que fait-elle?...

Oh! si elle est dehors par ce vilain temps,
De quelles histoires trop humaines rentre-t-elle?
Et si elle est dedans,
A ne pas pouvoir dormir par ce grand vent,
Pense-t-elle au Bonheur,
Au bonheur à tout prix
Disant: tout plutôt que mon coeur reste ainsi incompris?

Soigne-toi, soigne-toi! pauvre coeur aux abois.

(Langueurs, débilité, palpitations, larmes,
Oh, cette misère de vouloir être notre femme!)

O pays, ô famille!
Et l'âme toute tournée
D'héroïques destinées
Au delà des saintes vieilles filles,
Et pour cette année!

Nuit noire, maisons closes, grand vent,
Oh, dans un couvent, dans un couvent!

Un couvent dans ma ville natale
Douce de vingt-mille âmes à peine,
Entre le lycée et la préfecture
Et vis-à-vis la cathédrale,
Avec ces anonymes en robes grises,
Dans la prière, le ménage, les travaux de couture;
Et que cela suffise...
Et méprise sans envie
Tout ce qui n'est pas cette vie de Vestale
Provinciale,
Et marche à jamais glacée,
Les yeux baissés.

Oh! je ne puis voir ta petite scène fatale à vif,
Et ton pauvre air dans ce huis-clos,
Et tes tristes petits gestes instinctifs,
Et peut-être incapable de sanglots!

Oh! ce ne fut pas et ce ne peut être,
Oh! tu n'es pas comme les autres,
Crispées aux rideaux de leur fenêtre
Devant le soleil couchant qui dans son sang se vautre!
Oh! tu n'as pas l'âge,
Oh, dis, tu n'auras jamais l'âge,
Oh, tu me promets de rester sage comme une image?...

La nuit est à jamais noire,
Le vent est grandement triste,
Tout dit la vieille histoire
Qu'il faut être deux au coin du feu,

Tout bâcle un hymne fataliste,
Mais toi, il ne faut pas que tu t'abandonnes,
A ces vilains jeux!...
A ces grandes pitiés du mois de novembre!
Reste dans ta petite chambre,
Passe, à jamais glacée,
Tes beaux yeux irréconciliablement baissés.

Oh, qu'elle est là-bas, que la nuit est noire!
Que la vie est une étourdissante foire!
Que toutes sont créature, et que tout est routine!
Oh, que nous mourrons!

Eh bien, pour aimer ce qu'il y a d'histoires
Derrière ces beaux yeux d'orpheline héroïne,
O Nature, donne-moi la force et le courage
De me croire en âge,
O Nature relève-moi le front!
Puisque, tôt ou tard, nous mourrons...

*Derniers Vers*

Black northwind, howling downpour, and black river, and brothels, and parts of town sinister as a morgue, and a belated passerby in whose wake follows all the wretchedness of the heart and of things, and sullied innocence, crying to the storm, "Oh drench my burning heart, my so interesting flesh!" And she, *my* heart and *my* flesh, what is she doing? Oh, if she is out in this dreadful weather, what too human adventures is she coming back from? And if she is inside, finding it hard to sleep with the heavy winds, is she thinking of happiness, at any price, saying, "I will try anything, provided that my heart not remain as misunderstood as now." Take care of yourself, take care of yourself! poor heart up against the wall. (Languor, weakness, palpitations, tears, oh, this wretched determination to marry me!) O birthplace, O family! And her soul overwhelmed and tempted by heroic destinies above and beyond those of holy old maidens, and for this year! Black night, brothels, heavy winds, oh get thee to a nunnery, to a nunnery go! A convent in my native town of scarcely twenty thousand gentle souls, between the lycée and the prefect's offices and opposite the cathedral, with those anonymous beings in grey habits engaged in prayer, housework, and needlework—let that suffice for you. And despise without envy everything that's not the life of a provincial Vestal virgin, and walk forever indifferent to the heart, with your eyes cast down. Oh, I can't bear to see your little wounded, fateful scene, and your wretched air in a cloistered life, and your sad little instinctive gestures, and perhaps your being beyond sobs. Oh! it was not the case and it cannot be. Oh, you are not like the others, clutching the window curtains watching the setting sun wallow in its own blood. Oh! you are not old enough; listen, you will never be old enough: you promise me to remain good as gold? Night is forever black; the wind is terribly sad. Everything repeats the old story that there have to be two of you by the fireplace. Everything blurts out the same thoughtless fatalistic hymn. But you musn't give in to those ugly mating games! To those great waves of pity overwhelming you in November! Stay in your little room; go your way, indifferent to the heart, with your eyes irreconcilably cast down. Oh! she must be out there! How black the night is! What a deafening fair life is! How creaturely all women are and what a routine existence is! Oh, how surely we shall die! And so, that I may appreciate the complications behind the beautiful eyes of this orphan heroine, O Nature, give me the strength and courage to believe myself old enough to accept them; O Nature, lift me up, since, sooner or later, we shall die.

# SAINT-POL ROUX

## Golgotha

Le ciel enténébré de ses plus tristes hardes
S'accroupit sur le drame universel du pic.
Le violent triangle de l'arme des gardes
A l'air au bout du bois d'une langue d'aspic.

Parmi des clous, entre deux loups à face humaine,
Pantelant ainsi qu'un quartier de venaison
Agonise l'Agneau déchiré par la haine,
Celui-là qui donnait son âme et sa maison.

Jésus bêle un pardon suprême en la tempête
Où ses os tracassés crissent comme un essieu,
Cependant que le sang qui pleure de sa tête
Emperle de corail sa souffrance de Dieu.

Dans le ravin Judas, crapaud drapé de toiles,
Balance ses remords sous un arbre indulgent,
—Et l'on dit que là-haut sont mortes les étoiles
Pour ne plus ressembler à des pièces d'argent.

*Anciennetés*

## Golgotha

The sky darkening in its wretched old wraps crouches over the universal drama on the steep hill. The violent triangle at the end of the guards' pikes looks like an asp's tongue protruding from the wood. Amid nails, between two man-faced wolves, panting like a quarter of venison, the Lamb is in death throes, torn by hate, the Lamb, who gave his soul and his house. Jesus bleats a last word of pardon in the storm, as his tormented bones creak like an axle. Meanwhile, the blood weeping from his head empearls with coral drops his divine suffering. In the ravine, Judas, a toad clad in linen, weighs his remorse under an indulgent tree. And they say that in the sky the stars died, so as not to resemble pieces of silver.

## La Magdeleine aux parfums

Le Bel au front de sacre éventé par la palme
Honore de sa faim l'orthodoxe Simon.
L'olive et le raisin, son pressoir de dents calme
En fait l'offrande fraîche à son divin limon.

*

Depuis la Crèche où zézayaient les ailes blanches
Des séraphins éclos parmi l'avènement
Et depuis Nazareth où l'on sciait des planches,
Nombreux fut le voyage, aussi l'événement.

Il est allé, versant la pacifique obole
En les coeurs tourmentés de la frêle maison;
Il a passé, contant la claire parabole
Où se marient le grain, la plume, la toison.

Genoux et bras chargés de puériles joues,
Maintes fois il parut un humain oranger.
Les femmes de la plaine, analogues aux proues
Vers le salut, appareillaient vers l'Etranger.

Céramique des puits, jarres de Samarie,
Il vous enjolivait d'une phrase de ciel.
Du haut de la colline il prêchait la prairie,
Et ce n'était qu'épis, que bruit d'aile, que miel.

Par un geste efficace autant qu'une harangue,
Il raviva la perle en le chaton des cils.
Les muets à la main souple comme une langue,
Il leur mit dans la gorge un nid plein de babils.

Il conquit, moyennant le chanvre aux mille mailles,
Les joyaux savoureux qui vivent dans les eaux.
Il fut le boulanger sans four et sans semailles.
Il ralluma la lampe maigre des tombeaux.

Tel, il eût pu florir emmi la Galilée
Où les regards l'ornaient d'un hommage de paon,
Mais il n'oubliait point qu'à sa vie exilée
Fut prédit le trépas vilain du chenapan.

C'est pour cela qu'assis sur son trône qui marche,
Une mule docile aux prunelles de jais,
Il traverse la foule en jeune patriarche,
Emerveillant les gueux d'un espoir de palais.

Il porte aux funérailles sa splendeur de cygne
Afin de consommer le serment éternel.
Sur un farouche mont deux rameaux lui font signe,
Que n'a pas caressés le rabot paternel.

*

A table chaque bras, tel un cou de cigogne,
Alimente la bouche avec son bec de main,
Des disciples aux traits couleur de la besogne
Mangent, vieillis par la poussière du chemin.

Tandis que, pavoisé d'un air de fiançailles,
Le Bel ouvre son âme, harmonieux grenier,
A l'écart, sous l'auvent de ses torves broussailles,
L'Iscariote attise un oeil comme un denier.

Déjà se sont vidés les plats et les corbeilles
Quand survient une femme au visage de fard
Et dont la chevelure est un essaim d'abeilles.
Simon l'Amphitryon sursaille, aigre et blafard.

—"N'est-ce pas le Scandale qui sort de son antre
A l'heure oblique afin de marchander aux chairs
Veuves d'abri le vestibule de son ventre?"
Sur son épaule un vase empli de parfums chers,

Lentement la publique va vers le Messie
Avec tous les ramiers de l'angoisse en son sein.
Les convives ont peur sous ses yeux de cassie,
Car elle est belle ainsi que l'on est assassin.

Se fanant à genoux, elle épand la magie
De son urne d'albâtre sur les pieds du Bel
Pendant que de l'ardente face d'élégie
Crèvent éperdûment les réservoirs de sel.

La pécheresse enfin se tord entre la pieuvre
Enorme des remords qui la tenaille au sol.

On dirait qu'un marteau fit tomber un chef-d'oeuvre.
Une âme se lamente en le gracile col.

\*

Les parfums gravissant le sentier des narines,
C'est, au cerveau de tous, un prompt enchantement
Qui sous la cloche taciturne des poitrines
Fait se pâmer les coeurs délicieusement.

Dans les crânes, des anges tissent en mirage
Un spontané vallon de fenouil et de thym
Avec, à son mitan, un timide village
Symbolisant le repentir de la putain.

Etrange vision de candides miracles!
Brebis enseignant à bêler aux loups gloutons;
Ventres de monstres, purs comme des tabernacles;
Torrents à pic, plus doux que des dos de moutons.

Pâle, un corbeau roucoule un vieil air des légendes;
Une colombe endeuille ses plumes de lys;
Les serpents ne sont plus que flexibles guirlandes
D'oiseaux bleus aspirés par les faims de jadis.

Rompus, des tournesols, orphelins de ton charme,
O Magdeleine, effarent l'herbe d'encensoirs.
Là-bas, près d'un tronc mort, une tombe sans larme
Recèle, au lieu d'un corps, un rire et des miroirs.

\*

Alors, Celui tombé du pommier de Marie
Sur la paille parmi l'encens, la myrrhe et l'or,
Se lève, étend les mains sur la chair de féerie
Et dit ces mots pareils aux pièces d'un trésor:

—"Fille qui, suppliant le Fils à barbe d'astre,
As choisi pour miroir l'ongle de mon orteil,
J'admire l'hirondelle éclose en ton désastre,
Et la honte me plaît qui t'a peinte en soleil.

C'est bien de tendre ses vertèbres à la corde,
O toi qui me chaussas de suaves parfums
Pour que le bleu pardon, fleur de miséricorde,
Etoilât le fumier de tes péchés défunts.

Mon âme est maternelle ainsi qu'une patrie
Et je préfère au lys un pleur de sacripant.
Les regrets sont la clef bonne à ma bergerie,
Je fais une brebis du loup qui se repent.

Venez, tous les vaincus aux griffes du reptile,
Le faible sans sourire et le pauvre sans fleur,
J'ouvre l'amène auberge de mon évangile
Aux vagabonds fourbus des routes de douleur.

C'est pour vous seuls, gens de misère ou de rapines,
Que sous le fouet j'irai vers le mont des rachats,
Ayant sur mon génie un royaume d'épines
Et le long de ma peine un manteau de crachats.

Les malins m'y cloueront au sycomore infâme
Et leur regard de fer me percera le flanc,
Mais de ce large trou s'envolera mon âme
Et tout s'anoblira de son passage blanc.

Or je veux ici-bas, rosier des allégresses
En humiliation devant mon front d'azur
Je veux, avec les roses qui sont tes caresses,
Composer ta couronne d'archange futur.

Car j'applaudis à la détresse non pareille
Qui fait jaillir deux océans de tes grands yeux,
O Fille au nom joli comme un pendant d'oreille
Et dont le corps sera le diamant des cieux!

Ta beauté ne pouvait sombrer dans la tempête,
O tragique symbole de la charité,
Cueille donc une palme au palmier de ma fête:
Etre belle, vois-tu, c'est de l'éternité!

Souris! Par le chemin léger de ton haleine
Un ange s'est blotti sous ta peau de baiser.
Retourne vers le peuple et dis-lui, Magdeleine,
Qu'une larme a suffi pour te diviniser."

La chevelure en pleurs à la façon des saules
L'intruse se leva comme on sort de la mer.
Un frisselis subtil à fleur de ses épaules
Indiquait que deux ailes germaient de sa chair.

Tous enfin, revenus du magique village
Et se frottant les yeux comme après le sommeil,
Suivirent, à genoux dans le joli sillage,
La femme au coeur plus grand qu'un lever de soleil.

*Anciennetés*

## The Magdalene with Perfumes

The beautiful man, whose consecrated forehead the palm branch cools, does the honor of partaking of orthodox Simon's meal. Olives and grapes, under the calm winepress of his teeth, make a cool offering to his divine body of clay. Since the nativity, at which lisped seraphim blossoming for the Advent, and since the time in Nazareth when he sawed planks, his travels have been abundant and also the events of them. He went, giving the coin of peace to hearts tormented by the frailty of their clay; he passed, narrating the bright parables joining grain, feathers, and fleece. With his knees and arms laden with fresh-cheeked children, he often looked like a human orange tree. Women from the plain, like ships toward safety, set off to find the Stranger. O tiles on wells, Samarian water jars, he made you beautiful with a heavenly phrase. From high on the hill he preached to the meadow, all in images of ears of grain, rustling wings, and honey. By a gesture as effective as a harangue, he gave new life to the pearls in the setting of his hearers' eyes. When he met mutes with hands skillful as tongues, he put a nest of murmuring words in their throats. With thousand-knotted nets of hemp, he obtained the tasty jewellike fish that live in the water. He was the ovenless and flourless baker. He relit the meager lamps of tombs. In this way, he could have flourished in Galilee, where he was honored by the gaze of thousands of eyes, as on a peacock's tail. But he did not forget that his life in exile was destined to end with a rogue's ugly death. Thus, seated on the moving throne of a jet-eyed, docile mule, he goes through crowds like a young patriarch and dazzles beggars with hopes of a palace. He bears, at burials, his swanlike radiance, in order to fulfill the eternal promise. On a rough mountain, two branches beckon to him, which his father's plane had not smoothed down. At table, each of his arms like a stork's neck feeds his mouth with its beak; the disciples with their workaday-colored features eat, looking older under the dust from the road. While the Beautiful One, decked out as for a betrothal, opens the harmonious granary of his soul, apart from the others, under the eaves of his tawny, bushy eyebrows,

Iscariot's eye starts to shine like a coin. Already the platters and bowls have been emptied when a painted woman arrives, whose hair is like a swarm of bees. Simon the host starts, acidulous and pale. "Do we not see scandal coming from its den in the evening to bargain with shelterless bodies for the anteroom of her belly?" With a vase filled with costly perfumes on her shoulder, the prostitute slowly advances toward the Messiah, and all the doves of fear are in her breast. The guests are afraid under the gaze of her cassia-colored eyes, for she is beautiful naturally the way others are born murderers. Falling, like a withered flower, on her knees, she pours out the magic of her alabaster urn on the Beautiful One's feet, while in her burning elegiac face the salt reservoirs of tears burst. Finally, the sinning woman is twisted in the grasp of the great octopus of remorse, tearing her to pieces on the ground. It is as if, with a blow of a hammer, a masterpiece tumbled to the floor. A soul laments in her graceful throat. As the perfumes climb their path toward the nostrils of the guests, a sudden spell overcomes their minds: within the silent bell of their breasts, their hearts faint with rapture. In their brains, angels weave spontaneously, like a mirage, a valley of fennel and thyme with, in its center, a timid village symbolizing the whore's repentance. A strange vision of naïve miracles! Sheep teaching the gluttonous wolves to bleat, bellies of monsters becoming white as altars, precipitous waterfalls growing more gentle than sheep's fleece. A pale crow coos a legendary melody; a dove makes mourning of its lily-white feathers. Snakes have become nothing more than soft garlands of bluebirds which once had been attracted for assuaging their appetite. Broken sunflower heads, deserted by your enchantment, O Magdalene, terrify the grass with their censers. In the distance, by a dead treetrunk, a tearless tomb conceals, instead of a body, laughter and mirrors. Then He who had fallen from Mary's apple tree onto the straw with its incense, myrrh, and gold, stands up, spreads his hands over her fairy flesh, and says these words, each like a coin in a treasure: "Whore who, as a supplicant to the star-bearded Son, chose for your mirror the nail of my toe, I admire the swallow hatched in your ill-starred life, and I am pleased with the shame which has painted you sun-colored. It is good to offer one's neck to the rope, O you who shod me with delicate perfumes, so that blue forgiveness, the flower of mercy, might shine like a star in the dungheap of your past sins. My soul is maternal like a native country, and I prefer to the lily a rogue's tear. Regrets are the right key to my sheepfold; I make an ewe of the repentant wolf. Come all you defeated ones in the grasp of the snake, the smileless weak and flowerless poor; I open the lovely inn of my gospel to the wayfarers lame from the roads of sorrow. For you alone, people of poverty or plunder, I shall go under the whip to the mount of redemption, with a kingdom of thorns on my genius and a robe of spittle the length of my pain. The evil will nail me to the infamous cross of sycamore, and their iron gaze pierce my side. But from that great wound my soul will take flight and ennoble all in its white path. Now I wish on earth, O rosebush of joy humiliated before my azure brow, I wish with the roses of your caresses to weave the archangel's crown you will wear. For I applaud the incomparable distress which makes oceans of your great eyes, O whore, whose name is pretty like an earring and whose body will be the diamond of the heavens. Your beauty could not succumb to the storm. O tragic symbol of charity, gather now a palm from the palm tree of my rejoicing, for being beautiful, you see, belongs to eternity. Smile! Going along the light paths of your breath, an angel has hidden in your kisslike body. Return toward the people, and tell them, Magdalene, that a tear sufficed to make you divine." With her hair like a weeping willow, the intruder rose as one rises from the sea. A light shudder along her shoulders indicated the birth of two wings from her flesh. They all, then, having returned from the magic village of their dream and rubbing their eyes as after sleep, followed, on their knees in her lovely wake, the woman whose heart was greater than dawn.

# CHARLES VAN LERBERGHE

## La Jonchée

Ici repose sur la terre
Immortelle, en un lieu solitaire
Où ne pénètrent pas les souffles extérieurs,
L'adorable et subtile poussière
De ce qui fut jadis des fleurs.

En cette pourpre et lasse automne
De roses fanées et de lys mourants
Tombés de leurs couronnes,
Parmi les herbes et les fleurs des champs;
En ce velours profond et plus doux que des mousses,
Elles, en les foulant jadis, ont laissé
Des empreintes de pas nus et tissés
Comme de laines, des pointes de petits pieds
Qui vont et viennent,
Sinueux et gracieux,
Et s'entrecroisent en fils de chaîne,
En un rythme silencieux.

Là où toutes les lignes convergent,
Onduleuses traînes d'or,
Minces ruisseaux entre des berges,
Comme un baiser splendide dort
Le long et tiède et clair repos
De celles qui, voluptueuses et nues,
Leurs longues chevelures en gerbes
Blondes, entre les hautes herbes
Se sont étendues,
Laissant l'empreinte de leurs mains,
De leurs têtes lourdes et de leurs seins,
De tous leurs corps superbes,
Et le parfum de leur chair uni
Aux aromates rares
Que versaient sur elles, en souriant,
Les esclaves portant des amphores.

Et, toujours, en un cercle infini,
S'enlacent et se nouent, et s'entrelacent
Et se dénouent de petits pas qui courent,
Comme un pétillement dans le vent.
Ainsi revivent en un rêve
Aux tons assourdis et fanés
D'une automne qui s'achève,
Les rares et somptueuses heures
Où dans du soleil résonnaient
Des sons de harpe et de cithare.

*Entrevisions*

## Autumn-strewn Ground

Here lies on the immortal earth, in a solitary spot, untouched by breezes from afar, the divine and subtle dust of what once was flowers. In this crimson and weary autumn of withered roses and dying lilies fallen from their stems, among the grass and flowers of the field, in this deep velvet softer than moss, flower-women, as they once stepped, left the imprint of bare steps woven like wool, the imprint of the toes of small feet coming and going, sinuous and graceful, crossing in chain patterns with a silent rhythm. In this spot, where all lines converge like undulating golden trains, like slim streams between two banks, like a splendid kiss there sleeps the long and warm and bright place of repose of women, who, voluptuous and naked, lay down in the high grass, with their long hair in blond sheaves, leaving the imprint of their hands, their heavy heads and breasts, of their whole superb bodies, and the perfume of their flesh polished with rare aromatics, which smiling slaves with urns poured on them. And always in an infinite circle, there is an entwining and knotting and weaving and parting of little running steps like bubbles bursting in the wind. Thus in a dream, with the faded soft tones of dying autumn, there live again the rare and rich hours when the sound of harps and citharas echoed in the sun.

# MAX ELSKAMP

J'ai triste d'une ville en bois,
—Tourne, foire de ma rancoeur,
Mes chevaux de bois de malheur—
J'ai triste d'une ville en bois.
J'ai mal à mes sabots de bois.

J'ai triste d'être le perdu
D'une ombre et nue et mal en place,
—Mais dont mon coeur trop sait la place—
J'ai triste d'être le perdu
Des places, et froid et tout nu.

J'ai triste de jours de patins
—Soeur Anne ne voyez-vous rien?—
Et de n'aimer en nulle femme;
J'ai triste de jours de patins,
Et de n'aimer en nulle femme.

J'ai triste de mon coeur en bois,
Et j'ai très-triste de mes pierres,
Et des maisons où, dans du froid,
Au dimanche des coeurs de bois,
Les lampes mangent la lumière.

Et j'ai triste d'une eau-de-vie
Qui fait rentrer tard les soldats.
Au dimanche ivre d'eau-de-vie,
Dans mes rues pleines de soldats,
J'ai triste de trop d'eau-de-vie.

*La Louange de la vie*

I have the sadness of a town built of wood—turn, country fair of my rancor, turn, my wooden horses of misfortune—I have the sadness of a town built of wood. I hurt in my wooden clogs. I am sad from being lost in a bare shadow, nowhere for sure—but my heart knows all too well where I am—I am sad from being lost nowhere and cold and bare. I am sad on ice-skating days—Sister Anne, do you see anyone coming?—and from loving no woman; I am sad on ice-skating days and from loving no woman. I am sad from having a wooden heart and very sad in my stones and sad from houses where, in the cold, on Sundays of wooden hearts, the lamps cast little light. And I am sad from the brandy which makes the soldiers late to the barracks, on Sundays drunk on brandy, in my streets full of soldiers, I'm sad from too much brandy.

Et c'est Lui, comme un matelot,
et c'est lui, qu'on n'attendait plus,
et c'est lui, comme un matelot,
qui s'en revient les bras tendus

pour baiser ceux qu'il a connus,
rire à ceux qu'il n'a jamais vus,
et c'est lui, comme un matelot,
qui s'en revient le sac au dos.

Or, bonnes heures, bonnes heures,
laissez alors choir vos tricots,
or, bonnes heures, bonnes heures,
endormez-vous jusqu'à tantôt:

il fait si chaud dans vos demeures
et c'est fête de si bon coeur!
Mais, partances aux mâts d'en haut,
voici s'agiter les vaisseaux,

et c'est Lui, comme un matelot,
qui, vides les pots, partira,
et c'est lui, comme un matelot,
et Dieu sait quand il reviendra.

*Enluminures*

And it is Christ, like a sailor; it is he whom we no longer expected; it is he, like a sailor, who comes home with his arms stretched out to kiss those he knew, smile at those he has never seen; it is he, like a sailor, who comes home with his bag over his shoulder. Now, good old hours, drop your knitting; now, good old hours, doze for a while: it is so hot in your houses, and it's such a joyous celebration. But the departure flags are on the top masts; the vessels are underway, and He, like a sailor, when the drinks are drunk will leave; it is he, like a sailor, and God knows when he will return.

# Reykjavik

Or voici alors Reykjavik,
Là-haut et sur la mer arctique,

Et dans l'embrun, et dans les glaces,
Et dans le froid d'un gel qui mord,

Où se dit port lors d'âme lasse
Et qui semble attendre la mort,

C'est par la nef abordé,
Les pêcheurs qui quittent le bord,

Pour en les bars aller chercher
L'alcool blanc en le jour qui dort,

Et les femmes elles qui veillent
Pour la donner aux matelots

Leur chair et dite ou jeune ou vieille
Dans un amour un peu falot,

Sans plus, et comme il est d'amour,
Et fait d'une heure ou bien d'un jour

En le bien, le mal ou le pire,
Pour ceux et qui sont des navires.

Or boissons aussi qui se disent
Amères ou douces qui grisent,

Et qu'élisent les matelots
Pour trouver joie qui chante haut,

Whiskey anglais qui donne ivresse,
Saké japonais la tendresse,

Dans la fièvre parfois qu'on a
D'une amour que l'on porte en soi,

Puis anis grec qui dit amer
Le désir qu'on a de la chair

Après des jours trop de sagesse
Passé sur la mer sans liesse,

Quand c'est le sang alors qui bat
Comme un marteau au coeur qu'on a,

Et qui cherche à se satisfaire
N'importe de quelle manière.

Or femmes lors et qui sont là,
En robes rouges, gorge ouverte,

Dans la nuit qui se dit sans foi,
Au bord des quais sur de l'eau verte,

Femmes qui savent ce qu'il faut
Au pêcheur ou au matelot,

Musique alors meulant aux bars,
Dans un grand froid qui dit le soir,

Ce sont elles et sur le tard,
Qui se donnent blondes ou noires,

Aux marins alors et qui viennent
Boire, en elles, l'heure païenne.

*Chansons d'amures*

## Reykjavik

Here is Reykjavik, high on the arctic sea, in the spray and in the ice, in the cold of a biting frost, called the port of weary souls and seeming to await death. With their ship in port, the fishermen leave the deck and go to bars to seek, in the somnolent day, white spirits and women who are waiting to give sailors their flesh, young or old as it may be, in a droll kind of love, straightforward, the way it is with love, lasting an hour or a day, good, bad, or worse, for those who come from the ships. There are also drinks, those supposed to be bitter or sweet intoxicating ones, that sailors choose in order to find high-pitched joy, English whiskey leading to drunkenness, Japanese sake leading to tenderness, in the fever they sometimes have from the love they bear in themselves, then Greek ouzo which expresses the bitter love of flesh, after too chaste days spent on the joyless sea, when your blood beats like a hammer in the heart, searching for some way, any way of being satisfied. Then there are the women there, in red dresses, with bare bosoms, in the faithless-seeming night, on the edge of the docks by the green water, women who know what fishermen and sailors need, while music grinds away in the bars, in the great cold announcing evening. They are the women who, blond or brunette, give themselves at the end of the day to the sailors who come to drink from their flesh the pagan hour.

# RENE GHIL

## Dies Irae

Un soir l'Orgue d'église aux spasmes des Violons
Montait loin sa douleur sourde en les râles longs:
Voix de genèse, Amour et Trépas, ô pleurs longs!
Un soir l'Orgue montait dans l'horreur des Violons...

Horreur! la Terre pleure, et, grande Trisaïeule,
Par la vulve et l'ovaire aux ouvraisons de gueule
Ainsi qu'Une en gésine appelle et meugle seule:
Horreur! la Terre pleure et pousse, en sa Terreur,
Son sein de glaise rouge et l'immense dièse
De la genèse en pleurs qui la saigne et la lèse:
Horreur! la Mère pleure et du Tout la genèse
Dans le noir a vagi le grand et premier pleur:

Horreur! la Terre a mis au monde; et, pris de peur,
Le noir ivre—sonnez!—ulule à voix mauvaise:
Dans l'Inouï sonnez! ô vous que rien n'apaise,
Sonnez, horreurs du noir et dièse vainqueur!...

Sang des dièses! le Vague en musique ruisselle
Sourde ou mélodieuse, et pleure, universelle,
Dans le spasme ou le spleen l'angoisse de mamelle,
Quand hurle l'aise large ou meugle d'inespoir:
Sang des dièses! le Vague, eau de voix noire et pâle,
Voix de gorge se pâme; et, hors du sexe mâle,
Le pollen doux et rauque et qui du Tout s'exhale
Hurle un péan d'amour et de mâle vouloir:

Sang des dièses! l'Amour hurle son péan noir
Dans le noir qui—sonnez!—ulule au large et râle:
Dans l'Inouï sonnez, ô rauqueur animale,
Plaisir aigu qui pleure aux serres du pouvoir!...
Vide et Trépas! du Tout pleure au loin la nénie:
A la Terre au sein noir l'âme du Vague unie
Doloroso s'éplore: et le pleur de la pluie,
Vide et trépas! haut darde, et sous l'ire du nord
Troue, hélas! de grands Trous et des mares navrées,

Des mares et des mers aux immenses marées
Montant: A Toi, Nihil! ô vainqueur des durées,
A Toi gloire! ô Tueur sans aise et sans remords!

Vide et Trépas! la mer ample, en l'ire qui mord,
A des sourdeurs—sonnez!—de gorges éplorées:
Dans l'Inouï sonnez! ô voix enlangourées!
O noir primordial et soupirs sans essor!...

Oh pleurez! longues voix, sourdes voix, voix des larmes!
Voix du monde qui saigne et qu'aux ivresses d'armes
Traverse, pâle et noir, le long peuple en alarmes
Des dièses de l'Orgue et des âpres Violons!
Oh pleurez! longues voix de la lèvre animale:
Rien ne vaut la douleur et le plaisir qui râle;
Rien ne vaut l'Orgue sourd et l'émoi qui s'exhale
Apre et rauque, et damné, des Violons noirs et longs:

Un soir l'Orgue d'église aux spasmes des Violons
Montait loin sa douleur sourde en les râles longs:
Voix de genèse, Amour et Trépas, ô pleurs longs!
Un soir l'Orgue montait dans l'horreur des Violons...

*Légendes d'âmes et de sang*

## Day of Wrath

One evening the church organ with violin spasms raised high its muffled sorrow in long death rattles: voice of genesis, love and death, oh long tears! One evening the organ rose in the horror of violins. Horror! The earth weeps, the great ancestress, through her ovaries and vulva gaping like mouths, like a woman in childbirth calling and groaning alone. Horror! The earth weeps and in her terror heaves her breast of red clay and the great sharp notes of weeping genesis wounding her and making her bleed. Horror! The mother weeps, and the genesis of the cosmos has moaned in the dark with its first great tear. Horror! Earth has given birth, and drunken darkness, filled with panic, hoots evilly—ring out, horrors of the darkness and conquering sharp notes! Blood of the sharp notes! The cloud streams in music, muffled or melodious, and weeps, covering all, with the anguish of nursing, in spasms or depression, when vast ease roars or bellows with hopelessness. Blood of the sharp notes! The cloud, black and pale vocal wetness, grows faint like a voice from the throat. And out of the male sex organ the sweet raucous pollen, exhaling from the universe, roars a paean of love and male will. Blood of the sharp notes! Love roars its black paean in the darkness, which, ring out! hoots from afar and croaks. In the unknown ring out! O living hoarseness, O sharp pleasure weeping in the claws of power. Emptiness and death! The cosmic dirge weeps in the distance. The soul of the cloud joined to black-breasted earth weeps, doloroso: and the tear of the rain, emptiness and death! darts high and under the wrath of the north pierces, alas! great holes and sorrowful ponds, ponds and seas with immense tides rising. Glory to you, nothingness, oh conqueror of time, glory to you, O killer easeless and remorseless! Emptiness and death! The vast sea under the biting wrath has muffled sounds, ring out! from weeping throats. Ring out in the unknown! O languorous voices, O primeval darkness and sighs unsoaring! Oh weep, long voices, muffled voices, voices of tears! Voices of the world which bleeds and through which passes, intoxicated and armed, pale and black, the long procession, in its alarms, of sharp notes from the organ and harsh violins! Oh weep, long voices of the living lip! Nothing can equal sorrow and pleasure's death rattle. Nothing can equal the muffled organ and the excitement, harsh and hoarse and damned, emanating from long black violins. One evening the church organ with violin spasms raised high its muffled sorrow in long death rattles: voice of genesis, love and death, oh long tears! One evening the organ rose in the horror of violins.

# LOUIS LE CARDONNEL

## Ville morte

Lentement, sourdement, des vêpres sonnent
Dans la grand'paix de cette vague ville;
Des arbres gris sur la place frissonnent,
Comme inquiets de ces vêpres qui sonnent.
Inquiétante est cette heure tranquille.

Un idiot qui va, revient, et glousse,
Content, car les enfants sont à l'école;
A sa fenêtre une vieille qui tousse;
Un idiot qui va, revient, et glousse,
Elle fait des gestes, à moitié folle.

Murs décrépits, lumière décrépite
Que ce Novembre épand sur cette place:
Sur un balcon du linge froid palpite,
Pâle, dans la lumière décrépite.
Et puis le son des cloches qui se lasse...

Tout à coup plus de cloches, plus de vieille,
Plus de pauvre idiot, vaguement singe,
Et l'on dirait que la ville sommeille.
Plus d'idiot, de cloche ni de vieille...
Seul, maintenant, le blanc glacé du linge.

*Poèmes*

## Dead City

Vespers ring slowly, dully in the great peace of this vague city. Grey trees on the square quiver, as if ill at ease with these ringing vespers. Disturbing is this quiet hour. An idiot comes and goes, clucks; he is happy, for the children are in school. At her window a coughing old woman. An idiot comes and goes, clucks. She makes half-crazy gestures. Crumbling walls, a decrepit light that November casts on the square. The cold wash spread over a balcony shivers, pale in the decrepit light. Then the sound of the bells growing ever more weary. Suddenly no more bells, no more old woman, no poor idiot, vaguely monkeylike. And the city seems to doze. No more idiot, bells, nor old woman. All that is left now is the chilly whiteness of the wash.

# GREGOIRE LE ROY

## Musique d'ombre

Un peu de musique incolore,
Afin d'éterniser ce soir,
Et qu'il revive et dure encore
Aux tristes nuits de nonchaloir...

Résonnance lunaire et lasse,
Eclose d'ombre dans le rêve,
Et dont la phrase ne s'achève
Pour qu'à jamais elle s'efface...

Oh! doucement! Loin de mes yeux!
Un peu vers le coeur, mais dans
l'âme...
Près de l'amour, loin de la femme...
Que je m'en sente un peu plus vieux!

D'où vient ce baiser d'inconnue
Que ma lèvre n'a pas rendu?
Elle s'en va, la bienvenue!
Elle s'en va! Tout est perdu...

Tout est pourtant bien dans cette heure:
La mélodie éteinte en l'ombre,
Et plus de rhythme et plus de nombre
Et qu'elle meure... et qu'elle meure...

*La Chanson du pauvre*

## Shadow Music

A little colorless music to make this evening eternal, so that it will come back to life and still endure on sad nights of indifference. A weary lunar resonance, unfolding out of shadow in dream; its phrase does not end but grows ever more discreet. Oh, softly! Far from my eyes! Near my heart but in the soul; near love, but far from woman, making me feel vaguely older. Whence comes this kiss as from an unknown woman, unanswered by my lips? Though welcome, she is retreating; she is retreating, all is lost. Yet this is a fine hour: the melody dies in the shadow; no more rhythms, no more beat—and let it die, and let it die.

## La Chevauchée

A l'horizon des grises plaines
De mes pensées et de mes peines,
Là-bas, vers ce morne lointain
De lune sur des brumes pâles,
Oh! ce galop triste et sans fin!
Ce galop de blanches cavales.

Et mes princesses nuptiales,
Déjà lointaines, vespérales,
Les belles-au-bois de mon âme,
Ces inoubliables d'amour,
Vers qui mon coeur se plaint et brame
Pour un inutile retour;
Celles de là, mes Walkyries,
Toujours plus pâles et plus pâles,
Chevauchent au loin des prairies,
Le galop des blanches cavales.

*La Chanson du pauvre*

## The Ride of the Valkyries

On the horizon of the grey plains of my thoughts and troubles, in the distance toward the dreary far-away moon over pale mists, oh, the sad, endless galloping! The galloping of white mares. And my marriageable princesses, already distant and bathed in twilight, the sleeping beauties of my soul, the unforgettable loved ones, toward whom my heart laments and calls, imploring in vain their return; those princesses, my Valkyries, ever paler and paler, ride in the distant meadows, galloping on white mares.

## La Mort

Ce soir, la gueuse fatale,
La vieille livide et brutale
Aux mains calleuses, au front bas;

Celle qui marche au milieu des chemins,
    Tantôt ici, tantôt là-bas,
    Barrant la route au lendemain;
    Celle qui fait sonner les pierres
    De son bâton noué de fer,
    Et de ses deux sabots d'enfer;

    Ce soir, la mort a, sans raison,
    Passé le seuil de ma maison.

J'étais rêveur, au coin du feu,
    Lisant l'espérance et la vie
    Dans les yeux bleus de mon enfant.

    La vieille entra
Et vint s'asseoir entre nous deux...
Et je n'avais pas vu qu'une chaise était là...

*La Chanson du pauvre*

## Death

This evening the fatal beggarwoman, the pale, brutal old woman with calloused hands and a low forehead, the one who walks in the middle of the road, sometimes here, sometimes elsewhere, blocking the road to tomorrow, the one who dashes her iron-clad stick against clattering stones and kicks them with her hellish clogs; this evening, death, for no reason, crossed the threshold of my house. I was dreaming by the fire, reading hope and life in my child's blue eyes. The old woman came in and sat between us. And I hadn't seen a chair was there.

## La Pluie du soir

Il pleut si misérablement
Sur ma barque et dans l'eau qui pleure!
    Il pleut des larmes sur la terre,
        Et puis c'est l'heure,
    Et c'est l'universel mystère,
    Et puis il pleut si tristement
Sur ma barque et dans l'eau qui pleure!

    Et voyez la voile grelotte
Dans le vent qui geint et qui corne!
    Et j'ai vu passer la licorne

Comme une espérance falote...
Et toujours, oh! ce vent qui corne!

Viens dans ma barque de misère!
Nous voguerons sur l'eau qui pleure...
Nous irons au lac de mystère
Où s'entend la voix éperdue
D'une princesse légendaire
Qui pleure là, qui pleure
La barque à tout jamais perdue
Au fond des eaux,
Dans les roseaux.

*La Chanson du pauvre*

## Evening Rain

It is raining so wretchedly on my ship and in the weeping water. It's raining tears on the earth, and it's also the special hour, the hour of universal mystery, and it's raining so dismally on my boat and in the weeping water. And look, the sail shivers in the moaning blasting wind. And I saw the unicorn go by like a foolish hope. And still the wind blasting. Come into my wretched ship! We will sail on the weeping water. We will go to the mystery lake where you hear the desperate voice of a legendary princess who weeps there, who weeps for her boat lost forever down in the water among the reeds.

# MAURICE MAETERLINCK

## Hôpital

Hôpital! hôpital au bord du canal!
Hôpital au mois de juillet!
On y fait du feu dans la salle!
Tandis que les transatlantiques sifflent sur le canal!

(Oh! n'approchez pas des fenêtres!)
Des émigrants traversent un palais!
Je vois un yacht sous la tempête!
Je vois des troupeaux sur tous les navires!
(Il vaut mieux que les fenêtres restent closes,
On est presque à l'abri du dehors.)
On a l'idée d'une serre sur la neige.
On croit célébrer des relevailles un jour d'orage.
On entrevoit des plantes éparses sur une couverture de laine,
Il y a un incendie un jour de soleil,
Et je traverse une forêt pleine de blessés.

Oh! voici enfin le clair de lune!

Un jet d'eau s'élève au milieu de la salle!
Une troupe de petites filles entr'ouvre la porte!
J'entrevois des agneaux dans une île de prairies!
Et de belles plantes sur un glacier!
Et des lys dans un vestibule de marbre!
Il y a un festin dans une forêt vierge!
Et une végétation orientale dans une grotte de glace!
Ecoutez! on ouvre les écluses!
Et les transatlantiques agitent l'eau du canal!

Oh! mais la soeur de charité attisant le feu!

Tous les beaux roseaux verts des berges sont en flamme!
Un bateau de blessés ballotte au clair de lune!
Toutes les filles du roi sont dans une barque sous l'orage!
Et les princesses vont mourir en un champ de ciguës!

Oh! n'entrouvrez pas les fenêtres!
Ecoutez: les transatlantiques sifflent encore à l'horizon!

On empoisonne quelqu'un dans un jardin!
Ils célèbrent une grande fête chez les ennemis!
Il y a des cerfs dans une ville assiégée!
Et une ménagerie au milieu des lys!
Il y a une végétation tropicale au fond d'une houillère!
Un troupeau de brebis traverse un pont de fer!
Et les agneaux de la prairie entrent tristement dans la salle!

Maintenant la soeur de charité allume les lampes,
Elle apporte le repas des malades,
Elle a clos les fenêtres sur le canal,
Et toutes les portes au clair de lune.

*Serres chaudes*

# Hospital

Hospital, hospital beside the canal! Hospital in the month of July! The fire is lit in the ward! While the ocean liners whistle on the canal! (Oh, don't go near the windows!) Emigrants are going through a palace! I see a yacht in the storm! I see flocks of sheep on all the ships! (The windows had better stay closed; we are almost completely protected from the outdoors.) It seems like a hothouse in the snow, as if we were celebrating a churching on a stormy day; there appear to be plants scattered on a woolen blanket. There is a fire on a sunny day, and I am crossing a forest full of the wounded. Oh, here at last is the moonlight! A fountain is rising in the middle of the ward! A band of little girls is opening the door! I seem to see lambs in a meadowy island! And beautiful plants on a glacier! And lilies in a marble entry! There is a feast in a virgin forest! And oriental vegetation in a grotto of ice! Listen! They're opening the locks! And the ocean liners are churning the waters in the canal! Yes, but the nun is stirring the fire! All the beautiful green reeds on the banks are on fire! A boatload of wounded men is pitching on the canal in the moonlight! All the king's daughters are in a bark in the storm! And the princesses are going to die in a field of hemlock! Oh, don't open the windows! Listen! The ocean liners are still whistling on the horizon! Someone is being poisoned in a garden! A great feast-day is being celebrated by the enemy! There are stags in a besieged city! And a menagerie in the midst of lilies! There is tropical vegetation at the bottom of a coal mine! A flock of sheep is crossing an iron bridge! And the lambs from the meadow sadly enter the ward! Now the nun is lighting the lamps; she is bringing the patients' dinner. She has closed the windows giving onto the canal and closed the doors in the moonlight.

## Ame de serre

Je vois des songes dans mes yeux;
Et mon âme enclose sous verre,
Eclairant sa mobile serre
Affleure les vitrages bleus.

O les serres de l'âme tiède,
Les lys contre les verres clos,
Les roseaux éclos sous leurs eaux,
Et tous mes désirs sans remède!

Je voudrais atteindre, à travers
L'oubli de mes pupilles closes,
Les ombelles autrefois roses
De tous mes songes entr'ouverts...

J'attends pour voir leurs feuilles mortes
Reverdir un peu dans mes yeux;
J'attends que la lune aux doigts bleus
Entr'ouvre en silence les portes.

*Serres chaudes*

## Hothouse Soul

I see dream in my eyes, and my soul enclosed in glass, to illuminate its moving hothouse, presses against the blue windows. Oh, the hothouse of a warm soul, lilies against the closed panes, reeds sprouting under the water, and all my irremediable desires! I should like to reach, through the oblivion of my closed eyes, the once pink umbels of all my former dreams. I am waiting to see their dead leaves become a bit green again in my eyes. I am expecting the blue-fingered moon to set the doors silently ajar.

## Serre d'ennui

O cet ennui bleu dans le coeur!
Avec la vision meilleure,
Dans le clair de lune qui pleure,
De mes rêves bleus de langueur!

Cet ennui bleu comme la serre,
Où l'on voit closes à travers
Les vitrages profonds et verts,
Couvertes de lune et de verre,

Les grandes végétations
Dont l'oubli nocturne s'allonge,
Immobilement comme un songe,
Sur les roses des passions;

Où de l'eau très lente s'élève,
En mêlant la lune et le ciel
En un sanglot glauque éternel,
Monotonement comme un rêve.

*Serres chaudes*

## Hothouse Ennui

Oh this blue ennui in the heart! With the best vision in the weeping moonlight of my languorous blue dreams! This ennui, blue like the hothouse, where you see, through the deep green panes, great clumps of vegetation covered with moon and glass, whose nocturnal oblivion extends, without moving, as in a dream, to the roses of passion. This ennui, blue like the hothouse, where water slowly rises, mingling moon and sky in an eternal sea green sob, monotonously as in a dream.

## Ame

Mon âme!
O mon âme vraiment trop à l'abri!
Et ces troupeaux de mes désirs dans une serre!
Attendant une tempête sur les prairies!

Allons vers les plus malades:
Ils ont d'étranges exhalaisons.
Au milieu d'eux, je traverse un champ de bataille avec ma mère.
On enterre un frère d'armes à midi,
Tandis que les sentinelles prennent leur repas.

Allons aussi vers les plus faibles:
Ils ont d'étranges sueurs;
Voici une fiancée malade,
Une trahison le dimanche

Et des petits enfants en prison.
(Et plus loin, à travers la vapeur,)
Est-ce une mourante à la porte d'une cuisine?
Ou une soeur épluchant des légumes au pied du lit d'un incurable?

Allons enfin vers les plus tristes:
(En dernier lieu, car ils ont des poisons.)
Oh! mes lèvres acceptent les baisers d'un blessé!

Toutes les châtelaines sont mortes de faim, cet été,
    dans les tours de mon âme!

Voici le petit jour qui entre dans la fête!
J'entrevois des brebis le long des quais,
Et il y a une voile aux fenêtres de l'hôpital.

Il y a un long chemin de mon coeur à mon âme!
Et toutes les sentinelles sont mortes à leur poste!

Il y eut un jour une pauvre petite fête dans les
    faubourgs de mon âme!
On y fauchait la ciguë un dimanche matin;
Et toutes les vierges du couvent regardaient passer
    les vaisseaux sur le canal, un jour de jeûne et
    de soleil.
Tandis que les cygnes souffraient sous un pont
    vénéneux;
On émondait les arbres autour de la prison,

On apportait des remèdes une après-midi de juin,
Et des repas de malades s'étendaient à tous les
    horizons!

Mon âme!
Et la tristesse de tout cela, mon âme! et la tristesse
    de tout cela!

*Serres chaudes*

## My Soul

My soul! O my soul truly sheltered too much! And the flocks of my
desires in a hothouse! Expecting a storm over the meadows! Let us look
at the sickest ones: they have strange odors. In the midst of them I go
through a battlefield with my mother. A brother-in-arms is being
buried at noon, while the guards are eating their meal. Let us also look

at the weakest ones: they are sweating strangely. Here is a sick fiancée, a betrayal on Sunday, and small children in prison. (And farther on, through the haze,) is that a dying woman at a kitchen door? Or a nun peeling vegetables at the foot of a hopeless invalid's bed? Let us go see the saddest ones (last of all, for they have poisons.) Oh! my lips take kisses from a wounded man! All the ladies of the manors died of hunger last summer, in my soul's towers! Now dawn is penetrating the festivities! I glimpse sheep along the wharves, and there is a sail in the hospital windows. It is a long road from my heart to my soul. And all the guards have died at their post! One day there were humble festivities in the poor district of my soul! They were harvesting hemlock on a Sunday morning. And all the virgins in the convent were watching the ships pass on the canal, on a day of fasting and sunshine. While the swans agonized under a poisonous bridge, they were pruning trees around the prison; they brought medicine on a June afternoon, and the invalids' meals stretched out to infinity! My soul! And the desolateness of it all, the desolateness!

# STUART MERRILL

## Nocturne

La blême lune allume en la mare qui luit,
Miroir des gloires d'or, un émoi d'incendie.
Tout dort. Seul, à mi-mort, un rossignol de nuit
Module en mal d'amour sa molle mélodie.

Plus ne vibrent les vents en le mystère vert
Des ramures. La lune a tu leurs voix nocturnes:
Mais à travers le deuil du feuillage entr'ouvert
Pleuvent les bleus baisers des astres taciturnes.

La vieille volupté de rêver à la mort
A l'entour de la mare endort l'âme des choses.
A peine la forêt parfois fait-elle effort
Sous le frisson furtif de ses métamorphoses.

Chaque feuille s'efface en des brouillards subtils.
Du zénith de l'azur ruisselle la rosée
Dont le cristal s'incruste en perles aux pistils
Des nénufars flottant sur l'eau fleurdelisée.

Rien n'émane du noir, ni vol, ni vent, ni voix,
Sauf lorsqu'au loin des bois, par soudaines saccades,
Un ruisseau turbulent croule sur les gravois:
L'écho s'émeut alors de l'éclat des cascades.

*Les Gammes*

## Nocturne

The pale moon in the gleaming pond, the mirror of gold haloes, kindles a quivering conflagration. Everything is asleep. Alone, half-dead, a night nightingale modulates his soft melody into love sickness. No more do the winds pulsate in the green mystery of the boughs. The moon has silenced their nocturnal voices. But through the mourning gaps in the foliage rain the blue kisses of silent stars. The old voluptuous dreaming of death makes the souls of things drowsy around the pond. The forest makes a movement only now and then under the furtive quiver of its transformations. Each leaf grows dim in soft mists.

From the height of the azure firmament streams the dew, whose crystal makes incrustations of pearls on the pistils of the water lilies floating in the lily-strewn water. Nothing emanates from the darkness, nothing in flight, no wind, no voice, save when far in the woods, in sudden gushes, a turbulent stream pours onto gravel: then the echo is troubled by the roar of the falling water.

## Conte

Ce fut par un pays fleuri de lilas noirs
Où des Dames en deuil faisaient tinter des harpes
Sur les tours de granit des magiques manoirs.

Et dans les soirs d'azur où flottaient des écharpes,
Le Héros ingénu, sous son heaume d'argent,
S'en vint vers les viviers pleins de fuites de carpes.

Sur ses pas éclatait le tonnerre outrageant
Des trompes; les hérauts ceints de sanglantes toiles
Le sommaient de se rendre aux amours de la gent.

Mais lui, redressant haut vers les froides étoiles
Son épée au pommeau qu'enguirlandaient des lys,
Remémorait sa Reine invisible en ses voiles.

Et sur ses yeux des doigts lourds de pierres d'iris
Pesaient; et dans son coeur roulaient de tièdes larmes
Pour avoir trop aimé la Doulce de jadis.

Il tua les hérauts impurs; les nuits d'alarmes
Retentissaient d'appels mortels, et les vergers
S'allumaient aux éclairs bleus et verts de ses armes.

Or il advint ceci: qu'un soir de vents légers
Il vint vers une mer merveilleuse de rêve,
Où dans des îles d'or des flûtes de bergers

Sifflaient. Et laissant choir le fardeau de son glaive,
Il ploya les genoux et sanglota très bas,
Ses bras de fer en croix et le dos à la grève:

"Je suis venu mourir, las des mauvais combats,
Au leurre de vos voix lointaines, ô sirènes,
Que pleurent en riant les flûtes de là-bas.

Car je me sens l'élu des pâles souveraines
Du Sort; à vous ce corps qui n'a pu vous surseoir,
Mais mon âme, mon âme à la Reine des reines!

O Pure que mes yeux, même purs, n'ont pu voir,
O Forte que mes bras, même forts, n'ont pu ceindre,
Voici que tonne enfin le triomphe de l'Hoir!"

Et ses doigts à sa gorge, afin d'y mieux étreindre
Les affres, il sonna de l'olifant vermeil
Vers le soleil tardif, sur ces mers, à s'éteindre.

Par merveille surgit du fond des flots, pareil
Au rêve d'un poète ancien, le blanc cortège
Des naïades, nageant lentes comme au réveil.

Et l'une sous ses bras plus froids qu'aucune neige
Souleva le mourant, et l'autre l'enroula
Dans un linceul tissé pour un roi de Norvège.

Une nacelle d'or et de nacre était là,
Que traînaient des dauphins bleus et des hippocampes;
Lourde de mort, pour les exils elle cingla.

Le troupeau des Tritons soufflait, l'écume aux tempes,
Dans les conques; le vent, secouant son sommeil,
Soulevait l'algue échevelée au bout des hampes.

Et vers le crépuscule, en ce noble appareil,
La barque déroula son lumineux sillage:
Et le Héros entra dans l'orbe du soleil.

Seul, son glaive flambait sur l'argent de la plage,
Afin qu'un futur Preux, surgissant du millier,
L'empoignât quelque soir pour en sacrer son âge.

C'est ainsi que mourut le chaste chevalier.

*Les Fastes*

## Tale

It was in a country of flowering black lilacs, whose ladies in mourning plucked harps on the granite towers of magic manors. And in the blue evening with its floating veils, the innocent Hero under his silver helmet came toward the ponds full of darting carp. At his footsteps the insolent thunder of horns burst forth; heralds girded with bloody cloths ordered him to yield to the desires of the ruling race of women. But raising toward the cold stars his sword with its lily-entwined pommel, he remembered his Queen, invisible in her veils. And on his eyelids there pressed fingers heavy with rainbow-quartz, and in his heart there dropped warm tears because he had too much loved the Dulcet One of yore. He killed the unchaste heralds; nights of alarum rang with fatal cries, and the orchards were lit up by the blue and green flashing of his weapons. Now this happened: one evening full of breezes, he came toward a marvelous dream sea, where shepherds' flutes piped on golden islands. And letting his burdensome sword drop, he knelt and sobbed low, crossing his iron-clad arms, with his back to the shore: "I have come to die, weary of evil battles, drawn by your far-away voices, O Sirens for whom those distant flutes weep and laugh. For I have been chosen by the pale queens of Fate. Yours is this body which could not withstand you, but my soul belongs to the Queen of queens. O Pure One whom my eyes, though pure, could not see, O Strong One whom my arms, though strong, could not embrace, here is the Heir's thundering triumph!" And with his fingers at his throat, the better to grasp his death agony, he blew the golden horn toward the sun, which sets late in those seas. Miraculously there rose from the depths of the waves, like an ancient poet's dream, a white procession of naiads, swimming slowly as if just awakened. And one of them picked up the dying man under his arms, which were colder than any snow, and another wrapped him in a winding sheet woven for a Norwegian king. A boat of gold and mother-of-pearl was there, drawn by blue dolphins and sea horses. Death-heavy, toward lands of exile, it sailed. The flock of Tritons with foamy temples blew conch shells like trumpets; the wind, shaking itself from slumber, tossed the seaweed tangled around the poles. And toward twilight, in such great pomp, the boat unfurled its gleaming wake, and the Hero entered the sun's orb. Alone, his sword flamed on the silver shore, so that a coming gallant, rising one out of a thousand, might lay hold of it some evening and consecrate his age. Thus died the chaste knight.

## La Cité rouge

Or ce sera par un pays de crépuscule
Où le soleil de pourpre, au ras des horizons
Qu'exhaussent des volcans fauves de floraisons,
Présagera les jours lourds de la canicule.

Un fleuve de flamme y déroulera ses flots
Entre les archipels de lotus et la grève,
Où la vieille Chimère, en l'âpre rut du rêve,
Tordra d'un vain essor ses flancs gros de sanglots.

Parfois, carène noire et cordages funèbres,
Une galère, aux pleurs des tambours et des voix,
Exaltera, le soir, sur sa poupe en pavois,
Le simulacre d'or d'un monstre des ténèbres.

Puis déferlant sa voile au vent des mauvais sorts
Et battant les lointains de l'écho de ses rames
Sur un rythme barbare et bas d'épithalames,
Elle appareillera, pesante d'enfants morts,

Vers la Cité d'amour et de grande épouvante
Dont on ne dit le nom qu'avec des sacrements,
De peur de trépasser en les impurs moments
Où son désir d'enfer hanta l'âme fervente;

La Cité qui là-bas avec ses étendards
De deuil, ses bastions de basalte et ses morgues,
Leurrera de ses voix de théorbes et d'orgues
Les pas las des Damnés et leurs regards hagards.

Et quand viendront les jours lourds de la canicule,
Les volcans, éclatant en fauves floraisons,
Feront hurler d'horreur, au ras des horizons,
Sodome, la Cité Rouge du crépuscule.

*Les Fastes*

## The Red City

Now it will be in a twilight land, where the red sun, on horizons made high by volcanoes in their tawny florescence, will foretell the heavy days of August heat. A river of flame will unroll its waves between the lotus archipelago and the strand, where the ancient Chimaera, in bitter rut in its dream, will twist its heavy sob-filled body in a vain effort to soar. Sometimes, with its black keel and funereal riggings a galley filled with weeping voices and drums will hoist, toward evening, among the flags on the stern, the golden image of a night monster. Then, releasing its sail in the ill-fated winds, with its oars beating the muffled rhythm of a barbarous wedding chant and reverberating in the distant echo, the galley takes to the sea, weighted down with dead children, and heading for the City of love and horror, whose name is spoken only with an oath on all that is holy, for fear of perishing in the unclean moment when the fervent soul is haunted by its desire for hell—the distant City, which with its mourning banners, mortuaries, and basalt bulwarks, will lure, to the sound of organs and theorbos, the weary step of the damned and their haggard faces. And when the heavy days of August heat come, the volcanoes, with their tawny bursting florescence, will make Sodom, the Red City of the twilight, on the horizon, scream in horror.

## La Mystérieuse Chanson

Nous avons vu trois femmes rousses
Assises, le menton aux genoux,
Au bord des sources, sur la mousse.
Le désespoir pleurait dans leurs yeux doux
Et la rage secouait leurs voix rauques.
De leurs doigts prestes, en chantant, elles enfilaient
Les gemmes jaunes et les perles glauques
Qui plaisent aux filles des cités;
Et toutes répétaient, entêtées,
Cette strophe d'une antique chanson
(On aurait dit les Parques qui filaient,
Rousses contre le soleil de la moisson):

> *Siffle la faux, saignent les fleurs,*
> *Voici le soir de la grand'lune;*
> *Vienne la nuit, pleurent mes soeurs,*
> *Les fleurs ont chu l'une après l'une.*

Nous nous arrêtâmes sans comprendre,
Muets comme des enfants du soir
A qui l'on raconte une histoire.
Les nuages étaient roses de cendres
Et les peupliers lourds de murmures.
Tu penchas le front, et soudain
Je t'entendis sangloter dans tes mains,
Cependant que, graves sous leurs chevelures,
Les trois femmes aux yeux pleins de passé
Reprenaient le cours de leur chanson

(On aurait dit les Parques qui filaient,
Rouges contre le soleil de la moisson):

> *Tourne le rouet, dorment les vieux,*
> *C'est un linceul qu'on tisse en l'ombre:*
> *Tremblent les poings, clignent les yeux,*
> *Les morts sont là, mes soeurs, en nombre.*

Tu lanças, d'un geste haut, du cuivre
Aux chanteuses qui, voulant nous suivre,
Firent tinter leurs perles par terre.
Et comme en tes yeux soudain clairs
S'allumait la folie d'un remords,
Je t'attirai vers moi de mes bras forts,
De mes bras qui ceignirent ta taille pleine,
Et nous courûmes vers la nuit prochaine
Sans ouïr la suite de la chanson
Que debout les trois femmes nous lançaient
(On aurait dit les Parques qui filaient
Noires contre le soleil de la moisson):

> *Fume l'encens, veille l'amour,*
> *Dans son lit bleu la vierge est morte;*
> *Couve le feu, tombe le jour,*
> *L'Ange, mes soeurs, frappe à la porte.*

*Les Quatre Saisons*

## The Mysterious Song

We saw three red-haired women sitting, their knees drawn up to their chins, in the moss by the springs. Despair wept in their gentle eyes, and their hoarse voices shook with rage. With nimble fingers, while singing, they strung the yellow gems and sea green beads that city girls like. And together, stubbornly, they repeated this stanza of an old song (they looked like the spinning Fates, red-haired against the harvest sun): "Let the scythe whistle, the flowers bleed, here is the evening of the full moon; let the night come, my sisters weep, the flowers have fallen one after another." We stopped, without understanding, silent as children in the evening being told stories. The clouds were ashen pink, the poplars heavy with murmurs. You looked down and suddenly I heard you sob into your hands, while, serious looking beneath their long hair, the three women, their eyes reflecting the past, began again their song (they looked like the spinning Fates, crimson against the harvest sun): "Let the spinning wheel turn, the old people sleep, a winding sheet is being woven in the shadow; let closed hands tremble, eyes blink, the dead are there in a great number, my sisters." With a haughty gesture you threw pennies to the singers, who, starting to follow us, dropped their beads with a clatter. And, as the folly of remorse suddenly lit up your bright eyes, I drew you toward me with my strong arms, with my arms which encircled your body, and we ran toward the approaching night and did not hear the rest of the song, which the three women, on their feet, screamed at us (they looked like the spinning Fates, black against the harvest sun): "Let the incense smoke, love stand guard, in her blue bed the virgin died; let the fire smolder, night fall, the angel, my sisters, is knocking at the door."

## Chrysostome

Le Poète éperdu sanglotait sur les roses
Pour n'avoir pu cueillir, avec leur vain parfum,
Que pétales éparpillés au vent défunt,
Souvenirs de baisers au seuil de portes closes.

Le magicien vint qui connaît toutes choses
Et lui dit à genoux le secret opportun
Qui fait revivre, rouge en l'âme de chacun,
La rose plus réele, hélas! d'être sans causes.

Et depuis, dans la nuit où dort tout front mortel,
Pour recréer les fleurs aux mots du sortilège,
Le poète, priant sous la croix de l'autel,

Tend ses lèvres—baiser pour d'autres sacrilège!—
A la flamme des cieux dont son rêve s'éprit,
Comme un calice où Dieu déversera l'esprit
Qui perpétue avril au milieu de la neige.

*Le Jeu des épées*

## Goldenmouthed

The despairing poet sobbed over the roses because he could gather, along with their vanishing scent, only petals scattered in the dead wind—memories of kisses on the threshold of closed doors. The all-knowing magician came and told him, as he knelt, the timely secret which brings to life in our soul a red rose even more real, alas! because it has no natural cause. And since then, in the night when all mortal brows sleep, in order to recreate the flowers by the words of the spell, the poet, praying under the altar's cross, stretches his lips toward the celestial flame his dream cherishes—in a kiss that for another would be sacrilege—like a chalice in which God will pour the spirit that can perpetuate April in the midst of snow.

# ADOLPHE RETTÉ

Vêts-toi de deuil, Octobre, accourez, vents d'automne!
Où est l'Aurore? où, celui-là qui s'en allait
Charmant des oiseaux fous dont le ramage étonne?...
L'adolescent s'assied sur ton seuil, ô palais
Ecroulé parmi l'ombre déserte et l'automne.

Les arbres inquiets lui dictent sa tristesse,
Les flots indifférents chantent bizarrement
Et vers les lointains gris un fantôme se dresse
Qui parle...Est-ce une voix ou la plainte du vent?

"Insensé, quelle ardeur à te frapper toi-même!
La vie a dispersé tes Princesses de rêve:
Celles-là qui venaient, belles comme un poème,
S'en vont chassées, s'en vont boiteuses par les grèves;
Mais moi qui fus ton âme et moi qui fus leur âme,
Moi, le mensonge amer de la réalité
Je reste et je te dis: Prends garde, en vérité
*Le rameau s'est flétri—et me voici la Femme.*"

L'adolescent frissonne aux clameurs de l'automne,
Ses mains effeuillent des pavots morts sur les flots:
Désormais c'est la Vie et la Femme et l'Automne—

Et le soir sidéral tremble comme un sanglot.

*Une Belle Dame passa*

Put on mourning, October, hither, autumn winds! Where is dawn, where is he whose presence charmed mad birds and their astonishing song? The adolescent sits down on your threshold, O palace crumbling amidst the deserted shadow and autumn. Disquieted trees suggest to him his sadness. The indifferent waves sing strangely and in the grey distance a ghost rises up and speaks. Is it a voice or the waves' lament? "Madman, what a fury of self-inflicted blows! Life has dispersed your dream princesses: they came beautiful as poems and are driven away, limping over the strand. But I who was your soul and their soul, I, the bitter lie of reality, I remain and say, Beware, in truth, for the branch has withered and I am Woman." The adolescent shudders in the roaring autumn. His hands strip petals from dead poppies over the waves. Now is the reign of Life and Woman and Autumn—and the starry evening trembles like a sob.

Bâille la haute salle et ses portes funèbres,
s'esseule et sombre, en les tentures de ténèbres,
la haute salle, âme inerte du navré manoir
identique
         et l'Etre est unanime en sa veillée
vers Rien, tandis que l'amie—par les houles du noir—
discord battant des temps et des cloches fêlées,
l'horloge égoutte l'heure tôt éparpillée,
vacille ainsi flamme vaguante et va disant:
"—Lentement la Nuit s'éplore en pleurs d'étoiles, largement.—"

l'espace et l'ombre, ailes de Nuit, bruits familiers:
soit le vol confus de quelque songe étrange,
soit d'un réel ces reflets dansants du foyer
aux spires d'or des murs—tels ils dérangent
le tiède apaisement d'un qui veut s'ignorer.

Ah frisson d'inconnu si le rêve prend corps:
vitrail magique où de vieux saints branlent la tête,
cris de victime en la plainte des cors,
le vent d'hiver…et sa chanson s'arrête
au refrain douloureux qu'il ne dira jamais;
d'autres:—volez essaims sibyllins et muets,
rythmes défunts pour avoir trop sonné les cycles éphémères,
     (l'Etre a connu ses folles concordances)—
mais voici que le vaste des tentures s'éclaire—
soit reflet dans les ors qui miroite et qui danse
soit le désir spectral d'une âme envolée

                       *toute, c'est la Chimère.*

Sévèrement l'horloge va son long voyage et dit:
"—l'heure s'efflue en flocons étoilés dans la Nuit—"

*C'est la Chimère*: elle fulgure
floraison de soudaine aurore,
Affirmant l'investiture
de dieux omnicolores
Elle dit: "donne-moi ton rêve blessé,
saignant de l'étreinte des espoirs caressés,
et dis-moi ton rêve à venir, je l'emporte
hors de ce manoir sourd dont je brise les portes"

l'Etre enfiévré de sa parole répond:
Je veux la femme, gloire de la chair—sa forme

je la veux nue et qu'elle vole
parmi les cloches et leurs tumultes énormes"

Appel vain il est seul—
                le vent aux vitres se désole.
Portes closes, salle inerte, et, la Chimère évanouie,
Un souffle de tombe passe
                et quel est ce démon enfui
vers l'horreur des couloirs où il ricane à petit bruit?

L'espace et l'ombre processionnent aux gouffres de la Nuit;
froid silence—puis des pas se perdent plus lointains dans la Nuit.

Hélas! ce n'est plus la Chimère—peu à peu le foyer s'endort,
derniers reflets agonisants lovés au lacis des ors—
ah! non plus elle—voici l'ennui séculaire,
nimbe obstiné que le rêve maudit.

sonorante voix monotone, l'horloge dit et redit:
"—faible et calme l'heure stagne en solitude lunaire—"

L'Etre vague par la salle enténébrée
et sa fatigue et la haine de son présent
vaguent par les houles du Noir et ses âmes restent ancrées
au rivage désert d'un aride présent.

L'espace et l'ombre gisent ailes de nuit qui l'effleurent.

Mais lui craintif à cause des ors figés et de l'aiguille
   à la même heure:
"ce morbide reflet ne peut-on qu'il se meure?
si l'horloge a menti, son éclat n'est qu'un leurre."

Clame voix des morts, clame une âme est en partance
pour les récifs des océans de navrance
clame les naufrages—
              Mais toi, reste luisance:
cercle chimérique immuable aux tentures,
cercle bannisseur des instants d'aventures,
   dérision et torture.

L'espace et l'ombre gisent, épaves de Nul infini.—
Et la vieille amie d'illusion, l'horloge
compte tomber, tomber si pâlement les larmes de la Nuit.

*Cloches dans la nuit*

The high hall and its funereal doors gape open. In the draperies of darkness the high hall grows more solitary and sinks, the inert soul of the identical heart-broken manor. And the Figure is unanimous in his vigil toward Nothingness, while the friend—the clock—through black swelling currents—the clock, a discordant clapper of cracked bells and days, lets drip the soon fragmented hour, quivers like a wandering flame, and is saying, "Slowly and amply the Night weeps away in star tears." Space and shadow, wings of Night, familiar sounds: either the muffled flight of some strange dream or reflections of reality, dancing here in the hearth, on the golden spires of the walls; be what they may, they disturb the warm calm of one who is trying not to be aware of himself. Ah, a shudder of the unknown, if dream takes on body, a magic stained-glass window, where old saints nod, victims' screams in the wail of horns, the winter wind . . . and his song stops at the sorrowful refrain he will never utter. Other sounds: fly, sibylline and mute swarms, rhythms extinct from having too long tolled the daily cycles (the Figure has known their frantic harmonies). But now the vast expanse of hangings lights up—either from a glistening, dancing reflection on the gold ornaments or else from the ghostly desire of a vanished soul. *The Chimaera is all.* Austerely the clock continues its long journey and says, "Time flows away in starry snowflakes in the Night." *It is the Chimaera*: it shines like a sudden dawn flowering and affirming the office of many-colored gods. It says, "Give me your wounded dream, bleeding from the embrace of cherished hopes, and tell me your coming dream, so I can carry it off from this silent manor when I break down its doors." The Figure, on fire with his words, replies, "I want Woman, the glory of the flesh; I want her naked form soaring amid bells and their great tumult." A vain cry: he is alone; the wind laments at the windows. Doors closed, a motionless hall, and the Chimaera gone. A breath from the grave drifts by, and what is that demon who fled to the horrible corridors, where he quietly jeers? Space and shadow proceed in pomp in the chasms of Night; a cold silence— then steps fade away in the distance of Night. Alas, it is not the Chimaera; gradually the hearth falls asleep, with the last reflections dying away, curling around the golden fretwork. Ah, no longer the Chimaera—here age-old ennui descends, the obstinate halo cursed by his dream. With a resonant, monotonous voice the clock says over and over, "The hour, weak and calm, grows stagnant in lunar solitude." The Figure wanders through the darkened hall, and his weariness and his hatred of the present moment drift through the swelling current of darkness, and his ghosts remain anchored on the empty shore of an arid present. Space and shadow lie supine like night wings grazing him. But he is fearful because of the motionless golden reflections and the clock hand still pointing at the same hour. "Can I not make this dying reflection die? If the clock lied, its gleam is only a deception." Cry out, voice of the dead, cry out, a soul is departing for the reefs of the oceans of sorrow, cry for the shipwrecks. But you, gleam, remain, like a chimaerical and motionless circle on the hangings, a circle banishing all moments of adventure, a derision and torment. Space and shadow lie supine, the wreckage of a nonexistent infinity. And the old friend in illusion, the clock, counts the tears of Night falling so palely.

## Sillages

L'automne et la nuit et la pluie
—Volez noirs souffles par l'espace—
Et la froide plaine où trépasse
D'irrémédiable agonie
La ville de ruines et d'impasses.

Oh si vieille (en bâtisses neuves)
Et si penchante au bord d'abîmes,
Si prostrée, elle pleure en veuve
A cause de l'exil des cimes.

Des noyés vont flottant au fleuve.

Ville exilée il ne sera d'étoiles
Le lourd plafond de ton ciel
                    Reste terne,
Reste automnale et vouée aux lanternes
De tes songes fumeux et sous tes voiles
De pluie, de nuit, sois veuve et solitaire:

Ta plainte tu l'encloras de mystère
Car il n'est plus d'églises où la taire—
Larmes au ciel larmes aussi sur terre.

Par les rues, par les places en torpeur,
Tel éternel mendiant pour son coeur
Rôde et s'entête aux sourds marteaux des portes:
"Ouvrez, ouvrez, c'est un printemps, j'apporte
Ma grande faim de l'amer pain d'amour;

Le froid enroue ma chanson dans vos cours,
Ouvrez! mon coeur défaillant veut renaître."

Mais les magiciennes aux fenêtres:
"Non, le bissac de ton coeur est troué,
Va-t'en plus loin nous t'avons trop donné."

  Les girouettes sur les toits
  Ricanent toutes à la fois.

Monuments aux reflets d'or de défunts étés,
Ce sont les palais de Savoir et les portiques
Du Dire, et raides, des parvis d'autorité,
S'érigent les mages aux faces identiques,
La certitude aux miroirs pâles de leurs yeux...
Coeur en détresse, le mendiant anxieux
Clame: "Faites-vous pas l'aumône de l'Idée?"

"C'est ici son tombeau nous l'avons embaumée."

  Les lanternes se balancent
  En dix mille absurdes danses.
Seule et si seule la ville s'esseule
Au frôlis des pas de vagues passants,
Ombres qui se traînent lentes et veules
Aux accords mouillés du vent vagissant—

"O flambeaux éteints d'une vie entière!"

Le répons des voix chantonne aux gouttières
Et goutte à goutte filtre tristement:

"Tais-toi, nous sommes morts et dès longtemps."

  Les girouettes dans la brume
  Toutes droites se profilent
  Et les lanternes, qui fument,
  Valsent, valsent dans la brume,
  Un cortège file et défile
  Aux lointains troubles de la brume.

Le mendiant s'éternise en la ville hostile;
Ses sanglots universels grelottent dans la brume—
C'est la ville de pluie, c'est la ville de nuit,
La lugubre cité si croulante à l'automne,
Des cloches en cadence, et, par les rues d'ennui,

Un morne défilé de cercueils monotones...
Suis-les donc à jamais, spectre frustré d'espoir,
Nocturne vagabond furtif et qu'on renie:
Va, sombre dans la nuit et la pluie infinie,
Puisque tu voudrais croire et que tu voudrais voir
—Etrange destin de ta vieille âme honteuse
Et, destin, tes pas lourds, et la cité brumeuse—
Erre seul à jamais le Vide et le Noir
A jamais à jamais par le Vide et le Noir...

*Cloches dans la nuit*

## Wakes

Autumn and night and rain—fly, black gusts, through the air—and the cold plain where in irremediable death throes the city dies in ruins and obstructions. Oh, so old a city (of new buildings) and tottering so on the edge of the abyss, so prostrate it weeps like a widow for the vanished treetops. Dead men float in the river. Exiled city, your rooflike heavy sky will not be starry. Stay dreary, autumnal, and given over to the lanterns of your smoky dreams, and under your veils of rain and night, be widowed and lonely. You will hide your complaint in mystery, for there are no more churches in which to stifle it—tears in heaven, tears also on earth. Through the streets and somnolent squares a certain eternal beggar of his heart wanders and stubbornly pounds on the muffled knockers on the doors. "Open, open, it is spring; I bring my great hunger for the bitter bread of love; the cold makes my song hoarse in your courtyards. Open up, my failing heart wants to be re-born." But the witches in the windows reply, "No, there are holes in the knapsack of your heart; go farther on, we have given you too much." The weather vanes on the roofs all cackle at once. These monuments with their golden reflections of dead summers are the palaces of Knowledge and the gates of Affirmation, and from the official portals stiffly arise magicians with identical faces and certainty in the pale mirrors of their eyes. With distress in his heart, the anguished beggar cries, "Do you not make alms of the Ideal?" "This is its tomb, and we have embalmed it." The lanterns sway in a thousand absurd dancing movements. Alone and so alone, the city grows yet more alone as the feet of vague wanderers brush by in it. They are shadows dragging along slowly and weakly to the damp harmonies of the moaning wind. "Oh extinguished torches of a whole life!" The voices' response hums in the rain gutters and drop by drop sadly falls: "Quiet, we are dead, and have been so for a long time." The weather vanes in the mist stand erect and in profile, and the smoky lanterns dance, dance in the mist. A procession winds along in the distant distress of the mist. The beggar remains for eternity in the hostile city. His universal sobs shiver in the mist. This is the city of rain, the city of night, the mournful city so crumbling in autumn, rhythmic bells, and, through the dreary streets, a dismal procession of monotonous coffins. Follow them forever, specter frustrated of hope, rejected nighttime wanderer; come, sink into night and infinite rain. Since you would like to believe and would like to see (such is the strange destiny of your shameful old soul and destiny too, your heavy steps and the misty city), wander alone forever through emptiness and the dark, forever, forever, through emptiness and the dark.

# PIERRE QUILLARD

## Les Fleurs noirs

Au bord de quels sinistres lacs d'eau lourde et sombre,
O ténébreuses fleurs plus vastes que la mort,
Les dieux muets du soir et les dieux froids du nord
    Tissent-ils votre robe d'ombre?

Vos abîmes de nuit dévorent le soleil;
Le jour est offensé par vos voiles de veuves
Et vous avez puisé sans peur aux mornes fleuves
    L'onde farouche du sommeil.

O fleurs noires, le vent de l'aube vous balance:
Mais nul parfum d'amour ne s'exhale de vous,
Chères, et vous versez dans les coeurs las et fous
    L'incantation du silence.

La vie épand en vain ses perfides douceurs;
La pompe du printemps inutile flamboie:
Votre deuil rédempteur libère de la joie;
    Salut, impérieuses soeurs.

Je vous aime et je veux dormir, soyez clémentes:
Je ne troublerai pas votre calme immortel
Et, là-bas, j'oublierai, loin du jour et du ciel,
    La bouche rouge des amantes.

*La Lyre héroïque et dolente*

## Black Flowers

On the edge of what sinister lakes of heavy dark water, O shadowy flowers vaster than death, did the mute gods of evening and the cold gods of the north weave your robe of shade? Your chasms of night devour the sun; day is insulted by your widow's veils, and you have fearlessly drawn from dismal rivers the elusive draught of sleep. O black flowers, you sway in the dawn wind, but no scent of love comes from you, dear flowers, and you pour into weary and mad hearts the spell of silence. In vain does life spread her treacherous sweetness;

uselessly flames the pomp of spring. Your redemptive mourning re-
leases us from joy. Hail, imperious sisters! I love you and wish to sleep,
have mercy: I will not disturb your immortal calm, and on those banks,
far from the day and sky, I shall forget the red mouth of my lovers.

# HENRI DE REGNIER

## Le Salut à l'étrangère

Aux ruines de Vie antérieure et morte,
Au fronton dominant l'ombre cave de la porte
Où s'engouffrent les feuilles comme les ailes mortes
Des vols de crêpe épars sur les étangs de moire,
Face de doux relief et triste épiphanie
Double de Songe et Soeur de Mémoire,
Et sourire posthume qui se renie!

Masque pâle entre ses bandeaux et pour la mort
Sans funèbre laurier au front ni pierrerie,
Lèvres de pourpre stricte où le silence crie,
Et les yeux clos comme des yeux d'enfant qui dort;

Masque pâle sans au front une pierrerie
Ni funèbre laurier au delà de la mort,
Quelle parole est morte à la lèvre meurtrie
De quel aveu pour que la lèvre en saigne encor?

Masque éperdu vers les étoiles,
Son intacte blancheur de marbre a vaincu l'ombre
Et la face s'exhume éternelle de l'ombre
Blanche et grave sous les étoiles.

Masque plus pâle que l'aurore
Et la lune aux étangs mirée et faciale,
Étrange et fruste et d'une douceur faciale
Ainsi qu'une lune d'aurore.

Masque ébloui sous le soleil
Fixe et grave d'une candeur inaltérée,
Nulle soif n'a disjoint la lèvre inaltérée
Rouge fruit gorgé de soleil.

Masque sans larme sous la pluie
Où la pluie aux soirs d'ombre éperdument ruisselle,
Paupières closes d'où rien autre ne ruisselle
Que les froides larmes de pluie.

Masque muet au vent qui passe,
Au vent qui passe et joue en les lèvres aphones
A simuler la voix de ces lèvres aphones
Où le mensonge du vent passe!

Je t'ai connu vivant, hilare et nimbé d'or
Sous le triple laurier et sous la pierrerie,
Yeux à la vie et bouche éloquente et mûrie
Pour le baiser et pour la colère qui mord.

J'ai vu vivre tes yeux, tes yeux, ô pierreries,
Et je sais le passé que ton silence dort
Quand tu marchais vivante, en les idolâtries,
Parmi les palmes et le sang et parmi l'or!

## I

L'usurpateur mystérieux des destinées,
L'involontaire Amant qui chevauche et guerroie
A disparu dans l'ombre au détour des années.

Le cimier d'ailes au vent de la mer s'éploie,
L'éternelle aventure a ri comme une femme
Aux horizons d'aurore un visage de joie.

Il a vu, dans le ciel de pourpre et d'oriflamme,
Un masque douloureux pleurer parmi les nues
Du couchant saccagé comme une Ville en flamme.

Des antres et du lac les Nymphes sortaient nues;
Les Aegypans des bois ont guetté son passage
De leurs yeux clairs luisant en leurs faces cornues.

Sous l'invincible pas de l'Errant triste et sage,
Les charmes vains craquaient un bris de branches mortes
Ou fuites de noirs vols d'orfraies au ciel d'orage;

Le pennon et le glaive hauts en ses mains fortes,
Il traversa le val et la mer et la plaine
Et vit, un soir, la ville et les murs aux sept portes,

Et sur la tour de marbre fruste, assise, Hélène!

## II

Reine des seuils sacrés et des villes murales,
Salut à ta splendeur, par le glaive et le cor!
En tes cheveux, en tes robes, en tes opales,
En ton passé divin tout incandescent d'or.

Salut en ta douceur de femme et de fileuse,
En les aubes de paix de tes soirs véhéments,
Et d'être née ainsi dans la nuit fabuleuse
Pour resplendir au songe éternel des amants.

Sur la tour solitaire où trône ton prestige
De fleur mystérieuse et d'idole des soirs
Les ramiers douloureux roucoulent le vertige
Des âmes de jadis qui burent aux Styx noirs.

Eux qui vinrent du fond des terres sans merveilles
Vers ta face apparue en leurs songes déserts;
Et leurs riches désirs montaient comme des treilles
Aux murs où posaient nus tes pieds vainqueurs des Mers.

A genoux, comme pour pleurer leurs funérailles,
Les uns mouraient d'amour devant tes seuils sacrés,
D'autres ensanglantaient la herse des murailles
Qui trouait le poitrail de leurs chevaux cabrés!

Ils percèrent parfois de flèches sacrilèges
Ta chevelure en tiare, écroulée à demi,
Pareille à quelque tour qui domine les neiges,
Et ta chair palpitait comme un cygne endormi.

Salut en ton passé divin et dans mon âme,
Etrangère, debout sur les siècles haïs
Du paisible regard de ton deuil qui les blâme
Et pour ta face pâle en mes soirs éblouis!

## III

Etrangère! fatale enfant, espoir des Fées,
Le geste de ta main où luit la fleur d'Endor
Destine les héros à la Gloire ou la Mort
Et les voue au travail des bêtes étouffées.

C'est par toi que de sang se payent les trophées
Et se crispe la chair sous la dent qui la mord
Et qu'au Bois noir où l'arc de frêne vibre encor
Une odeur de tuerie éclate par bouffées.

Si le pied triomphal parmi l'ache et la flouve
Foule hors de l'antre un crin de laie ou de louve,
Le cri de l'Oliphant qui vocifère, au soir,

L'angoisse de rubis dont s'orne l'âpre corne,
Du fond du passé fabuleux t'appelle à voir
La hure bestiale au point du Tueur morne!


### IV

Un fard exalte encore un peu d'ivresse morte
Aux lèvres que sa flamme ardente pourpre et brûle
Et le sourire est plus triste qu'un crépuscule
Où souffre le sanglot d'un blessé qu'on emporte
Mourir sanglant et douloureux au crépuscule!

L'antique amour a ri sur ta lèvre, ô Vivante,
L'écho des forts désirs à qui la chair accède
Et les lourds midis nés à la vie éclatante
Ont plu leur clarté d'astre sur ta nuque tiède
D'où croulait ta toison chevelue et vivante.

L'impérieuse ivresse est brève comme un songe,
Sang des lèvres tari par le soleil avide;
Le fard mystérieux qui supplée et prolonge
Sourit plus las qu'un soir stérile en le ciel vide,
Et la Vivante est pâle et triste comme un songe.

Ennemie, étrange Morte, Guerrière morne,
Ombre de la forêt, masque de l'aventure,
Oh va, pour l'invisible Chimère dont s'orne
Le casque d'or cimé que fut ta chevelure,
Abjurer ton mensonge au noir flot d'un Styx morne!


### V

Que n'es-tu l'Exilée, hélas, ou l'Etrangère
Cachant pour vrai trésor sous sa robe en lambeaux

Une pierrerie immortelle et messagère
De quelque astre levé derrière les tombeaux!

La voix d'enfant est douce en les chansons d'aïeules
Et le glaive du père mort ou massacré
Sied aux mains des filles errantes qui vont seules
Loin de la Nuit sanglante où leur âme a pleuré.

Le vent a dispersé les oiseaux et les nues,
Les feuilles volent sur le fleuve vert et noir
Et jonchent le morne sable des grèves nues
Où des iris fleuris éclatent dans le soir.

M'apportes-tu sous tes haillons de Voyageuse
A qui sourit l'étoile en la forêt sans fleurs,
L'opale que la grotte avare et ténébreuse
Mit cent ans, goutte à goutte, à germer de ses pleurs?

Si le glaive est toujours l'ornement du trophée
Où luit l'opale prise à trois griffes d'accord,
Quel talisman s'exalte en tes cheveux de fée
Pour que je croie à ta promesse d'un trésor?

Nul signe que tu sois Celle pour qui dédie
La magique forêt ses arbres merveilleux
Et ses paons triomphaux dont la roue irradie
Une extase de plume où rayonnent des yeux.

Qui sait si le flot sombre ainsi qu'une herbe mûre
Ouvrira ses sillons devant tes pas divins?
Qu'importe de n'avoir pour preuve et pour augure
Que ta simple beauté des pays d'où tu vins.

Prends ma main! le Soir apaise l'onde fatale
Du fleuve où nous entrons comme dans un tombeau
Jusqu'à ce qu'elle monte à ton sourire pâle...

Nul talisman en ses cheveux flottant sur l'eau!

*Poèmes anciens et romanesques*

## Salute to the Foreign One

By a former and dead life's ruins, by the pediment standing over the door's hollow shadow, where leaves are engulfed like the dead wings of crepe flights scattered over the watered-silk ponds: a face in gentle relief and sad epiphany, double of the face in a dream and sister of memory, and a posthumous smile denying itself! Between her tresses a mask pale for death with no funereal laurel on her brow nor gem; with lips of tightly closed crimson from which silence cries out; and with eyes closed like a sleeping child's. Pale mask without a gem on her brow or funereal laurel outlasting death—what word died away on her lips bruised by what avowal, such that they still bleed from it? Mask looking desperately toward the stars—her untouched marble whiteness has vanquished the shadows and her visage rises eternally from the shadows, white and grave under the stars. Mask paler than dawn or the facelike moon reflected in ponds, strange and worn, with a facelike gentleness like a dawn moon. Dazzled mask under the sun, staring and grave with a candor untouched by the elements—no thirst has disjoined her unblemished lips like a red fruit engorged with sunlight. Tearless mask under the rain, on which the rain streams torrentially in shadowy evenings, closed lids from which nothing streams but the rain's cold tears. Mask silent in the passing wind, the wind passing over her wordless lips, playing at imitating the voice of these wordless lips, over which the lying wind passes! I knew you alive, mirthful, and haloed with gold under the triple laurel and the gems—with eyes cast on life and an eloquent mouth ripe for kisses and biting anger. I saw your eyes alive, your eyes, O gems, and I know the past stifled by your silence—when you walked, living, amid idolatrous rites, through the palms and the blood and the gold! I. The mysterious usurper of destinies, the unintentional Lover who rides and wages war, has disappeared into shadow at some turn in time. The winged helmet crest opens in the sea wind; eternal adventure laughed like a woman laughing, on dawn horizons, with a joyous face. He saw, in a sky of purple and golden flames, a sorrowful mask weeping among the clouds of sunset torn like a city in flames. From caves and the lake the Nymphs emerged naked; aegypans from the woods watched him pass, with their bright eyes gleaming in their horned faces. Under the sad and wise Wanderer's invincible steps, vain spells brought about no more than a crackling of dead branches or a black flight of ospreys in the stormy sky. With his banner and sword raised high in his strong hands, he crossed the valley and the sea and the plain and saw, one evening, the city and the walls with seven gates, and, on the tower of worn marble, Helen sitting. II. Queen of sacred thresholds and walled cities, I salute your splendor, by my sword and horn! I salute you in your beauty—hair, robes, and opals—in your divine past burning with gold, I salute you in your gentleness befitting a woman and spinner, in the peaceful dawns of your vehement evenings, and because you were born thus in the fabulous night to shine in lovers' eternal dream. On the tower, where you are enthroned with the prestige of a mysterious flower or of evening's idol, the sorrowful doves tell in their cooing of dizzied souls of long ago, who drank from the black Stygian streams. Those souls of men coming from the far reaches of wonderless lands toward your face, which appeared in their sterile dreams—and their rich desires climbed like vines on walls where your sea-conquering feet stepped bare. Kneeling, as if weeping at their own interment, some died of love before your sacred thresholds; others reddened with blood the portcullis in the walls, which pierced the breast of their rearing horses. Sometimes they shot sacrilegious arrows through the half-undone tiara of your hair, like some tower overlooking snowfalls, and your flesh throbbed like a sleeping swan. I salute you in your divine past and in my soul, Foreign Woman, standing over ages hated by your peaceful, reproachful, mourning features, and I salute you in my inner radiant evenings for your pale face! III. Foreign Woman! Child of fate, the fairies' hope! The gesture of your hand, bearing the witch of Endor's flower, sends heroes to Glory or Death and designates them for the task of strangling wild beasts. Because of you, trophies are bought with blood, and flesh tenses as teeth bite it, and in the black wood, where the bow of ash still quivers, the smell of slaughter breaks out in gusts. If, in the vernal grass and wild celery, the conquering foot tramples outside its lair a wild sow or a she-wolf's pelt, the trumpet's cry in the evening, which tells of the tracery of ruby blood coloring the beast's horns, calls you, from the depths of the fabled past, to see the great severed head in the dejected killer's clenched fist! IV. Paint still heightens on her lips a touch of vanished intoxication, with its ardent, purpling, burning flame, and her smile is more melancholy than the sobbing, in the twilight, of a wounded man being taken off to die, bleeding and suffering, in the twilight. Age-old love laughed on your lips, O Living One; the echo of powerful desires, to which the flesh consents, and the heavy noons born for vibrant life poured their sunlight on your warm neck and shoulders, from which fell your streaming, living hair. Overwhelming intoxication is brief as a dream: full-blooded lips dried up by the consuming sun. The mysterious red lip-paint, which intensifies and prolongs such intoxication, smiles more wearily than a sterile evening in the empty sky, and the Living One is pale and melancholy like a dream. O enemy, strange dead woman, morose amazon, shadow of the forest, mask of adventure, for the sake of the invisible chimaera on the pointed golden helmet, once your hair, oh, go abjure your lie in the black waters of a mournful Styx! V. Why are you not the Exiled Woman or the Foreign Woman hiding under her ragged dress the treasure of an immortal gem, bearing witness of some star risen beyond the grave! The child's voice is sweet in her grandmothers' old songs, and the dead or slaughtered father's sword is becoming in the hands of wandering girls who roam alone, far from the bloody night when their souls wept. The wind has dispersed birds and dark clouds; leaves fly over the green and black river and pile up on the dreary sand of the barren shores, where iris in flower burst forth in the evening. Are you the Wayfarer on whom the star in the flowerless forest smiles? Are you bringing me under your wayfarer's rags the opal which the dark and jealous grotto took a hundred years to create, drop by drop, from its tears? If the sword is still the ornament of a trophy in which figures the gleaming opal held by three prongs together, what talisman is borne high in your fairy hair, that I should believe in your promise of a treasure? There is no sign that you are the one to whom the magic forest consecrates its marvelous trees and its triumphant peacocks, whose tails radiate shining eyes in an ecstacy of feathers? Who knows whether the dark waves like ripe grass will open their ripples before your divine feet? What matters that the only proof of it and presage is your simple beauty from the lands whence you came? Take my hand! Evening quiets the fateful water of the river, which we will enter like a tomb, until it rises to your pale smile... There is no talisman in her hair floating on the water!

## Motifs de légende et de mélancolie

### I

L'essieu des chars se brise à l'angle dur des tombes
Où nos âmes de jadis reviennent s'asseoir
Et des gestes qu'ont fui des exils de colombes
Jettent à pleines mains des roses au ciel noir.

Le crépuscule pleut un deuil d'heure et de cendre
Qui courbe les fronts pâles de cheveux trop lourds
Dont le poids mûr s'effondre et croule et va s'épandre
Sur la dalle où dorment les songes des vieux jours.

L'éternelle Toison, par delà les mers sombres,
Au fond des soirs, se dresse, étrange en son poil d'or,
Et les cornes d'émail allongent leurs deux ombres
Sur le flot fabuleux qui gronde et saigne encor.

Le flot saigne à jamais de l'éperon des proues
Qui coupaient le reflet des étoiles dans l'eau;
Le roc rompt la carène et la pierre les roues,
Et le vent à l'écueil pleure comme au tombeau.

Les Arianes, aux îles de fleurs et d'astres,
Qui veillaient dans la nuit sur leur sommeil fatal,
Attendent le Héros de leurs tristes désastres
Qui les doit reconduire au vieux Palais natal.

La Chimère accroupie aux gorges de l'attente
Crispe ses ongles durs où luit le sang des forts,
Et notre âme a tenté l'aventure éclatante
Du mensonge immortel pour qui d'autres sont morts.

Dormez, Princesses au manoir, nul cor, ô Mortes,
N'éveillera vos rêves et nul glaive clair
Ne heurtera de son pommeau vos hautes portes
Où le béryl magique incruste son éclair.

Le vent de la Mer vaste a déchiré les voiles
Des nefs que l'albe aurore égara vers la nuit,
Et l'essieu s'est brisé dans l'ombre sans étoiles;
La Licorne vers la forêt, d'un bond, a fui!

La Mémoire pleure sur la pierre des tombes,
Gloriole éternelle et très antique espoir,
Et ces songes sont comme un exil de colombes
Emportant à leurs becs des roses au ciel noir.


II

"Et la Belle s'endormit"

La Belle, dont le sort fut de dormir cent ans
Au jardin du manoir et dans le vaste songe
Où le cri né des clairons sacrés se prolonge
Pour sonner son sommeil jusqu'à l'aube des Temps!

La Belle, pour l'éveil victorieux d'antans
Que son intacte chair proclamera mensonge,
A chargé de joyaux sa main qui gît et plonge
En un flot de crinière où les doigts sont latents.

Et tandis que des toits, des tours et des tourelles
Les Colombes ont pris essor et qu'infidèles
Les Paons mystérieux ont fui vers la forêt,

Couchée auprès de la Dormeuse, la Licorne
Attend l'heure et là-bas guette si reparaît
L'annonciateur vol blanchir l'aurore morne!

                              "Et le Chevalier ne vint pas."
Les paons bleus l'ont cherché dans la forêt. Nul soir
N'a rougi son cimier d'ailes et de chimère,
Les Colombes blanches dont l'aurore est la mère
Ont vu la tour déserte et vide le manoir.

Et les Aïeux, dès jadis morts, n'eurent pas d'hoir
Avide d'aventure étrange et de mystère,
Nul héros à venir, pour l'honneur de la terre,
Vaincre d'un baiser le magique sommeil noir.

L'endormie à jamais étale ses mains pâles
Où verdit une mort annulaire d'opales;
Et la Princesse va mourir s'il ne vient pas.

Plus n'a souci, Nul, de dissoudre un sortilège,
Et la Licorne hennit rauque au ciel lilas
Où frissonne une odeur de mort, d'ombre et de neige.

                              "Et la Belle mourut"
La Licorne ruée en fuite hume et croise
Les vents qui du midi remontent vers le nord,
Et sa crinière éparse ruisselle et se tord
Que nattait de rubis la Princesse danoise.

Loin des glaciers et des neiges roses que boise
La verdure des pins où gronde comme un cor
L'écho du marteau lourd des Nains qui, forgeurs d'or,
Façonnent le hanap où l'on boit la cervoise,

La Princesse aux doux yeux de lac, d'astre et de mers,
Est morte, et la Bête fabuleuse à travers
Les gels glauques, la nuit vaste, l'aurore morne,

Folle d'avoir flairé les mains froides de mort,
Se cabre, fonce et heurte et coupe de sa corne
Les vents qui du midi remontent vers le nord!

### III

Ce fut par delà le fleuve aux rives d'iris
Que le vent agite en papillons d'hyacinthe
En un silence doux que je la conduisis,
Joyeuse du grelot d'un bracelet qui tinte.

L'étonnement de son regard parmi l'aurore
Etait au fleuve clair tout violet d'iris
Où s'aile en vol de fleurs la nuit pour fuir l'aurore,
Et la ville était belle où je la conduisis:

Aux escaliers d'onyx un lé d'antique soie,
Des paons veilleurs rouant des gloires de saphyr,
Des textes graves et des légendes de joie
Aux banderoles brusques de pourpre de Tyr!

La maison vide était sonore comme en rêve
Et j'entendais battre son coeur, tout bas, de joie
D'être vêtue ainsi selon un voeu de rêve
De robes d'or ouvré de rosaces de soie.

### IV

Errantes aux grèves des mers parmi les roches,
Leur grâce puérile minaude en reproches:

"Nous avons dans la mer trempé nos mains comme des folles
Et cueilli des bouquets d'écume et d'algues rousses;
Nos amants ont glané les fleurs de nos paroles
Et vont là-bas humant le miel des lèvres douces
Dont le parfum flotte au soir pavoisé de nos paroles!

Voici toute la mer qui croule aux plages douces
En floraison d'écume éparse et d'algues folles.

Nos beaux amoureux sont vêtus de soie et d'écarlate,
Ils ont des colliers d'ambre et des bagues d'opales

Et l'orgueil par un rire à leurs lèvres éclate
D'avoir cueilli l'aveu de nos avrils, fleurs pâles
Qu'ils portent en grappes aux pans de leur robe écarlate.

La mer déferle et pleure au long des grèves pâles
Et le rire des flots aux dents des rocs éclate.

Nous n'irons plus au bord des mers, nous n'irons plus, ô folles,
Sur les sables stellés de lagunes d'opales...
Les oiseaux de passage ont volé nos paroles
Qui parfumaient le soir ainsi que les fleurs pâles,
Les infidèles sont partis, nous n'irons plus, les folles!

Les saphyrs de nos yeux s'attristent en opales
Et l'écho des coeurs morts est sourd à nos paroles."

*

Ils ont heurté les portes d'or
Du pommeau rude de leurs glaives
Et leurs lèvres étaient encor
Amères de l'embrun des grèves.

Ils entrèrent comme des rois
En la ville où la torche fume,
Au trot sonnant des palefrois
Dont la crinière est une écume.

On les reçut en des palais
Et des jardins où les dallages
Sont des saphyrs et des galets
Comme on en trouve sur les plages;

On les abreuva de vin clair,
De louanges et de merveilles;
Et l'écho grave de la mer
Bourdonnait seul à leurs oreilles.

*

Elles diront quand, las des jardins de la ville,
Leurs amoureux appareilleront vers quelque île:

"Leur nef rasa de près les rocs du promontoire
Où ne plus rire fut toute notre tristesse
Et d'être assises en cette pose qui laisse
Pendre ses mains avec des brisements de lis,
Et leur départ hésite aux rocs du promontoire
Et s'enfonce en voguant aux occidents pâlis.

Vogue, ô Navire, et va sans nous chercher des îles
Mystérieuses où les grèves sont désertes;
Nos chevelures valaient les algues inertes
Que tressera, là-bas, l'ennui de leurs doigts las
D'avoir si loin ramé vers le port et les îles
Où les fruits doux mordus ne leur suffiront pas.

Et si quelque tempête un soir te désempare,
Tu n'auras pour franchir le piège des parages
Nos lourds cheveux à tordre en guise de cordages
Et nos chants pour calmer le tumulte des flots
Submergeurs des vaisseaux que le vent désempare,
Ni nos yeux pour guetter l'embûche des îlots.

Plus tard ils rêveront en l'exil misérable
A des retours vers nous vogués à toutes voiles,
Et nous serons pour eux des souvenirs d'étoiles
En le passé stellé du feu de nos yeux clairs.
Ils pleureront vers nous dans l'exil misérable
Comme on pleure à des levers d'astres sur les mers!"


                              V

La Vie étrange et douce et lente va mourir
En vigne qui s'effeuille au temps des grappes mûres.
La chevelure est toute aux prises du saphyr
Et le désir s'entrave aux boucles des ceintures.

La voix du vieil amour qui riait à l'aurore
Sanglote dans le soir et suffoque et larmoie,
Et la fontaine pleure en la forêt sonore
Encore des échos de notre antique joie.

La ceinture agrafe son étreinte mauvaise
Et de sa boucle griffe les robes meurtries,
L'aile du vent s'acharne en les cheveux où pèse
L'emprise d'ongles d'un joyau de pierreries.

Oh! dans l'aurore, après l'affre de la vigile
Où mon âme saigna son angoisse au désert,
La robe s'allongeait en rite d'Evangile
A l'entour des pieds nus et lavés par la Mer.

La terre d'ocre et de stérile Samarie
Fêta Celle qui vint, par miracle, sa joie!
Et le pli de sa robe étalée et fleurie
Secoua des roses prises parmi la soie.

Crispée en amas roux aux griffes d'un saphyr
Ruissela du joyau maître la chevelure
Et les seins divulgués jaillirent pour s'offrir
Au désir qui s'irrite au noeud de la ceinture.

Et l'amour a dormi sous l'averse des roses
Et nue et douce et plus rieuse qu'une enfant
En qui revit l'âme grave d'antiques choses
Qu'apporte du fond des vieux royaumes, le vent.

Le vent chargé d'exils, de songes et d'années
Et de voix mortes aux oublis de la mémoire...
Elle a dormi selon les vieilles destinées
Qui la voulaient soumise au gré de ma victoire.

Pour railler par échos la clarté de ses rires
Sourdirent des douceurs de flûte et de fontaines;
De glorifiantes et laudatrices Lyres
Chantèrent par delà les arbres de la plaine.

A travers ses cheveux épars dans le soleil,
J'ai vu monter des forêts hautes et des terres
Où passait dans le soir violet et vermeil
La harde des Désirs cabrés en Sagittaires,

A travers l'odeur chaude dont sa chair endort,
J'ai vu des ciels clairs où grimpaient des fleurs étranges
A vaincre d'un parfum la folle et vieille Mort
Titubant du vin bu de ses tristes vendanges.

La rumeur des grands flots aux caps des péninsules
Apaisés sous le soir et sous les vols d'oiseaux,
Fut au rythme de ses seins, et des crépuscules
Stellèrent vaguement ses yeux larges et beaux.

L'antique Samarie où pria ma vigile
Sur la terre déserte et sous les oliviers,
A fleuri son miracle à la voix d'Evangile
Qui vint du pays des Songes émerveillés.

Le vent a balayé les roses éphémères
Au marais par le soir élargis dans les nues;
Les joyaux aigus sont des griffes de Chimères
Et les boucles des dents de Bêtes inconnues;

La robe lourde et longue et grave est une armure
Et l'or des cheveux roux un casque de guerrière;
Le désir s'entrave aux boucles de la ceinture
Qui s'agrafe en rigueurs d'étreinte meurtrière.

L'ample robe a vêtu d'un mystère vorace
La chair nue à jamais pour mon rêve et reprend
Sa rigidité de hiératique cuirasse
Où darde le soleil futile et fulgurant;

Et le vent de l'Automne exfolie et saccage
La vigne nue et jusques vers la Mer emporte
Le sanglot éperdu qui pleure le passage
De Celle qui s'en va parmi la Forêt morte.

## VI

Les fleurs sont mortes sous ses pas
De la plaine aux collines pâles
Et le ciel est d'un rose las
Comme les roses automnales,

Les fleurs sont mortes en ses mains
De la maison aux jardins pâles
Et le vent chasse à pleins chemins
Un tiède sang de purs pétales.

La voici seule et nue en le soir de mon songe!
Les oiseaux en passant sur sa tête ont pleuré,
Le vent en emportant sa voix douce a pleuré,
La source en reflétant son visage a pleuré;
Elle va seule et nue en le soir de mon songe.

La porte est fermée et les fenêtres,
Et nul phare de lampe aux vitres mortes
Et la maison, parmi les vieux hêtres,
A la tristesse des demeures sans maîtres,
Et dans le puits on a jeté la clef des portes.

Les grands Cerfs roux viendront flairer aux serrures
Et fuir au bruit léger des faînes sur le toit,
Et les oiseaux mangeront seuls les grappes mûres
Comme de lourds rubis au manteau d'un vieux roi.

Je sais la forêt sombre où s'en va l'enfant nue;
Sa main est froide encor du cuivre du heurtoir,
Etrangère qu'ont méconnue
La maison taciturne et l'hôte sans espoir.

Les vents accroupis comme des chiens voraces
Du seuil des antres sourds hurleront sur ses pas
Et pour la Fille en pleurs des royales terrasses
Les Portes du palais ne se rouvriront pas;

Ses las cheveux en proie aux souffles du ciel morne
Flotteront dans l'aurore et le soir, à jamais!
La forêt et le mont où la lune s'écorne
Ignoreront le prix de leurs ors parfumés.

Le triste Maître de la maison déserte pleure;
La hêtraie immobile ou folle, selon l'heure,
Se balance ou s'endort, s'apaise ou murmure;
Une à une les faînes tombent sur les toits,
Les grappes s'égrènent dans l'herbe mûre,
Et par la vitre, vers le bois
Et la plaine et le jardin que la mousse ronge,
Le triste Maître en deuil du mal de quelque songe
Regarde et songe:

"En l'antique forêt des hêtres et des houx
Sur qui le crépuscule expire en mort de mauves,
Les arbres bercent sur les branches des hiboux
Dardant une pierrerie étrange d'yeux fauves.

Forêt vaste qui croît sur ma terre de songe,
Cache au moins dans ta vie un pan du dur tombeau
Où gît ce que mon âme a cru du vieux mensonge
Et mêle l'aube et l'ombre à mon rêve plus beau.

Si les anciens désirs volent de cime en cime
Avec de longs cris doux de tristesse et de nuit,
Epanche la douceur de tes voix unanimes
Sur la maison déserte à qui quelque astre a nui.

Hélas! les arbres sont hantés comme mon âme
Et des yeux vigilants s'irritent dans le soir,
Et voici par le bois où le cerf rôde et brame
Luire des griffes d'or en le feuillage noir."

## VII

Que t'importe? Je sais le mot, le charme et le signe!
Les bois clairs sont oisifs de brises et d'oiseaux
Et les grappes des hautes vignes
S'égrènent, une à une, dans les eaux
Tranquilles où dans les roseaux
Dorment les cygnes.

Les loups méchants dans les chemins de ma forêt
Fuiront furtifs et roux comme mes vieilles haines;
Ma mémoire pareille aux fontaines
Oubliera le passé qui s'y mirait
Pour y pleurer ses peines
Avec sa pâle face de Geneviève aux tristes Ardennes
Parmi l'exil de la forêt.

Les biches blanches qui broutent l'ache et le cytise
Et grimpent aux rochers de mousse et sont rieuses
De gaîtés mystérieuses
Viendront, selon tes clairs regards qui les motivent,
Manger en mes mains oisives
A l'ombre des saules ensoleillés et des yeuses.

Ton regard n'est-il pas tous les passés en moi,
Ta voix tous les oiseaux du bois qui dort
Et garde un lac de mort
Sous les grappes s'y égrenant, une à une, en rides d'émoi?
Celui qui t'exila dans les grottes du Nord
C'était Moi,
Puisque je sais le mot, le signe et l'endroit
Où paissent dans la nuit les palefrois,
Nous reviendrons un jour vers le Palais du Roi!

## VIII

Ce vent triste qui vient du fleuve et des prairies
En aromes de fleurs, d'îles et d'oseraies,
Et qui passe à travers les arbres des futaies,
Où veut-il donc mourir las de ses rôderies,
Vent de prés et d'arbres
Qui chuchote aux lèvres de mousse des vieux marbres,
Voix en exode, voix en peine et vague?

Il était un bois noir, comme une âme, ombre et songe.

Les mille feuilles en coeurs vivants des lierres,
Jours d'antan clairs et brefs comme des clairières,
Mousses du vieux silence aux lèvres qu'elles rongent,
Ruisseaux qu'on suit longtemps sans les voir
A leur murmure sous les branches,
Chênes plus vieux que le manoir
Au bout de l'avenue issu, dormant et noir,
Avec les filles du vieux Seigneur en robes blanches!

Le vent aux feuilles déjà rousses papillonne,
Le vent aux feuilles a des soupirs de vierge,
Les glaïeuls défleurissent leur flamme de cierge;
Le vent va-t-il mourir en la forêt d'automne?

Il courbe les fléoles et les hautes herbes
Et semble une main qui flatte des cheveux fins.
Ah! notre meule était toute de bonnes gerbes
Et nos greniers d'hiver lourds d'orges et de grain
Et les gais étains clairs riaient à notre faim.

Le vent agite follement les campanules
De la fenêtre ouverte aux fièvres du lit blanc.
Souvenances des passés en fleurs carillonnant,
Troupeaux du doux jadis au gué bêlant,
Et les voix de la barque nous hélant...

Du fond du vent et de parmi les crépuscules.


## IX

Un si pâle pastel qu'il semble être un miroir
Où tu fus rose et blonde et douce, et qu'un espoir
De sourire illumine en sa poudre ancienne;

Une fleur en un cristal noir
Où semble avoir brûlé par la magicienne
Le vieux philtre d'amour qui rend pâle au miroir.

Un satin froid qui meurt sa flore cueillie
En des Jardins que savaient les Tisseurs du vieux temps
Casse à ses grands plis durs les lys et les glaïeuls
Au dossier des fauteuils
Etoffe vaine, faux printemps
Dont s'était parée, ô Jolie,
Ta folie
D'avoir ri de ces lèvres de fruits éclatants.

Un fin collier qui pleure en perles, une à une,
Sur le tapis et roule en grêle jusqu'au parquet
Où miroite un lac de cygnes enfuis la lune,
Et le fard, l'éventail, la mule et le bouquet.

Pastel, fleurs et satin, collier, et la mémoire
Des roses de la barque éparses sur l'eau noire
Qui mire le tombeau de bronze et de basalte,
C'est tout ce qui demeure et tout ce qui s'exalte
Du grand délice mort par qui mon âme est chaste.


# X

Au royaume oublié des Nefs et des Vigies,
Les grands Oiseaux plus lents que les vagues
Rasent la côte avec des ailes élargies
Et cherchent la Morte dont les bagues
Luisent au sable qui couvre ses mains pâlies.

Le flot de la Mer n'a plus d'écume,
Les roses s'ouvrent comme des lèvres mortes
Sans espoir de quelque Avril posthume
Où refleurir encor les vitres et les portes
Du palais-perdu parmi la brume.

Flot sans écume et crépuscule aux ailes lasses
Dont l'ombre est légère aux grèves d'ombre
Et flûte suraiguë à l'angle des terrasses,
Dont l'ombre déborde aux jardins d'ombre
Où les clefs sont aux serrures des portes basses.

## XI

Des songes du plus beau des soirs
Rien ne survit en l'aube aride
Qui ne montra dans les miroirs
Que sa morte pâleur d'Armide.

Jardins, portiques de portor,
Iles, eaux, fleurs, grottes, prairies
Où les paons gardaient un trésor
Dont ils semblaient les pierreries.

Le sortilège enseveli,
Cendres sans phénix par la flamme,
Isole sous le ciel pâli
La face triste de la femme.

Voici mort le royaume faux
Croupir en la nuit ancienne.
Tombez, sourires triomphaux
Et fard de la Magicienne.

Des songes du plus beau des soirs,
O victime et dépositaire,
Confronte à tes mornes miroirs
Un éveil d'Amant solitaire!

*Poèmes anciens et romanesques*

## Legendary and Melancholic Themes

I. The axle of the chariots breaks against the hard corner of the tombs, where our former souls have come back to sit; and with those gestures which sent into exile fleeing doves, they cast handfuls of roses into the black sky. Twilight weeps mournful, ashen evening tears, bending brows pale and heavy with hair, which, with its ripe weight, tumbles and pours down, spreading over the marble floor under which sleep the dreams of the old days. The eternal Fleece, beyond the dark seas, deep in the evening, rises up, a strange sight with its golden wool. And the enamel horns cast their two long shadows over the fabulous, roaring, and still bleeding sea. The waves bleed forever from the spur on the prows which once cut the reflection of stars in the water. A rocky shoal breaks the keel, and stone shatters the wheels; wind over the reef weeps as over a grave. Ariadnes on isles of flowers and stars, who kept watch at night over their destined sleep, are awaiting the Hero of their sad disasters, who is to lead them back to their old native palaces. The Chimaera crouching expectant in gorges curls its hard nails shining with the blood of the strong. And our souls have attempted the immortal lie's famous adventure, in which others have died. Sleep in your manor, dead Princesses; no horn will wake you from dreams, and no bright sword will beat with its pommel against your high gates incrusted with magic beryl's glint. The vast seawind has torn the sails on the ships which white dawn led off course toward night, and the axle broke in the starless shadow. With one bound, the unicorn has fled toward the forest. II. "And the Beauty Fell Asleep." The beauty— whose fate it was to sleep a hundred years in the manor garden, with her dream in which the sacred trumpets still echoed, to prolong her sleep till the dawn of time—the beauty, for the victorious awakening that long ago was to have happened and which her still intact flesh proclaims to have been a false prophecy, had laden her hand with jewels, her hand lying covered and hidden by her long mane. And while from roofs, towers, and turrets the doves have flown away and the faithless and mysterious peacocks fled toward the forest, the unicorn, lying by the sleeping princess's side, awaits the hour of wakening and watches in the distance for the annunciatory flight of doves whitening the dawn. "And the Knight Did Not Come." The blue peacocks looked for him in the forest. No evening light reddened the wings and dream beast on his crest. The white doves, children of dawn, have only seen the tower deserted and the manor empty. And the ancestors, dead long ago, had no heir eager for strange adventure and mystery; there was no hero to come and do the world honor by releasing with a kiss the black magic slumber. The sleeping princess spreads forever her pale hands, where death takes the form of an opal ring, turning green, and the princess is going to die if he does not come. There is no one who cares to break the spell, and the unicorn hoarsely whinnies at the lilac sky, where quivers an odor of death, shadow, and snow. "And the Beauty Died." The unicorn fleeing at a gallop smells and passes through the winds rising from the south to the north, and its sparse mane streams and tangles, which once the Danish princess braided with rubies. Far from the glaciers and pink snow wooded with green firs, where like a horn roars the heavy hammer of gold-forging dwarfs, fashioning the mead-drinkers' cup, far from here the princess with gentle eyes like lake, star, or sea has died; and the fabulous unicorn passing through green ice floes, vast night, and mournful dawn, frantic from having smelled death on her cold hands, rears, charges, and beats with its horn against the winds rising from south to north. III. Beyond the river and its banks of iris, looking like hyacinthine butterflies as they waved in the wind, in a gentle silence I led her, and she was happy with the tinkling bell on her bracelet. Her eyes in the dawn were astonished at the bright river violet with iris, where winged night flees from dawn in a flight of flowers, and the city to which I led her was beautiful. There were hangings of antique silk on the onyx staircases, vigilant peacocks spreading their glorious tails of sapphire, solemn texts and joyous legends inscribed on flapping pennants of Tyrian purple. The empty house echoed as in a dream, and I heard her heart beat softly with joy at being dressed, as if to satisfy a dreamed-of wish, in gold robes embroidered with silk rose patterns. IV. As they wander among the rocks on the seashore, they make mincing reproaches in their childishly graceful way: "We have dipped our hands in the sea like madwomen and gathered bouquets of foam and reddish seaweed! Our lovers have gathered the flowers of our words, and go off with the scent in their nostrils of sweet honeyed lips, whose smell drifts through the evening bedecked with our words! Now the whole sea is spreading out on the sweet shores with scattered flowers of foam and wild seaweed. Our handsome lovers are dressed in silk and scarlet; they have amber necklaces and opal rings, and on their lips pride bursts forth in laughter, pride at having gathered the avowal of our April, pale flowers which they wear in clusters on the skirts of their scarlet robes. The sea unfolds its waves and weeps along the pale strand, and the waves' laughter breaks forth in the rocks' teeth. We shall never again, madwomen that we are, we shall never again go along the seashore, on the sands starred with opal lagoons. The passing birds have stolen our words which perfumed the evening like pale flowers; the faithless lovers have left, and we shall go no more like madwomen to the sea. Our sapphire eyes grow opalescent in sadness, and the echo of dead hearts does not answer our words." The men knocked on golden gates with the rough pommel of their swords, and their lips were still bitter with the salt spray of the strand. They entered like kings in the city with its smoking torches, with the ringing trot of their horses, whose mane is like foam. They were welcomed in palaces and gardens paved with sapphires and smooth rocks such as are found on the shore. They were given in abundance bright wine, praise, and marvelous entertainments. And the deep echo of the sea alone rang in their ears. The madwomen will say, when, tired of the city's gardens, their lovers set forth toward some island:

"Their ship grazed the jutting rocks where our whole sadness was expressed in not laughing, in sitting in a posture with our hands hanging like broken lilies, and they hesitate to set forth from the jutting rocks and to sink with their sails into the pale west. Sail, O ship, and without us seek for mysterious islands with empty shores. Our hair was more precious than the lifeless seaweed which they will plait with their tired fingers on those islands, weary at having rowed toward a harbor and islands whose sweet fruit, once tasted, will not satisfy them. And if some storm some evening strips your ship of its riggings, you will not be able to cross the treacherous water to the shore by twisting our heavy hair to serve as ropes, and you will not have our song to calm the tumultuous waves, which sink ships stripped of their riggings, nor our eyes to watch for half-concealed islets. Later in their wretched exile, they will dream of returning toward us at full sail, and we shall be for them like the memory of stars in the past, gleaming with the light of our bright eyes. In their wretched exile they will weep toward us, as one weeps when stars rise over the sea." V. Life, strange and sweet and slow, is going to end, like a vine losing its leaves when the grapes are ripe. Her hair is caught by a sapphire clasp, and desire for her is checked by belt buckles. The voice of old love, which laughed at dawn, sobs in the evening and chokes and weeps, and the fountain in the sonorous forest still weeps with the echoes of our old joy. The belt tightens its evil embrace and with its buckle has its claws in the wounded robe! The wind's wing tears at her hair weighed down by the clutching nails of an ornament of gems. Oh in the dawn, after the horrible vigil when my soul bled with anguish in the desert, the robe spread out, as in some rite from the Gospel, around her bare feet laved by the sea! Ochreous and sterile Samaria grew festive around her, its joy, when she miraculously came. And from the fold of her robe, flowing and florid, fell roses caught in the silk. Held tight in reddish piles by a sapphire clasp, suddenly her hair streamed from the jeweler's masterwork; and her breasts became visible and burst forth in response to desires held in check and sharpened by the belt's knot. And love has slept under a shower of roses, naked and sweet and laughing more than a child in whom relives the grave soul of ancient things which the wind brings from the depths of old kingdoms—the wind bearing exiles, dreams, years, and voices dead in the forgetful memory. She has slept in accordance with the old decrees of destiny which willed her submissive, as my victory demanded. To mock in echoes the brightness of her laugh, there arose the sweetness of flutes and springs. Glorifying and praising lyres sang

beyond the trees on the plain. Through her hair loose in the sun I saw
rise high forests and lands where in the gold and violet evening there
passed by the herd of desires rearing like centaurs. Through the hot
soporific odor of her flesh I saw bright skies with strange climbing
flowers such as to vanquish with their scent crazy old death, staggering
from the wine of his sad grape harvest. The roar of the great waves
around the peninsular headlands, grown quiet in the evening under
flights of birds, matched the rhythm of her breasts, and twilight put
vague stars in her large beautiful eyes. Ancient Samaria, where I prayed
in my vigil on the deserted earth and under the olive trees, has flowered
in a miracle at the voice of the Gospel which came from the land of
astonished dreams. The wind has swept away the ephemeral roses in
the lakes opened in the clouds by evening. The sharp jewels are the
claws of Chimaeras, and the buckles are the teeth of unknown beasts.
The long and heavy and solemn robe is a suit of armor and the golden
red hair an amazon's helmet. Desire is checked by the belt buckles
hooked tight in a murderous embrace. The ample robe has clad with
devouring mystery the flesh forever bare in my dream and takes on
again the stiffness of a priestly breastplate, with the sharp glints of a
futile and brilliant sun. And the autumn wind rips and strips the leaves
from the bare vine, and, as far as the sea, carries off the wild sob weep-
ing the passing of her who goes off now into the dead forest. VI. The
flowers died under her steps from the plain to the pale hills, and the sky
is a weary pink like autumn roses. The flowers died in her hands from
the house to the pale gardens, and the wind fills the paths with warm
pure bloodlike petals. She is now alone and naked in the evening of my
dream! Passing birds have wept over her head; the wind carrying off
her voice wept; the spring reflecting her face wept. She goes alone and
naked in the evening of my dream. The door is closed and the win-
dows. And no lamp serves as a guide in the dead windows, and the
house, among the old beech trees, has the sadness of a masterless dwell-
ing, and in the well the door key has been thrown. The great red stags
will come sniff at the locks and flee at the light sound of beechnuts
dropping on the roof, and birds alone will eat the ripe grapes like heavy
rubies on a king's old mantle. I know the dark forest into which the
naked child goes. Her hand is still cold from the touch of the copper
knocker. She is a stranger whom the silent house and hopeless master
have refused to recognize. The winds, crouching like hungry dogs, will
roar after her from the entrance of their dull-echoing caves. And for the
weeping girl from the royal terraces the palace gates will not open

again. Her weary hair disarrayed by gusts in the dreary sky will blow about in the dawn and evening forever! The mountain and forest where the moon wanes will never know the treasure of her perfumed hair. The sad master of the deserted house weeps. The beech grove motionless or wild, according to the hour, waves in the wind or sleeps, grows quiet or murmurs. One by one the beechnuts fall on the roofs; the grapes fall one by one in the ripe grass; and through the window, toward the wood and the plain and the garden invaded by moss, the sad Master mourning from some dream, gazes and plunges into revery: "In the ancient forest of beech and holly, over which the twilight dies like dying mallows, trees rock owls in their branches, whose wild eyes dart like some living gem. O vast forest growing in my dreamland, in your living midst conceal at least in part the grave of what of the ancient lie my soul believed! and mingle dawn and shadow with my most beautiful dream. If ancient desires flutter from treetop to treetop, with their long sweet cries of sadness and night, pour forth the sweetness of your blended voices over the deserted house, ruined by some star! Alas the trees are haunted like my soul, and watching eyes grow excited in the evening; and now in the wood where the stag roams and bellows, golden claws are gleaming in the black foliage." VII. What does it matter? I know the word, the spell, and the sign. The bright woods are idle under the breezes and birds, and the grapes on the high vines are dropping one by one in the calm water where swans sleep in the reeds. The wicked wolves in my forest paths will flee, furtive and red, like my old hatreds. My memory, like the springs, will forget the past once reflected there and will weep in the springs over its troubles, like pale-faced Genevieve of Brabant in the sad Ardennes, in the midst of her forest exile. The white does who feed on wild celery and laburnum and clamber on the mossy rocks and frolic with a mysterious gaiety will come, as your bright eyes move them, to eat in my idle hands, in the shadow of sunny willows and ilex. Is not your look all the pasts within me, your voice, all the birds of the sleeping wood with its death lake rippling with excitement under the grapes falling one by one? It was I who exiled you to the northern grottoes. Since I know the word, sign, and spot where palfreys pass in the night, we shall return one day toward the King's palace. VIII. Where will this wind die, weary of roaming, sad wind from the river and meadows with the odor of flowers, islands, and willow groves, passing through clusters of trees, a wind of meadows and trees, whispering in the moss lips of old tombstones, an exiled wind, in travail and wandering? There was a

black wood, like a soul, all shadow and dream. The thousand leaves,
like living hearts, of the ivy; bright, short days of yesteryear like clear-
ings in a forest; the mosses of old silence on the lips they eat away at;
invisible streams you follow for a long time by their murmuring sound
under the branches; oaks older than the manor house appearing at the
end of the avenue of trees, the house sleeping and black with the
daughters of the old lord in white dresses. The wind flutters in
the already russet leaves; the wind in the leaves sighs like a virgin; the
gladioli have lost their flower like the flame of a taper; will the wind die
in the autumn forest? It bends down the timothy and the high grass and
seems like a hand caressing fine hair. Ah, for our mill we took only the
best of the harvest, and our winter granaries were heavy with barley
and wheat, and bright pewter welcomed us at meals. The wind wildly
shakes the bellflowers, from the open window to the fever-ridden white
bed. Recollections of past days ringing in bellflowers, the flocks of
sweet yesteryear bleating at the ford, and the voices hailing us from the
boat. From the deep reaches of the wind and from within the twilight.
IX. A pastel so pale it seems like a mirror in which you were pink and
blond and gentle, a pastel illuminated in its ancient chalk by the hope of
a smile; a flower in a black crystal vase in which the sorceress seems to
have burnt the old love philter which makes the image in the pastel-
mirror seem pale. A cold, dying satin, whose flowers were once
gathered in the gardens known to the weavers of old, breaks, as it falls
in hard folds, the lilies and gladioli against the chairbacks. Vain cloth,
false spring, with which, pretty one, your folly adorned itself, your
folly of laughing with lips like bursting fruit. A delicate necklace weeps
its pearls one by one onto the carpet and rolls like tiny hailstones as far
as the parquet, where gleams the reflection of a lake of swans fled from
the moon, and the rouge, the fan, the slipper, and the bouquet. Pastel,
flowers, and satin, necklace, and the memory of roses from the boat
scattered on the black water in which the tomb of bronze and basalt is
reflected—that is all that remains, exalted in my memory, of the great
dead delight which makes my soul chaste. X. In the kingdom forgotten
by ships and men in crow's-nests, the great birds slower than waves
graze along the coast with widespread wings and seek the dead one
whose rings gleam in the sand covering her hands. The sea wave has no
more foam; roses open like dead lips without hope of any posthumous
April in which color would return to the panes and gates of the palace
lost in the fog. Foamless wave and weary-winged twilight, whose
shadow is light on the shadowy strand, and high-pitched flute at the

corner of the terraces, whose shadow pours into the shadowy gardens, where the key remains in the garden gates. XI. Of the dreams of the most beautiful evening nothing survives in the arid dawn, which in the mirrors revealed nothing but its dead Armida-like pallor. Gardens, black and green marble porticoes, islands, water, flowers, grottoes, meadows, where the peacocks guarded a treasure of which they themselves seemed the gems. The vanished spell, ashes from which no phoenix will arise, isolates under the pale sky the sad face of the woman. The false kingdom is dead and buried in ancient night. Fall, triumphant smiles, and fall the sorceress Armida's painted face! From the dreams of the most beautiful of evenings, O victim and repository, rise and confront your solitary lover's awakening in the dismal mirrors.

# EPHRAIM MIKHAEL

## Le Mage

C'est fini: tout le jour les chevaux des Barbares
Ont marché dans le sang des Mages massacrés,
Et des clairons vainqueurs insultent de fanfares
Les portiques du temple et les jardins sacrés.

Dans les champs lumineux et parfumés de menthes,
Au fond des bois hantés d'aegipans et de dieux,
Les flèches des castrats ont percé les amantes;
Les muets ont vaincu les rois mélodieux.

Voici qu'ils sont tombés, les beaux gardiens du Verbe
Qui veillaient le trésor des secrets fabuleux.
On les a prosternés la face contre l'herbe
Pour ravir à leur mort l'amitié des soirs bleus.

Et des mains de bouffons se traînent sur la lyre;
Les hymnes sont souillés par des voix de valets,
Et tous, chiens offusqués par le nard et la myrrhe,
Hurlent d'horreur devant la splendeur des palais.

Fugitif et donnant à la terre natale
La bénédiction de son sang précieux,
Le survivant de la tribu sacerdotale,
Le dernier des voyants jette un cri vers les cieux.

"Dieu de la nuit, le ciel est plein de mauvais astres
Dont le regard haineux fait mourir les cités.
Voici le jour sanglant des suprêmes désastres,
Et je vous parle seul dans des champs dévastés.

"Cependant, comme au soir des jeunes allégresses,
Je m'enivre en fuyant des parfums vespéraux,
Et le coeur tout meurtri de divines tendresses,
J'ai peur de pardonner, Seigneur! à mes bourreaux.

"Je suis le prisonnier de la forêt magique;
J'adore malgré moi les horribles vergers
Dont les rameaux ont bu dans le printemps tragique
Le sang mystérieux des justes égorgés.

"Et je souffre d'aimer encor la gloire infâme
De la terre déchue et du ciel avili.
Je pleure de sentir descendre sur mon âme
Comme une brume d'or le pacifique oubli.

"O mon Dieu! sauvez-moi des fleurs crépusculaires
Et laissez-moi m'enfuir des pays bien aimés.
Je veux savoir la joie immense des colères,
La royale rancoeur des lions enfermés.

"Comme un chasseur qui vient raviver sous sa lance
L'ancienne cruauté des monstres endormis,
Irritez-moi, troublez ma bonne somnolence,
Que je puisse à la fin haïr mes ennemis.

"Et quand ils sortiront des demeures pillées,
Emplissez-moi le coeur de désirs ténébreux,
Pour que je veuille enfin, de mes mains réveillées,
Faire crouler les rocs des montagnes sur eux."

Il dit; et le jour vient, et le honteux cortège
Des étrangers remplit la plaine et le ravin;
Et le conquérant dort, stupide, sur le siège
Du char royal sali de poussière et de vin.

Mais ces hommes sont beaux sous le soleil qui dore
Les cuirasses de bronze et les riches cimiers
Dans la campagne en fleurs où le vent de l'aurore
Incline devant eux les lys et les palmiers.

Alors, respectueux et doux, le dernier Mage,
Contemplant les chevaux cabrés dans la moisson,
Semble un vieux serviteur courbé pour rendre
    hommage
Au maître vénéré qui rentre en sa maison:

"Salut, voleurs épris de gloires insensées,
Lachés dans les blés mûrs comme de lourds taureaux!
Gloire à vous, meurtriers des blanches fiancées,
Car le soleil levant vous égale aux héros.

"Vous chevauchez pareils aux dompteurs des
    Chimères,
Aux blonds libérateurs des princesses en deuil,
Et plus haut que le bruit des peuples éphémères
Vous faites résonner le cri de votre orgueil.

"Et les hommes, au fond de leurs villes lointaines,
Troublés par la rumeur de vos chars merveilleux,
Vous prêteront, muets, des paroles hautaines,
Castrats, vous salueront comme de grands aïeux.

"Allez! moi seul, j'ai vu vos mauvaises épées;
Seul je sais le secret de votre coeur banal.
Mais je veux être aussi pour les foules trompées
Complice de l'aurore et du vent matinal.

"Je veux laisser en paix la splendeur des mensonges
Eclore sous les pieds de vos chevaux impurs;
Car vous êtes élus pour passer dans les songes,
Car le destin vous livre aux aèdes futurs.

"Et vaincu je bénis les ennemis immondes,
Puisque aux appels de leurs clairons retentissants
Un éphèbe surgit à l'orient des mondes,
Qui sacrera leur roi par les rhythmes puissants."

Il parle ainsi, tendant sans haine des mains calmes;
Et dans les champs, émus d'un frisson de réveil,
Parmi les gerbes d'or et les tranquilles palmes,
Ces brutes, dieux nouveaux, marchent vers le soleil.

*Oeuvres*

## The Priest

It is over: all day long the Barbarians' horses have stepped in the blood of the massacred priests, and conquering trumpets now insult with their fanfares the porticoes of the temple and the sacred gardens. In the brilliant fields smelling of mint, deep in the woods where gods and aegypans lurk, the castrates' arrows have pierced women in love; mutes have conquered the melodious kings. Now they have fallen, splendid guardians of the Word, who watched over the treasure of fabulous secrets. They have been stretched out with their faces against the grass to take away from their dying moment the sympathy of the blue evening. And buffoons' hands fumble on the lyre; hymns are sullied by valets' voices. And all of them, like dogs repelled by myrrh and spikenard, howl in horror before the splendid palaces. Like a fugitive, giving his fatherland the blessing of his precious blood, the survivor of the priestly tribe, the last of the seers, cries out toward the heavens. "God of night, the sky is filled with evil stars, whose hateful glance kills cities. This is the bloody day of the ultimate disaster, and I speak to you alone in ravaged fields. Nevertheless, as on the nights of youthful joy, I intoxicate myself, though in flight, with evening scents, and, because my heart is bruised by divine inspirations of tenderness, I am afraid, Lord, of pardoning my tormentors. I am a prisoner of the magic forest; despite myself, I worship the horrible orchards, in which the tree branches drank, in this tragic spring, the mysterious blood of the slaughtered just. And I am pained that I still love the dishonored glory of the earth depraved and of heaven debased. I weep when I feel peaceful oblivion descend into my soul like a golden mist. O my God, save me from the twilight flowers and let me flee from these beloved lands. I want to learn the immense joy of anger, the royal rancor of caged lions. Like a huntsman who comes to reawaken with his lance the old cruelty of sleeping monsters, exasperate me, disturb my satisfying drowsiness, so that I can finally hate my enemies. And when they will emerge from pillaged dwellings, fill my heart with shadowy desires, so I will want to roll mountain rocks down on them with my two revived hands." He spoke and day comes, and the shameful procession of foreigners fills the plain and the ravine. And the conqueror sleeps, in a stupor, on the seat of the royal chariot sullied with dust and wine. But these men are beautiful under the sun, which gilds the bronze cuirasses and rich crests in the flowering countryside, where the dawn wind bows down the lilies and palm trees before them. Then, respectful and mild, the last priest, gazing at the horses rearing in the harvest, seems like some old servant bowing to do homage to his venerated master on his return home. "I salute you, thieves enamoured of demented and glorious projects, running wild in the ripe wheat like great bulls! Glory to you, assassins of pale betrothed maidens, for the dawn sun has raised you to the place of heroes. You ride like chimaera tamers, like liberators of mourning princesses, and louder than the murmur of ephemeral peoples you make your cry of glory echo. And men within their distant cities, disturbed by the sound of your marvelous chariots, will attribute to you, though you are mute, haughty speeches, and greet you, who are castrated, as great ancestors. Come, I alone have seen your evil swords; I alone know the secret of your dreary hearts. But I also want to be, for the deluded throngs, the abettor of dawn and the morning breeze. I want to let the splendor of lies peacefully open like flowers under the hooves of your profane horses; for you are chosen to figure in dreams, and destiny will set you before future rhapsodists. Though conquered, I bless my foul enemies, because, at the call of the echoing trumpets, a youth is rising in the east of the cosmos, who will consecrate their king in powerful rhythms." Thus he speaks, stretching forth his calm hands without hatred, and in the fields, excited by their tremulous awakening, among the golden sheaves and peaceful palms, these brutes, the new gods, march toward the sun.

# Florimond

Les tueurs de dragons et les rois chevaliers
Dont le pennon de pourpre est brodé d'une guivre
Heurtèrent tout le jour avec de lourds béliers
Le rempart de sardoine et la porte de cuivre.

Ils se pressaient devant la magique prison
Où leur frère asservi s'enivre d'amours vaines.
Les chars guerriers lâchés sur le calme gazon
Fauchaient au loin les fleurs de sauge et de verveines.

Les durs soldats campés dans les champs saccagés
Meurtrissaient pesamment l'herbe surnaturelle:
Les hérauts effrayaient de leurs cris étrangers
Les fabuleux oiseaux qui gardaient la tourelle.

Et des cavaliers dans l'occident enflammé,
Secouant les crins d'or des casques héroïques,
Semblaient en élevant au ciel leur bras armé
Attiser le soir rouge avec leurs longues piques.

Des troupeaux de lions et des griffons domptés
Leur faisaient une horrible et fastueuse escorte.
Des tigres bondissaient sous leurs fouets enchantés,
Et des lionnes se ruèrent sur la porte.

Maintenant les guerriers anxieux et les rois,
Las d'assaillir en vain des pierres merveilleuses,
Du haut de la colline appellent par trois fois
Le prince prisonnier des fleurs victorieuses.

"Nous sommes, disent-ils, tes frères oubliés,
Ceux que ta voix, pareille au clairon des archanges,
Guidait jadis, par les landes et les halliers,
Vers la moisson guerrière et les rouges vendanges.

"Souvent, quand tu chantais tes puissantes chansons,
Nous vîmes dans le ciel de la nuit froide et noire
Au loin resplendir l'or fabuleux des toisons,
Et nous sentions dans l'air une odeur de victoire.

"C'est toi qui nous menais délivrer des cités;
Et debout sur ton char constellé d'améthystes,
Tu nous montrais les grands pays épouvantés
Par les sphinx accroupis sur les collines tristes.

"Et pourtant te voici prisonnier! Et tes mains,
Tes folles mains, laissant tomber l'epée ancienne,
Effeuillent des glaïeuls frêles et des jasmins
Dans les cheveux épars de la magicienne.

"O frère, nous venions rompre l'enchantement,
Te sauver des jardins et des honteuses roses,
Mais nous sommes vaincus mystérieusement;
Toi seul, tu peux ouvrir les belles portes closes.

"Prince, prince captif dans les vergers impurs,
Prince qui dors auprès des fontaines fleuries,
N'entends-tu pas devant tes tours, devant tes murs,
La royale rumeur de nos cavaleries?

"Souviens-toi des chemins rudes que nous foulions
Joyeusement au bruit des conques éclatantes,
Et de nos camps sacrés veillés par des lions,
Et des sommeils virils sous les loyales tentes.

"Viens! le vent de la plaine et l'embrun de la mer
Ont de meilleurs parfums que les fleurs des parterres.
Viens! tu respireras encor le charme amer
Des farouches forêts et des grèves austères.

"Evade-toi! Secoue, en franchissant le seuil,
Tous tes désirs ainsi qu'une infâme poussière,
Et chasse de ton coeur, jadis riche d'orgueil,
L'inavouable amour de la Reine sorcière."

Ils disent; dans le soir, de sauvages senteurs
Montent des bois et des campagnes endormies,
Et vers les hauts remparts les rois libérateurs
Tendent leurs étendards et leurs armes amies.

Mais voici que, penché sur les balcons en fleurs,
D'un geste de ses mains indulgentes et lasses,
Le doux captif épris de divines douleurs
Ecarte ces guerriers des paisibles terrasses:

"Hommes, pourquoi ce bruit d'armes et de buccins?
Ma féerique prison est à jamais fermée;
Je ne veux plus vers les chemins libres et sains
Ouvrir le lourd vantail de la porte charmée.

"Car un sombre bonheur me retient en exil;
Frères, l'amour surgi dans mon âme dormante,
Ce n'est pas le désir joyeux et puéril
D'ensoleiller mes doigts à des cheveux d'amante.

"Je ne suis point pareil au faune maraudeur
Qui ravit en chantant les dryades frivoles,
Et ce que j'aime, hélas! ce n'est pas la splendeur
Des bras blancs, ni le rire ardent des lèvres folles.

"Une soif de souffrance et de renoncement
Seule m'a fait chercher la mauvaise amoureuse,
Vers qui mon âme épanche intarissablement
Comme une eau triste sa tendresse douloureuse.

"Autrefois, ô guerriers, une étrange langueur
Me glaçait au soleil des heureuses mêlées;
Un dégoût surhumain se levait en mon coeur,
Et je pleurais d'ennui dans les villes brûlées.

"Et peut-être au matin des triomphes haineux
Rêvais-je seulement de mort expiatoire;
J'étais l'aventurier morose et dédaigneux
Qui méprise la guerre à cause de la gloire.

"Voici que j'ai trouvé l'atroce paradis
Où des poisons sacrés corrompent les fontaines,
Et celle qui me garde en ces jardins maudits
Sait bien me déchirer avec ses mains hautaines.

"Elle a pris à mon bras, par un charme blessé,
L'anneau de fer forgé par les nains, et, rieuse,
Elle a jeté dans l'herbe immonde du fossé
L'étendard imprégné de brise glorieuse.

"J'aime mystiquement ses jeunes cruautés,
J'aime ses mains souillant ma pourpre solennelle;
Agenouillé parmi les lys ensanglantés,
Je sens mon coeur princier s'anéantir en elle.

"Et je connais ma honte immense, et j'y consens.
Vous n'aviez pas besoin d'assaillir les murailles
Et d'éveiller les fleurs par vos appels puissants,
Je me souviens assez des antiques batailles.

"Mais nul renom de roi conquérant et de preux
Ne vaut l'orgueil amer des secrètes tortures!
L'amour seul peut remplir mon grand coeur
    ténébreux,
Divinement élu pour les douleurs obscures."

Tel le captif, parmi les roses des balcons,
Parle aux guerriers. L'armée invincible recule.
Les casques d'or cimés d'aigles et de faucons
S'éloignent. Des hérauts, dans le fier crépuscule,

Proclament le départ vers des combats nouveaux,
Et le prince enfermé dans son palais de rêve
Regarde au loin, parmi les furieux chevaux,
S'enfuir le char désert où se rouille son glaive.

*Oeuvres*

## Florimond

The dragon killers and knight-kings, whose red pennant is embroidered with a serpent, beat all day with heavy battering-rams against the sard rampart and the copper gate. They thronged before the magic prison in which their enslaved brother gets drunk on vain love. Their war chariots, scattered over the calm turf, crushed wide around the sage and verbena flowers. The tough soldiers camping in the ravaged fields bruised under their weight the magic grass: heralds with their unfamiliar shouts terrified the fabled birds guarding the turret. And horsemen in the flaming west, tossing the golden plumes of their heroic helmets, seemed, when they raised their arms, to stir up the red evening with their long pikes. Whole troops of lions and tame griffins provided them with a horrible, grandiose escort. Tigers leaped under their magic whips, and lionesses rushed at the gate. Now the worried warriors and kings, weary of besieging wonder-bearing stones in vain, call three

times, from the top of the hill, the prince emprisoned by victorious
flowers. "We are," they say, "your forgotten brothers, those whom
your voice, like the archangels' trumpet, once led through heaths and
thickets toward the gathering of the warrior's crop and the red wine
harvest. Often when you sang us your powerful songs, in the night
sky, cold and black, we saw afar the fabled gold fleece shining, and we
smelled victory in the air. You led us to the deliverance of cities, and
standing on your amythest-studded chariot you pointed out great lands
terrified by sphinxes crouching on the dismal hills. And yet you are
now a prisoner. And your hands, your foolish hands, dropping their
old sword, cast one by one the petals of frail gladiolus and jasmine into
the sorceress's disheveled hair. O brother, we were coming to break the
spell, to save you from the gardens of shameful roses, but we are mys-
teriously overcome. You alone can open those beautiful closed gates.
Prince, captive prince of the unchaste orchards, prince sleeping by
flowering fountains, do you not hear before your towers, your walls,
the kingly thunder of our cavalry? Remember the rough roads we
trampled joyously, to the sound of bursting conch-horns, and our sa-
cred camps watched over by lions, and virile slumber under the loyal
tents. Come, the wind on the plain and the sea spray have a better scent
than garden flowers. Come, you will again breathe in the bitter charm
of wild forests and barren strands. Make your escape; as you cross the
threshold, cast off your desires like vile dust and drive from your heart,
once rich in pride, the unspeakable love of the sorceress queen." They
speak; in the evening air wild scents rise from the sleeping woods and
countryside, and the kingly liberators hold out their standards and
friendly arms toward the high ramparts. But now leaning over flower-
ing balconies, the gentle captive enamoured of divine pain, with a wave
of his weary and indulgent hands, motioned the warriors from the
peaceful terraces: "Men, why this noise of arms and trumpets? My fairy
prison is closed forever; toward free and wholesome roads I will not
again open the heavy double doors of the enchanted gate. For a dark
happiness holds me in exile. Brothers, the love which arose in my sleep-
ing soul is not the joyful and boyish desire to run my fingers through a
lover's sunny hair; I am not like the marauding faun, ravishing dryads
while singing a song, and what I love, alas, is not the splendor of white
arms nor ardent laughter on giddy lips. The thirst for suffering and
renunciation alone drove me to seek the evil lover, toward whom my
soul pours out without end, like melancholy water, its sorrowful ten-
derness. In times past, O warriors, a strange languor chilled me in the

sunlight of happy battles; a superhuman distaste rose in my heart, and I wept with ennui in burned cities. And perhaps in the morning of hatred and triumph I dreamt only of expiatory death; I was the morose and disdainful adventurer who despises war because of the glory. Now I have found the horrible paradise where sacred poisons taint the springs, and she who keeps me in these cursed gardens knows well how to lacerate me with her haughty hands. She took from my arm, wounded by a spell, the iron ring forged by the dwarfs and with a laugh threw my standard, waving in a breeze of glory, into the filthy weeds of the moat. I have a mystic love for her cruel young ways; I love her hands defiling my solemn purple glory. On my knees among the bloody lilies, I feel my princely heart annihilated in her. And I know my vast shame and allow it. You did not need to besiege the walls and to awaken the flowers with your loud cries; I remember well enough our ancient battles. But no conquering king or valiant's fame is so precious as the bitter pride of secret torments! Love alone can fill my great shadowy heart, divinely chosen for dark sorrows." Thus the captive, among the roses on the balcony, speaks to the warriors. The invincible army falls back. The gold helmets surmounted by eagles and falcons move away. Heralds, in the haughty twilight, proclaim their departure toward new battles, and the prince, shut up in his dream palace, watches in the distance the empty chariot, where his sword lies rusting, vanish among the furious horses.

# PIERRE LOUYS

## Emaux sur or et sur argent

### I

O gloire et nuit des eaux! mare aux lueurs livides!
Vol de nénufars blancs entre deux ciels le soir
Immobiles, crépusculaires... O miroir
Orageux du soleil couchant sur les champs vides.
Ombre d'eau corrompue, éblouissement noir...

O fauve amas d'inextricables longues pailles.
Lumière en floraison dans la lumière. Essor
D'aurore frissonnante aux flammes des broussailles
Fumantes parmi la sueur de messidor.

O, silence!—rayons dardés hors du mirage
Où des éclats d'étoile ont gravé leur sillage
Car c'est l'immense paix du ciel nocturne, encor.

Et voici qu'en mes bras de brume, soulevée,
Réfléchissent la gloire et l'étoile arrêvée

Tes longs yeux verts stagnants sous des frondaisons d'or.

### II

C'est un lys, une fleur vivante, une corolle
Chaude, et qui respire, et qui palpite, et qui bat.
O rougeur que nul midi de feu n'étiole!
C'est la fleur turgescente et jeune qui tomba
Des cheveux de la Nuit sur ta beauté d'Idole.

Sa volupté nocturne a gardé pour les sens
La féminine odeur des corolles sacrées
Et dans l'air où fraîchit la douceur des soirées
Je rêve errer sur elle un bleu brumeux d'encens.

C'est pourquoi, de ta fleur de chair endolorie
Je veux faire un lys froid comme une pierrerie,
Pourpre comme la lune à l'horizon naissant

Calice de rubis comme une fleur d'étoile
Chair de vierge fouettée avec des flots de sang

Ta bouche rouge et blanche et toute liliale.

### III

Pour cuirasser ton coeur contre ma faible main,
Telle que les Vertus des hautes mosaïques
Tu dresses fortement sur ton torse hautain
Deux grands casques de guerre aux crêtes héroïques
Et ton poitrail surgit comme bardé d'airain.

Mais parfois tes fureurs durant les nuits cruelles
Se couchent au niveau de mes lèvres d'enfant,
Et tu daignes fléchir sur ton corps triomphant
L'éclosion sereine et vaste des mamelles.

Je te regarde alors sous ton bras indolent,
Et je cherche, étendu devant tes chairs païennes,
Vierge! quelle Amphitrite aux mains céruléennes,

Quelle Thétis distraite, avec un geste lent, —
De ses doigts bleus encor des glauques empirées

Stria l'or de tes seins d'artères azurées.

*Astarté*

## Enamel Work on Gold and Silver

I. O glory and night on the water! Pond with livid glowings! A flight of white water lilies between different colored parts of the evening sky, immobile and crepuscular. O stormy mirror of the sun setting over empty fields. Corrupt water shadow, black dazzlement! O tawny heap of straw inextricably knotted. Light flowering in light. Soaring dawn quivering in the brush on fire and smoking in September sweat! O silence! Beams emanating from the mirage where star shards have engraved their wake! For it is still the immense peaceful night sky! And now in my arms of risen mist, your long, green, stagnant eyes under their golden foliage reflect the brilliance of the dreamed-of star. II. It is a lily, a living flower, a warm, breathing corolla, beating, palpitating. O redness withered by no burning noon! It is the young, swelling flower fallen from night's hair on your idollike beauty. Its nighttime voluptousness has kept for our senses the feminine scent of sacred corollas, and in the air filled with evening's sweet coolness, I dream I see drift over it a misty incense blue. That is why from your flower of sorrowful flesh I want to make a lily cold as a gem, red like the moon appearing on the horizon. A ruby chalice like a star flower, virgin flesh whipped with waves of blood is your red and white and quite lilylike mouth. III. To arm your heart against my weak hand, you bear on your haughty torso, like images of the virtues in high mosaics, two great war helmets with heroic crests, and your chest rises, as it were, plated with bronze. But sometimes during cruel nights, your furious bosom reclines beside my childish lips, and you deign to release on your triumphant body the vast, serene unfolding of breasts. I look at you then, under your indolent arm, and I try to imagine, before your pagan flesh, what blue-handed Amphitrite, what distracted Thetis—in a slow gesture with her fingers still blue from sea green heavens—streaked the gold of your breasts with azure arteries.

## Le Geste de la lance

Naïf, aux yeux à fleur de tête et grands ouverts
Il a taché de sang le vol sacré du Cygne
Mais il pleure, le Fou, le Pur...
Une procession lente de chênes verts
S'ébranle vers la nuit où va rougir le Signe.

Sur le lys qui descend d'avoir regardé Dieu
Ne prévaudront les roses ni les chairs fleuries.
Il sait par la pitié la Blessure, et le Feu
Jailli des trous d'enfer par les sorcelleries.

Et la Femme aux yeux d'ombre en qui vivait l'effroi
D'avoir étreint dans ses genoux dressés le Roi,
Se prosterne entre ses cheveux de Madeleine.

Sanctus et hosanna vers le preux Parsifal
Qui, marchant sur les fleurs dans le soir triomphal,

Brandit à bout de bras vers le Graal la Lance!

*Astarté*

## Stretching forth the Lance

Ingenuous, with his flat face and wide-open eyes, he spotted with blood the Swan's sacred flight, but he weeps, the Fool, the Pure One. A slow procession of holm oaks sets off for the night in which the Sign will glow red. Over the lily, humble from having seen God, neither roses nor flowering flesh will prevail. He knows through pity the Wound and the Fire sprung by magic from hellholes. And the shadowy-eyed Woman, living in terror from having held between her legs the King, prostrates herself in her Magdalene's hair. Cry Sanctus and Hosanna to the courageous Parsifal, who, walking on flowers in the triumphal evening, brandishes the Lance at arm's length toward the Grail!

# PAUL VALERY

## Blanc

La lune mince verse une lueur sacrée,
Comme une jupe d'un tissu d'argent léger
Sur les degrés d'ivoire où va l'Enfant songer,
Chair de perle que moule une gaze nacrée.

Sur les cygnes dolents qui frôlent les roseaux,
—Galères blanches et carènes lumineuses—
Elle effeuille des lys et des roses neigeuses
Et les pétales font des cercles sur les eaux.

Puis—pensive—la fille aux chimères subtiles
Voit se tordre les flots comme de blancs reptiles
A ses pieds fins chaussés d'hermine et de cristal;

La Mer confuse des fleurs pudiques l'encense
Car elle enchante de sa voix, frêle métal,
La Nuit lactée et douce et le pâle silence.

*L'Ermitage,* 1890

## White

The slim moon sheds a sacred glow, like a skirt made of some light silver fabric, onto the ivory steps where the child goes to dream, with her pearl flesh outlined by nacreous gauze. Over the sorrowful swans brushing against the reeds—white galleys and luminous keels—she strips the petals from lilies and snowy roses, and the petals make circles in the water. Then, pensive, the girl with subtle and fantastic thoughts sees the water ripple, sinuous as white reptiles, at her delicate feet shod in ermine and crystal. The dumbfounded sea of chaste flowers offers her incense, for with the fragile metal of her voice, she charms the sweet milky night and the pale silence.

# HENRY BATAILLE

## Le Mois mouillé

Par les vitres grises de la lavanderie
J'ai vu tomber la nuit d'automne que voilà...
Quelqu'un marche le long des fossés pleins de pluie...
Voyageur, voyageur de jadis qui t'en vas,
A l'heure où les bergers descendent des montagnes,
Hâte-toi! Les foyers sont éteints où tu vas,
Closes les portes au pays que tu regagnes.
La grande route est vide et le bruit des luzernes
Vient de si loin qu'il ferait peur... Dépêche-toi:
Les vieilles carrioles ont soufflé leurs lanternes...
C'est l'automne: elle s'est assise et dort de froid
Sur la chaise de paille au fond de la cuisine...
L'automne chante dans les sarments morts des
    vignes...
C'est le moment où les cadavres introuvés,
Les blancs noyés, flottant, songeurs, entre deux ondes,
Saisis eux-mêmes aux premiers froids soulevés,
Descendent s'abriter dans les vases profondes.

*La Chambre blanche*

## The Wet Month

Through the grey panes of the laundry shed, I saw this autumn night fall. Someone is walking along the ditches full of rain. Wayfarer, onetime wayfarer, marching along, at the time when the shepherds come down from the mountains, make haste! The hearths you are heading for have gone out; closed are the doors in your native village. The highway is empty, and the sound of the wind in the alfalfa comes from so far away it is frightening. Hurry! The old wagons have put out their lanterns. It's autumn: she has sat down and sleeps from the cold on the rush-bottomed chair in the back of the kitchen. Autumn sings in the dead vine branches. It is the time when the unrecovered bodies, the white drowned corpses, floating, pensive, between two ripples, risen with the first cold, are, even they, seized by the chill and sink to shelter in the deep mud.

## Les Villages

Il y a de grands soirs où les villages meurent.
Après que les pigeons sont rentrés se coucher,
Ils meurent, lentement, avec le bruit de l'heure
Et le cri bleu des hirondelles au clocher...
Alors, pour les veiller, des lumières s'allument,
Vieilles petites lumières de bonnes soeurs,
Et des lanternes passent, là-bas, dans la brume...
Au loin le chemin gris chemine avec douceur...
Les fleurs dans les jardins se sont pelotonnées
Pour écouter mourir leur village d'antan,
Car elles savent que c'est là qu'elles sont nées...
Puis les lumières s'éteignent, cependant
Que les vieux murs habituels ont rendu l'âme,
Tout doux, tout bonnement, comme de vieilles femmes.

*Le Beau Voyage*

## Villages

There are vast evenings when villages die. After the pigeons have come home to roost, they die, slowly, with the striking of the hour and the swallows' blue cry in the steeple. Then, for their wake, lights are lit, little old lamps such as nuns have, and lanterns go by, there, in the mist. In the distance the grey road moves gently on; flowers in gardens have folded up tight to hear their old village die, for they know it was there they were born. Then the lights go out, after the familiar old walls have given up the ghost, gently, simply, like old women.

# OSCAR-VENCESLAS DE MILOSZ

## Salomé

—Jette cet or de deuil où tes lèvres touchèrent,
Dans le miroir du sang, le reflet de leur fleur
Mélodieuse et douce à blesser!
La vie d'un Sage ne vaut pas, ma Salomé,
Ta danse d'Orient sauvage comme la chair,
Et ta bouche couleur de meurtre, et tes seins couleur de désert!
—Puis, secouant ta chevelure, dont les lumières
S'allongent vers mon coeur avec leurs têtes de lys rouges,
—Ta chevelure où la colère
Du soleil et des perles
Allume des lueurs d'épées—
Fais que ton rire ensanglanté sonne un glas de mépris,
O Beauté de la Chair, toi qui marches drapée
Dans l'incendie aveugle et froid des pierreries!
Ton oeuvre est grande et je t'admire,
Car les yeux du Prophète, lacs de sang et de nuit
Où le fantôme de la tristesse se mire,
Comme l'áutomne en la rosée des fleurs gâtées
Et le déclin des jours dans les flaques de pluie,
Connaîtront, grâce à toi, la volupté d'Oubli!
—Ah! tournant vers ce front sinistre, que saccagent
Les torches mal éteintes de l'hallucination,
Tes yeux ensoleillés comme les fleurs sauvages
Et les flots de la mer poignardée de rayons,
Tu peux battre des mains, et le faire crier bien fort
Ton rire asiatique amoureux de la mort!
Car, les pensers d'orgueil et les pudeurs de vanité,
Qui tombèrent pour ta gaîté
Avec un bruit d'idole creuse et un râle de bijoux faux,
Ne valent, ni tes bras luisants et recourbés
Comme les glaives et les faux,
Ni tes cheveux amers et durs comme l'herbe brûlée,
Salomé, Salomé
Glorieuse qui sus chasser

Le sarcoramphe noir Ennui du coeur d'Hérode,
Et qui fis en dansant l'aumône de la mort!
La sagesse mûrit pour la faim de la Terre,
Et toi tu vis! et tu respires, ô Beauté,
Et ta chair réelle a des brises de santal
A la place où ta voix s'effeuille en accords rares,
Et le Monde s'abreuve à tes veines barbares
Où la pourpre charrie un délice brutal!

—Et nous qui connaissons la certitude unique,
Salomé des Instincts, nous te donnons nos coeurs
Aux battements plus forts que les soirs de panique,
L'appel désespéré des airains de douleur,

Et nous voulons qu'au vent soulevé par ta robe
Et par ta chevelure éclaboussée de fleurs
Se déchire enfin la fumée
De l'Idéal et des Labeurs,

O Salomé de nos hontes, Salomé!

*Le Poème des décadences*

## Salome

Cast that mourning-gold salver your lips touched into the mirror of blood, a reflection of their melodious flower which gently invites wounding. A wise man's life, my Salome, is not worth the price of your Eastern dance, wild like the flesh, and your murder-colored mouth and your desert-colored breasts. Then, shaking your hair, the rays of which curl their red-lily heads toward my heart—your hair in which the angry sun and pearls kindle gleams as on a sword blade—make your bloody laugh sound a knell of scorn, O Beauty of the Flesh, you who proceed draped in the cold, blind conflagration of gems! Your works are great, and I admire you, for the Prophet's eyes, lakes of blood and night reflecting the ghost of sadness, as dew on withered flowers reflects autumn or rain puddles the end of the day, will know, thanks to you, voluptuous oblivion. Ah! as you turn your eyes toward this sinister brow, ravaged by the still smouldering torches of hallucination—your eyes gleaming with sun like wild flowers and the waves of the sea stabbed by light beams—you can clap your hands and make shrill your Asiatic laugh enamoured of death! For the haughty thoughts and vain modesty which fell, as if to amuse you, with the sound of a hollow idol and the rasp of false gems, cannot compare with your gleaming arms curved like swords and scythes or your hair bitter and hard as burnt grass, Salome, Salome, O glorious one, who succeeded in driving Ennui, the black bird of prey, from Herod's heart and gave death as alms with your dance. Wisdom only ripens further to famish man. And you live and you breathe, O Beauty, and your real flesh wafts sandalwood there where your voice scatters petals of rare harmony, and the world drinks from your barbarian veins where brutal delight is borne by the crimson stream! And we who know the one certainty, Salome, all Instinct, we give you our hearts beating harder than does, on panic evenings, the desperate summons of sorrowful brass trumpets, and we long that, in the gusts of air raised by your robe and by your hair splashed with flowers, the smoke of the Ideal and its Labors be rent and dispelled. O Salome of our shames, Salome!

# GUILLAUME APOLLINAIRE

## L'Ermite

Un ermite déchaux, près d'un crâne blanchi,
Cria: "Je vous maudis, martyres et détresses,
Trop de tentations malgré moi me caressent.
Tentations de lune et de logomachies.

Trop d'étoiles s'enfuient quand je dis mes prières.
O chef de morte! O vieil ivoire! Orbites! Trous
Des narines rongées! J'ai faim! Mes cris
    s'enrouent.
Voici donc pour mon jeûne un morceau de
    gruyère.

Tu es un crâne féminin, certainement,
Car le gruyère est fait avec du lait de vache,
O crâne dont j'ai peur en mon âme bravache!
O tête, j'ai baisé tes dents comme un amant.

Entendez-vous, Seigneur, quand d'horreur je
    l'écrase,
Craquer comme une noix le crâne féminin?
Ayez pitié, Seigneur, de mes soupirs bénins.
Doux Seigneur, pardonnez au printemps qui
    viédaze.

Flagellez, flagellez les nuées du coucher
Qui tendent sans espoir de si jolis culs roses.
Et, c'est le soir, les fleurs de jour déjà se closent
Et les souris dans l'ombre incantent le plancher.

Les humains savent tant de jeux: l'amour, la
    mourre.
L'amour, jeu des nombrils ou jeu de la grande
    oie.
La mourre, jeu du nombre illusoire des doigts.
Seigneur, faites, Seigneur, qu'un jour je
    m'enamoure.

J'attends celle qui me tendra ses doigts menus.
Combien de signes blancs aux ongles? Les
    paresses,
Les mensonges. Pourtant j'attends qu'elle les
    dresse
Ses mains enamourées devant moi, l'Inconnue.

Seigneur, que t'ai-je fait? Vois, je suis unicorne.
Pourtant, malgré son bel effroi concupiscent,
Comme un poupon chéri, mon sexe est innocent
D'être anxieux, seul et debout, comme une
    borne.

Seigneur, le christ est nu. Jetez, jetez sur lui
La robe sans couture. Eteignez les ardeurs.
Au puits vont se noyer tant de tintements
    d'heures,
Quand, isochrones, choient des gouttes d'eau de
    pluie.

J'ai veillé trente nuits sous les lauriers-roses.
As-tu sué du sang, Christ, dans Gethsémani?
Crucifié, réponds! Dis non! Moi, je le nie,
Car j'ai trop espéré en vain l'hématidrose.

J'écoutais à genoux toquer les battements
Du coeur. Le sang, toujours, roulait en ses
    artères
Qui sont de vieux coraux ou qui sont des
    clavaires,
Et je sentais l'aorte avare éperdument.

Une goutte tomba. Sueur? et sa couleur?
Lueur! le sang est rouge! et j'ai ri des damnés!
Puis enfin j'ai compris que je saignais du nez
A cause des parfums violents de mes fleurs.

Et j'ai ri du vieil ange qui n'est point venu
De vol très indolent me tendre un beau calice.
J'ai ri de l'aile grise et j'ôte mon cilice
Tissé de crins soyeux par de cruels canuts.

Vertuchou! riotant des vulves des papesses,
Des saintes sans tétons, j'irai vers les cités

Et peut-être y mourir pour ma virginité,
Parmi les mains, les peaux, les mots et les
    promesses.

Malgré les autans bleus, je me dresse divin
Comme un rayon de lune adoré par la mer.
En vain, j'ai supplié tous les saints aémères,
Aucun n'a consacré mes doux pains sans levain.

Et je marche, je fuis, ô nuit, Lilith ulule
Et clame vainement et je vois de grands yeux
S'ouvrir tragiquement. O nuit, je vois tes cieux
L'étoiler calmement de splendides pilules.

Un squelette de reine innocente est pendu
A un long fil d'étoile en désespoir sévère.
La nuit, les bois sont noirs et se meurt l'espoir
    vert
Quand meurt le jour avec un râle inattendu.

Et je marche, je fuis. O jour, l'émoi de l'aube
Ferma le regard fixe et doux de vieux rubis
Des hiboux et voici le regard des brebis
Et des truies aux tétins roses comme des lobes.

Des corbeaux éployés comme des tildes font
Une ombre vaine aux pauvres champs de seigle
    mûr,
Non loin des bourgs où des chaumières sont
    impures
D'avoir des hiboux morts cloués à leur plafond.

Mes kilomètres longs, mes tristesses plénières,
Les squelettes de doigts terminant les sapins
Ont égaré ma route et mes rêves poupins
Souvent et j'ai dormi au sol des sapinières.

Enfin, ô soir pâmé, au bout de mes chemins
La ville m'apparut, très grave, au son des
    cloches,
Et ma luxure meurt à présent que j'approche.
En entrant j'ai béni les foules des deux mains.

Cité, j'ai ri de tes palais tels que des truffes
Blanches, au sol fouillé de clairières bleues.

Or, mes désirs s'en vont tous à la queue leu-leu.
Ma migraine pieuse a coiffé sa cucuphe.

Car toutes sont venues m'avouer leurs péchés,
Et, Seigneur, je suis saint par le voeu des
    amantes,
Zélotide et Lorie, Louise et Diamante
Ont dit: Tu peux savoir, ô toi, l'effarouché.

Ermite, absous nos fautes jamais vénielles,
O toi, le pur et le contrit que nous aimons,
Sache nos coeurs, sache les jeux que nous aimons
Et nos baisers quintessenciés comme du miel.

Or, j'absous les aveux pourpres comme leur sang
Des poétesses nues, des fées, des fornarines.
Aucun pauvre désir ne gonfle ma poitrine
Lorsque je vois, le soir, des couples s'enlaçant.

Et je ne veux plus rien, sinon laisser se clore
Mes yeux, couple lassé, au verger pantelant
Plein du râle pompeux des groseillers sanglants
Et de la sainte cruauté des passiflores."

La Revue Blanche, 1902

## The Hermit

A barefoot hermit by a whitened skull cried, "I curse you, martyr-dom and distress. Do what I will, too many temptations caress me, moonlight temptations and temptations to devious casuistry. Too many stars flee when I say my prayers. O female skull, old ivory! Eyesockets! Gnawed away nostril holes! I am hungry. My cries grow hoarse. Here, to content my fast, is a piece of Swiss cheese with holes like a skull! You are most certainly a female skull, for Swiss cheese is made with cow's milk! O skull, whom I fear in my blustering soul! O head, I have kissed your teeth like a lover. Can you hear it, Lord, when in my horror I crush the female skull and it cracks like a nut? Take pity, Lord, on my harmless sighs. Sweet Lord, pardon the springtime in me for rutting like an ass! Whip, whip the sunset clouds, which in vain thrust out such pretty pink buttocks! And it's evening; the daytime flowers close, and in the shadow mice cast a spell on the floor. Humans know many a game: amor, a mora game! A-mor: the bellybutton game or game of the ultimate favors! Mor-a: the game where you guess how many fingers are held up. Let me, Lord, one day fall in love. I am expecting her who will extend to me her slim fingers. How many white marks on her nails? Marks of laziness, lies. Yet I am waiting for her, the unknown woman, to hold up her enamored hands before me. Lord, what have I done to you? Look, I have a horn. Yet, despite its great lustful terror, like a cherished baby my penis is innocent in its anxiety, alone and upright like a milestone. Lord, christ is naked. Cast, cast on him the seamless robe. Extinguish my ardors! In the well drown so many ringings of the hour, when raindrops fall rhythmically. I have made a thirty-night vigil under the oleanders. Christ, did you sweat blood in Gethsemane? Reply, O crucified one! Say you didn't! I, for one, deny it, for I have waited too long in vain for a sweat of blood. Kneeling I listened to my heartbeats. My blood continued to pour through its arteries, which are branches of old coral or ramous wild mushrooms, and I felt the frantic movement of my avid aorta! A drop fell. Sweat? And what color? Revelation! Blood is red! And I have laughed at the damned! Finally, I realized my nose was bleeding because of the violent scent of my flowers! And I laughed at the old angel who didn't come, flying indolently, to offer me a beautiful chalice! I laughed at his grey wing, and now I take off my hairshirt, woven of soft prickles by cruel silkworkers. 'Sblood! Chuckling over papesses' vulvas and titless female saints, I shall go toward the cities and perhaps die there for my virginity, amid the hands, flesh, words, and promises. Despite the blue wind I stand divinely erect like a moonbeam worshipped by the sea! In vain have I called on all the saints without saint's days; none has consecrated my sweet unleavened bread. And I set off walking, I flee; O night, Lilith is howling and demanding in vain, and I see great eyes open tragically. O night, I see your skies calmly cover her with starlike globules. An innocent queen's skeleton is hanging from the long thread of a star desperately severe. At night the woods are black and green hope dies, when day dies with an unexpected death rattle. And I set off walking, I flee. O day, the thrill of the dawn closed off the gentle, steady, old-ruby gaze of the owls, and now the ewes are looking about and sows with pink nipples like lobes. Ravens outspread like tildes cast a vain shadow on poor fields of ripe rye, not far from villages where cottages are polluted by dead owls nailed to their ceilings. My long kilometers, my plenary sadnesses, skeletal fingers topping the pines have often misled my steps and my infantile dreams, and I have slept on the ground of fir thickets. Finally, O languorous evening, the city appeared to me, grave, in the sound of bells, and my lust dies as I now approach it. Entering the city, I blessed the crowd with both hands. City, I laughed at your palaces like white truffles, on a soil deep with blue clearings. Now my desires all are leaving one by one. My devout migraine has put on the hood of beheaded Saint Cucufa. For all the women have come to confess to me their sins, and Lord, I am sanctified by the lovers' vows. Zelotida, Loria, Louisa, and Diamantina have said, 'You can know our secret, O shy one. Hermit, absolve us of our never venial sins, O pure and contrite one, whom we love! See into our hearts, know the games we love and the distillate of our kisses like honey.' Now I give absolution to the confessions, red as their blood, of naked poetesses, fairies, and women beautiful as Raphael's model. No faint desire even begins to swell in my breast when, in the evening, I see couples entwine. And I want nothing anymore but to close my eyes, the weary pair, in the panting orchard, full of the majestic throaty breathing of blood red gooseberries and the holy gore of passionflowers!"

# NOTES ON POETS

Only the poets' more important volumes for symbolism are mentioned, and the poems sometimes considerably antedate their appearance in a collection. For detailed bibliographies of each poet's work see *Poètes d'aujourd'hui,* ed. Adolphe Van Bever and Paul Léautaud, 3 vols. (Paris: Mercure de France, 1947). Suggestions for further reading are confined to general studies.

GUILLAUME APOLLINAIRE (WILHELM KOSTROWITZSKY) (1880–1918), the great modernist of the pre-World War I era in Paris, was born in Rome of a Polish mother but raised in France. His very symbolist early work is included in *Alcools* (1913). See Margaret Davies, *Apollinaire* (New York: St. Martin's Press, 1964) and Francis Steegmuller, *Apollinaire: Poet Among the Painters* (New York: Farrar, Straus, 1963).

HENRY BATAILLE (1872–1922) became famous above all as a playwright. His chief volume of poems was *Le Beau Voyage* (1904).

TRISTAN (EDOUARD-JOACHIM) CORBIERE (1845–1875) did not move in literary circles and spent most of his short adult life in Roscoff, Brittany, for his health. An important part of *Les Amours jaunes* (1873), however, has reference to Paris and his stays there. His elliptic, often slangy style has been especially admired in the English-speaking world. See Albert Sonnenfeld, *L'Oeuvre poétique de Tristan Corbière* (Paris: Presses universitaires de France, 1960).

MAX ELSKAMP (1862–1931) wrote song-like poems, mostly about life in his native Antwerp, travel, and religious subjects. *La Louange de la vie* (1898); *Enluminures* (1898).

RENE GHIL (1862–1925) was especially interested in the symbolism of sounds or "verbal instrumentation," about which he wrote a *Traité du verbe* (1886). *Légende d'âmes et de sang* (1885).

ALBERT GIRAUD (1860–1929), a Belgian symbolist, is best known for *Pierrot Lunaire: Rondels bergamasques* (1884), which Schönberg set to music in a German translation. *La Guirlande des Dieux* (1910).

REMY DE GOURMONT (1858–1915) was one of the most important critics of his day, admired by Pound and Eliot. Many of his poems reflect his interest in medieval Latin literature. *Litanies de la rose* (1892); *Les Saintes du paradis* (1898); *Divertissements* (1912).

GUSTAVE KAHN (1859–1936), whose literary activities were largely confined to his youth, founded the important periodical *La Vogue* and claimed to have invented free verse. *Les Palais nomades* (1887). See John Clifford Ireson, *L'Oeuvre poétique de Gustave Kahn* (Paris: A. G. Nizet, 1962).

JULES LAFORGUE (1860–1887), the greatest talent among the younger poets of the 1880s, is credited with reinventing free verse; he influenced Eliot and other English-speaking poets. *Les Complaintes* (1885); *Imitation de Notre-Dame la lune* (1886); *Derniers Vers* (1890). See Warren Ramsey, *Jules Laforgue and the Ironic Inheritance* (New York: Oxford University Press, 1953).

LOUIS LE CARDONNEL (1862–1936), after a youth spent in symbolist circles, became a priest. *Poèmes* (1904).

GREGOIRE LE ROY (1862–1914), born in Ghent, was one of a number of Belgian symbolists associated with that memorable, atmospheric city by birth, upbringing, or education. He was a friend of Van Lerberghe and Maeterlinck. *La Chanson du pauvre* (1897).

JEAN LORRAIN (DUVAL) (1856–1906) was most famous as a decadent novelist. *Modernités* (1885); *Les Griseries* (1887); *L'Ombre ardente* (1897).

PIERRE LOUYS (1870–1925), a close friend of Valéry's, is best known for the neo-antique strain in his verse and prose. *Poésies* (1927).

MAURICE MAETERLINCK (1862–1949), before his fame as a dramatist and essayist, wrote verse. *Serres chaudes* (1889).

STEPHANE MALLARME (1842–1898) was both a precursor of symbolism and a fellow poet of younger men, publishing his later verse in the 1880s and '90s along with them. *Poésies* (1899). See Robert Greer Cohn, *Toward the Poems of Mallarmé* (Berkeley: University of California Press, 1965) and Guy Michaud, *Mallarmé* (New York: New York University Press, 1965).

STUART MERRILL (1863–1915), an American raised in Paris, belonged to a group of poets who had gone to the same lycée and which included Mikhaël, Ghil, and Quillard. He was a student of medieval French texts and an admirer of Swinburne. *Les Gammes* (1887); *Les Fastes* (1891).

EPHRAIM MIKHAEL (1866–1890) set out to be a professional scholar but died young. *Oeuvres* (1890).

OSCAR-VENCESLAS DE MILOSZ (1877–1939), a Lithuanian raised in Paris, began his work under symbolist influence. *Le Poème des décadences* (1899).

JEAN MOREAS (PAPADIAMANTOPOULOS) (1856–1910), a Greek, showed a striking philological bent in his poetry and was one of the well-known literary figures of Paris in his day. *Les Syrtes* (1884); *Les Cantilènes* (1886); *Le Pèlerin passionné* (1891). See Robert A. Jouanny, *Jean Moréas, Ecrivain français* (Paris: Minard, 1969).

PIERRE QUILLARD (1864–1912) was a professional scholar. *La Lyre héroïque et dolente* (1897).

HENRI DE REGNIER (1864–1939) was famous in his later years as a novelist. *Poèmes anciens et romanesques* (1890); *Tel qu'en songe* (1892).

ADOLPHE RETTE (1863–1930) was a truculent member of symbolist groups in his youth. *Cloches dans la nuit* (1889); *Une Belle Dame passa* (1893).

ARTHUR RIMBAUD (1854–1891), after moving from regular verse to *vers libérés* and then to the prose poem, gave up poetry at the age of twenty; he was in Africa and had lost all interest in literature by the time his work was revealed to the public. *Illuminations* (1886); *Le Reliquaire* (Poésies) (1891). See Wilbur M. Frohock, *Rimbaud's Poetic Practice: Image and Theme in the Major Poems* (Cambridge: Harvard University Press, 1963) and John Porter Houston, *The Design of Rimbaud's Poetry* (New Haven: Yale University Press, 1963).

GEORGES RODENBACH (1855–1898) used imagery largely of Bruges and his native Ghent, although he lived in Paris. *Le Règne du silence* (1891); *Les Vies encloses* (1896); *Le Miroir du ciel natal* (1898).

SAINT-POL ROUX (PAUL ROUX) (1861–1940), a rather eccentric figure, became best known as a highly metaphoric writer of prose poems. *Les Reposoirs de la procession* (1893); *Les Roses et les Epines du chemin* (1901); *Anciennetés* (1908).

ALBERT SAMAIN (1858–1900), a quiet civil servant, is usually represented in anthologies as a much tamer poet than he actually was. *Au jardin de l'infante* (1893).

PAUL VALERY (1871–1945) was active in symbolist circles in his youth. His verse of that period, much rewritten, was published in *Album de vers anciens* (1920). See Henry Alexander Grubbs, *Paul Valéry* (New York: Twayne, 1968).

CHARLES VAN LERBERGHE (1861–1907) was a member of Belgian symbolist circles. *La Chanson d'Eve* (1904) is an atheist interpretation of the story of Adam and Eve. *Entrevisions* (1898).

EMILE VERHAEREN (1855–1916), the most famous and prolific Belgian poet of his day, wrote for a time in a symbolist style. *Les Soirs* (1887); *Les Débâcles* (1888); *Les Flambeaux noirs* (1890); *Au bord de la route* (1891); *Les Apparus dans mes chemins* (1891); *Les Campagnes hallucinées* (1893); *Les Villages illusoires* (1895); *Les Villes tentaculaires* (1895); *Poèmes* (1899).

PAUL VERLAINE (1844–1896) had a noteworthy early career but became persona non grata in the world of letters after being imprisoned for trying to shoot Rimbaud in 1873. In the 1880s he became famous as one of the two masters (the other was Mallarmé) of the symbolists. *Poèmes saturniens* (1866); *Fêtes galantes* (1869); *Romances sans paroles* (1874); *Sagesse* (1881); *Jadis et Naguère* (1884); *Amour* (1888). See Alfred E. Carter, *Verlaine: A Study in Parallels* (Toronto: University of Toronto Press, 1969) and Eléonore M. Zimmerman, *Magies de Verlaine* (Paris: José Corti, 1967).